I WILL NEVER LEAVE YOU

I WILL NEVER LEAVE YOU

How Couples Can Achieve the Power of Lasting Love

HUGH AND GAYLE PRATHER

BANTAM BOOKS

New York   Toronto   London   Sydney   Auckland

I WILL NEVER LEAVE YOU

PUBLISHING HISTORY

Bantam hardcover edition / February 1995
Bantam trade paperback edition / February 1996
For permissions, please see page 375.
To protect privacy, many names and other identifying details
of the people's lives discussed in this book have been changed.

ISBN 0-553-37531-8
Published simultaneously in the United States and Canada

Bantam Books are published by Bantam Books, a division of Bantam Doubleday Dell
Publishing Group, Inc. Its trademark, consisting of the words ''Bantam Books'' and the
portrayal of a rooster, is Registered in U.S. Patent and Trademark Office and in other
countries. Marca Registrada. Bantam Books, 1540 Broadway, New York, New York 10036.

PRINTED IN THE UNITED STATES OF AMERICA

BVG   10 9 8 7 6 5 4

Contents

Part III Protecting and Perfecting a Real Relationship

NINE AFFAIRS

Acknowledgments

For their rich contribution of ideas and insights, and especially for their inspiring personal example, we are grateful to Terrianne Jacobson, Jerry Jampolsky and Diane Cirincione, Karron and Randy Jorgen, Bonnie Knickerbocker, Catherine McKinzie, Donovan and Jill Porterfield, Scott Prather, Mark Ramirez and Bonnie Beaty, Cindy and Julian Silverman, Barry and Joyce Vissell, and David and Susan Wilkinson. We want especially to thank Stacy Smith, who contributed her wisdom, her considerable editorial skills, and her creative design. The love, the courage, and the devotion to their children that she and her husband, Jeffrey Arlt, have exhibited over the years has blessed our family deeply.

I Will Never Leave You

O N E

The Twenty-first Century Relationship

What went wrong with our relationships in the twentieth century?

We live in a world that is out of control. Actually, the world was never controlled or controllable, but a fundamental shift occurred in the twentieth century—we became aware of this fact. Anyone who reads or watches television now knows that there is no end to the things that can hurt or kill you. Our reaction to this daily deluge of problems is understandable: Regardless of how utterly we have failed in the past, we still want to gain some measure of control. Anything that promises that possibility—from a new political movement to a new approach to health, from a new religion to a new gun—will inevitably appeal to many people.

The first line of defense against our recognition of chaos has been to withdraw into the smallest possible definition of ourselves. Large nations are breaking up into smaller ones. Religions and races are pulling in their boundaries and rejecting anyone who is dissimilar. Men and women, gays and straights, are preoccupied with their differences. And even neighborhoods of one culture now use arms against the neighborhoods of another.

Obviously relationships have not been immune to this atmosphere. Breakups and divorce are epidemic, even among the elderly. Those couples who do stay together may face addiction, infidelity, disease, financial uncertainties, sexual incompatibility, psychological and physical abuse, and problems with children, in-laws, and schools. Our relationships are as out of control as the world itself. This fact is now inescapable, and its recognition has brought a tide of anxiety and confusion that has engulfed most couples.

A little over a century ago, a person needed a partner just to share the labor involved in mere survival. Families were larger, with older children often helping to raise their younger siblings. Marriage was permanent; life expectancy was shorter; and it was not uncommon for children to remain at home throughout the lifetimes of their parents. Those who already had wealth looked at marriage as a practical means of increasing it, and for both the poor and the privileged, marriage was needed to continue the family name. In other words, marriage was a simple necessity, a part of life, and not something that had to be singled out and carefully watched, like some strange bank of clouds on the horizon that could bring either a miracle rain or a disaster.

Today there are no obvious reasons for getting married, and so, thinking that a reason is required, we have invented new ones. Now you need a partner in order to be supported and fulfilled, in order to be "all that you can be." Concepts such as the "soul mate" have been invented, and mysticism has been injected into sex. If you add to this the fact that we no longer have a moral objection to divorce, then potentially one can have anyone at any time. Little wonder that today most people are probing every aspect of their romantic relationships for inadequacies. If you can have *anyone,* is your present partner really giving you everything you could get? Or if there is a person with whom you are already mystically matched, the one right person for you, have you in fact found this individual?

Now couples who come to us for help believe that simply by

having a relationship, the hurt and loneliness of their past should be healed. *They weren't happy before they got married,* but now that they have a partner, their continued unhappiness is their partner's fault. It doesn't occur to them that except for "owning" their "mistake" in choosing each other (an arrogant rationalization for passing judgment), undoing their present unhappiness will require a joint effort.

When you get married, you simply become like the majority of adults: You are married. That in itself changes nothing. But how you react to it can change everything. Most people still believe that getting married is the most important event in their lives, but *being* married has become like test-driving a new car. They really think that it doesn't matter whether they reject it or not and that they can make their decision quickly, conveniently, and in accordance with the latest Blue Book of spouse ratings. Many marriage-denigrating concepts such as the throwaway "starter marriage" are now in vogue.

The enormous spiritual cost of betrayal and abandonment is presently being so miscalculated that an entire generation is in danger of becoming emotionally and spiritually bankrupt.

A couple we counseled for three years—we will call them Ben and Mary—developed a deep bond early in their freshman year of college. They got married on the very evening of graduation day. Mary, who had won several titles in synchronized swimming, began teaching at a large racquet and swimming club to support them and to help pay Ben's way through law school. Two children and twelve years later, they came to us with a family on the verge of a breakup.

At the time we met them, they had basically everything that couples long for: wonderful children (two girls), successful careers (Mary was now a prominent hydrotherapist for the physically disabled, and Ben periodically gave expert testimony before Congress on the legal issues affecting the elderly), good health, a beautiful home, and a normal, if not above average, sex life.

At any other time in history, the issues that had arisen between them probably would not have threatened their marriage. Neither of them had ever had an affair, not even an emotional one; neither was abusive to the other or to the children, not even verbally; neither was addicted to anything; they had no in-law problems; they had no money problems; they shared common political and religious philosophies; and they liked most of the same activities. Above all, they had one of the deeper bonds we have seen between two people.

Basically their issues with each other arose out of the new selfishness in which they had both become steeped, primarily through the books they had read and the separate groups they regularly attended. (Mary went to one of the twelve-step spin-off groups, while Ben attended a large men's group.) To enhance their sex life, to be "a better physical example" to their children, and to avoid "embarrassing" her, Mary wanted Ben, who was prematurely gray, to dye his hair and lose twenty pounds. This Ben refused to do. He said that if Mary truly loved him, she would accept him as he was.

For Ben's part, he wanted Mary either to quit her job or to stop bringing home the "wrenching stories" of her handicapped patients and the soap-opera politics of the hospital where she worked. Mary insisted that she had to have a partner who would listen to whatever she had to say.

We have never worked harder with any couple than we did this one, nor have we ever felt our failure to keep a family together more acutely. These two definitely loved each other, and they loved their children, but weighed against the advice they were getting from their friends and separate groups—that above all, they must not give in—love was not enough. Or to state it more accurately, although love was unquestionably present, they chose to heed their "emotional needs" (Mary) and their "integrity as an individual" (Ben) rather than the bond between them.

When Ben found himself back on the singles market, he lost a total of thirty-eight pounds and dyed his hair, his beard, and his eyebrows. Mary found that the stress of the divorce, added to the stress of her job, was too much, and within three months of their separation she had left it. Their oldest girl now comes to us for counseling.

Thousands if not millions of stories like this one indicate why a new kind of relationship is now needed, one founded on a radically different set of values. Not a perfect relationship, not one that fits the picture of who we want and what that person should do for us, but a relationship that can go through fire and survive. Nor is this a call to return to the all-form, no-content standard of the 1940s and 1950s, when many marriages were held together by the fear of divorce and the censure that could come from breaking the rules, yet contained little love and almost no equality between the sexes.

Ironically, at this time in the world's history when we need each other most, when feelings of recrimination, separateness, and discontent are so deep that they have driven out almost all other emotions, and when present world trends offer surprisingly little hope, the therapeutic philosophy that so many have turned to justifies selfism and withdrawal and tends to characterize most loving efforts as symptoms of a pathology. Certainly this is not the goal of many individuals who have been writing and teaching in this area, but as so often happens with new approaches, a shadow teaching develops that becomes more widely accepted than the original. In this book we will refer to that teaching as **separation psychology.**

As a people, what we desperately need now are young, old, and middle-aged partners who understand what a real relationship is, who are unwilling to give up on a friend, unwilling to back away from a sacred commitment, unwilling to abandon the gentleness of their own hearts, regardless of pressure from those around them and influences from popular philosophies. To attain this, we must stop scanning our partner's every act and utterance for signs of abusiveness, suspecting every generous impulse we have of betraying some inner pathology, weighing every gift we give against those we receive, and judging our relationship by an impossible and selfish standard. Let us simply admit that we are flawed, that our families were flawed, that their families were flawed, that we have many unhappy traits, but that nevertheless we have agreed to see this through together. Like a parent with a flawed child, we refuse to stop loving and to stop trying. Let us dare to believe in the possibility that two highly imperfect people can come together and, through patience and creativity and ordinary devotion, heal each other deeply.

In the twenty-first century the real frontier will not be space, or the oceans' floors, or telecommunications, or genetic engineering, or a thousand other external pursuits. It will be human relations. Everything we achieve as a species will be torn down again and again, and men, women, and children will be reduced to living as animals of prey—as they already are today in numerous areas of the world—unless we honestly deal with what is destroying us.

At this time we do not love each other. We don't even act as if we love each other. We are consumed by an epidemic far more virulent than the black plague, cholera, polio, tuberculosis, or AIDS, and it is composed of simple hatred and fear.

The answer is not for everyone to start trying to save the world. The *heart* of humanity must be saved. We have tried attack for tens of thousands of years, and it has gotten us nowhere. The question "What can I do right?" rather than "What are you doing wrong?" points to the one area where progress is still within our control. Attack is the problem, not the answer, because attack is a form of procrastination. It is the decision to focus on what separates us, to the total exclusion of what joins us.

Surely it's obvious by now that "Whose mistake is it?" will never unite us, never bring us peace. The revolution must take place within our own circle of acquaintances. We must light the room where we stand. The inherent peace and integrity of our mind must be allowed to shine forth. We begin with our own partner, our own children, our own family, and personally become the answer. How else can we bind up the world's wounds and begin the healing?

As ministers and counselors, we can tell you unequivocally that after more than two decades of helping couples with their marriages and almost three decades of working on our own, **we have rarely encountered anyone whose life was made happier by the act of abandoning his or her partner.** Certainly situations exist in which a child is being sexually or physically abused, or someone's life or sanity is being threatened, and separation becomes a clear and immediate necessity. But even during the many years when we helped both battered women and batterers, those men and women who personally came to us for help did not prove an exception to our experience that most problems can be worked out, and that it's happier in the long run to complete the task.

We will not dwell on the exceptions, because it's unlikely that many of our readers are in an environment that is unsafe. If you are, then leave—or step away from the relationship temporarily and continue working on it from a distance. But if you are not, stay, and we will do our best to point to at least a few ways that you can gradually heal your marriage, even if at present you don't have the cooperation of your partner.

This book is devoted to relationships in which breakup and divorce are unnecessary—which is probably 90 percent of all relationships. Unlike our two other books on couples, our focus here is on how the peculiar set of forces that has come into play at the end of the twentieth century has affected potentially permanent relationships, and what you as a couple can do to recognize these and move beyond them. We think of this book as an emergency manual to deal with an ongoing disaster.

We know from experience that there are sound reasons for you to have hope. As you will see, our own path has not been an easy one. The problems we have had to work through include a previous divorce, long-term infidelity, financial difficulties, an adolescent child from another marriage, and children of our own late in our marriage. And yet because we have never stopped building it for thirty years, we now have an unshakable friendship. It is possible for you to have this also—and with far fewer delays and mistakes along the way.

Naturally, a book can't prevent your partner from abandoning you. But the principles we will outline, if you live them, can keep you from separating from your core if your partner should leave— provided that until such time comes, you stay where you have pledged to stay, work as hard and creatively as you can, and be willing to start over as often as necessary.

There is a strong current of destiny running through every life. You, like all of us, are not where you are by accident. Before you make a life change, it is in your interest to communicate deeply with your quiet knowing. This place of stillness is so deep and so connected to reality that it can be safely called a part of God. Whether you choose this or another word, or no word at all, it remains in consciousness to guide and assure you, and it is never a mistake to draw any decision about your relationship from this peace.

Such an approach will obviously increase the chances of your having a permanent and satisfying relationship, but just as important, it will gradually transform *you*. And it will empower and define you far more than any ego-centered approach ever could. Just as turning against your partner will imprint your heart with a sense of failure and self-betrayal that is very hard to shake, so dedicating yourself to the good of your relationship will connect you more deeply with your intuition and your core and will point a path to a greater peace.

PART I

Separation Psychology and Other Indirect Influences to Break Up

THE CLOSING DECADES OF THE TWENTIETH CENTURY HAVE SEEN THE development of an entire psychological movement based on preserving separateness. In many ways, and possibly in all ways, separation psychology was well intentioned. Despite its broad misapplication of sound ideas, it enabled many people to make attitudinal gains that can be built upon in the twenty-first century. It is good that psychology, instead of merely classifying and theorizing about disorders, has been pushed into being more practical and is now concerned with real people and their problems. For example, almost any form of substance abuse can now be understood and handled, thanks in part to separation psychology. It is also good that we have been encouraged to recognize and develop our creative and spiritual potential and been shown ways to do this. It has been useful to see more clearly, through codependence theory, some of the patterns in which our own ego reactions call forth ego reactions in others, and how theirs affect ours. It is important that the danger of ignoring our needs has been pointed out. Certainly, it has been tremendously helpful that our attitudes toward our children have been more closely examined and that patience and compassion are now seen as effective parental tools and that fear and shame are recognized as ineffective ones. We are also more aware of the childhood antecedents of our problems and of the need to relinquish these obsolete lessons from the past. And perhaps most encouraging of all is the official recognition that we have a spiritual core and that this too must not be neglected. These are only a few of the gains brought about by separation psychology, and if the movement had been able to rest with these accomplishments, our relationships would be strong, our children would be cherished, and our individual potentials would be actualized.

However, it could not be more painfully clear that strong relationships are usually not the outcome when couples immerse themselves in the philosophy of this movement, become members of its groups, read its books, listen to its tapes, attend its workshops, and seek counsel from its therapists. Many individuals have been helped, but why have so many *relationships* been destroyed?

Obviously not all of the difficulties that relationships are currently experiencing can be laid at the feet of this one movement, and we will point out other contributing factors in the course of this book. But never in our work with couples in the last three decades have we witnessed such an across-the-board impact from a set of *ideas* as we have in the last several years. We have seen this coming since the 1960s, but in the eighties and early nineties it reached a peak that few could have imagined.

The problem that we have gotten ourselves into as a culture is that we are now oriented toward individual focus and accomplishment, to the exclusion of relationship focus and accomplishment. **Thinking in relationship** is a very different mental process from the need-centered process we have been teaching each other for the past several decades. And ironically, relationship thinking has the potential of meeting *individual* needs far more quickly than me-first thinking. We are now a people so consumed with fear and blame, so separate from each other, and so clearly unhappy, that you would think that the inadequacy of "the new selfishness" would be obvious to most people.

What we call in this book a **real relationship** is similar to a joint bank account into which money is given. The deposits are not lost or sacrificed. They remain in safekeeping. They even earn interest and grow. Likewise, a real relationship, being a mental account rather than a financial one, holds safe every act of generosity, every gentle laugh, every forbearance, every kindness, every understanding, every moment of peace—whether it is matched by one's partner or not. And this spiritual investment becomes our inheritance—provided we don't withdraw it and try to spend it on ourselves alone.

Unlike money, spiritual gifts can be spent only in relationship, in love. You simply can't think of yourself as an isolated, solitary body, whose thoughts affect no one but yourself, and still spend your spiritual capital. But if through a real relationship you have discovered that you are more than a body, the inner wealth to which you have been contributing will remain intact even if your partner leaves you. It is our hope, though, that this book will make leaving less likely.

To be happy, most of us now think we must focus on the small needy part of ourselves, the part that knows only **what it was not given, what it does not have, and what it must get now.** "If I don't think about me, who will?"—what a small lonely "me" that is! We forget how much more we are, but a real relationship can help us remember.

TWO

How to Swim Against the Tide

ARE YOU A PART OF THE GENERAL PICTURE?

today's tide of opinion   This is not an easy time to build a relationship. On all sides, people feel the need to contrast themselves, and especially their opinions, with everyone else. It's not having a deep belief, but a *different* belief, that is now important. Separation is strongly valued and universally practiced. Not only do most families have running battles within them, they also reverberate to the drumbeat of angry talking heads on television, the constant discord on radio talk shows, the war of words in newspapers and magazines, the battle over values between religious and political groups, men and women, blacks and whites, straights and gays, and the sickening average of fifty to a hundred armed conflicts raging at all times between or within nations. We live and move in a documentary of separateness.

Although at present this discord is particularly egregious, it is a very old and sad theme in human history. You can take steps to lessen its influence on your relationship, and we will be discussing a number of them, but as a couple you are never completely immune to this atmosphere. For this reason each of you must reach within for a different picture of reality from the one the world is continually holding up. The stillness of the spirit—where the fact of your oneness is still known—must be repeatedly touched so that a basis for healing other than mere opinion can be practiced.

Perhaps the strongest tide of opinion you will have to swim against in order to remain focused on the well-being of your relationship is separation psychology. In the last several years it has begun to be questioned, but those aspects of it that are particularly damaging to relationships are usually not the ones singled out for examination. The so-called "culture of victimhood" may indeed be worth looking at, but even more questionable is the assumption that to build and nourish your ego ("to individuate") leads to increased self-esteem, empowerment, and the capacity to form an intimate relationship; in short, that "you must love yourself before you can love another."

As a result of the remarkable dissemination and acceptance of this concept, not only are we looking at relationships in a one-dimensional way, we are also making unrealistic assumptions about what contributes to our growth as a person.

In a workshop we gave recently in Montana, a man whose wife was confined to a wheelchair said that he wanted to "check out" his attitude toward her. In the workshop we were demonstrating how you can work through issues even if your partner won't cooperate, and we had asked for volunteers. This man's wife was not in the workshop, and so we set up two empty chairs facing each other and invited the man to sit in one of them.*

Just as we were finishing our demonstration, a psychiatrist in the audience asked if she could work with the man for a moment. He agreed, and the woman came up and began using a therapeutic approach that encouraged him to admit his anger toward his wife. Seeing that the psychiatrist was not making much headway, a

---

* Our modification of the gestalt therapy technique is explained more fully in Chapter Nine, under "The Two- and Three-Chair Approach."

colleague of hers in the audience joined her. Switching now to another technique, they together tried to get the man to "vent his rage." They even asked him to shout out certain angry sentences to see "if they fit." Obviously they didn't, and finally they both gave up, declaring that the man had "deadened himself."

After the workshop, he came up to us and apologized for not having much anger at his wife. "I've spent years working through all of that, and I just don't have any real judgments of her anymore. I really love her." This was what he had tried to tell the two psychiatrists several times and what was clear to most of the audience, judging from what they said to us later. However, during their demonstration one of the psychiatrists had played the part of the man's wife, and when he had been instructed to confront her in anger, a number of people in the audience had shouted out such things as "Yeah, let her [his wife] have it!" "Tell her you resent all this shit you have to do!" "Yell at her!" "Tell her you hate her guts that she does nothing!"

In talking to some of these people afterward, it was clear that they didn't believe the man's basic peace; they thought it wasn't a healthy attitude for anyone to have in that kind of situation; and above all, they thought he was stuck, that he wasn't growing.

is power the source of fulfillment?   Whether the man was actually peaceful could be argued.* But whether peace is appropriate and whether love and acceptance lead to growth are fundamental questions that go to the heart of the new psychology. **Basic to the appeal of separation psychology is the assumption that separation gives you power, and that from power comes fulfillment.** Unquestionably some forms of distancing make you more powerful in the world. The most violent and sepa-

---

* The first psychiatrist later wrote us a letter of apology in which she said that she had misread the man because her husband had filed for divorce the day before the workshop and that she had projected her own anger onto the man.

rating news usually gets the highest ratings; the most ruthless child usually controls the playground; the angriest speaker usually motivates the crowd; the most adversarial radio and TV commentators are usually the most popular. We have heard several Little League coaches advise children to "get angry at the ball," and at times this has resulted in a more powerful swing. And perhaps everyone has been in a group in which just one silently judgmental person dominated the mood. At a party, for example, even though this person may say very little, everyone else tiptoes around him and the overall atmosphere is slightly depressed. To separate yourself from others can give you a certain power—certainly not spiritual power, but a force that can be easily recognized. But does it lead to fulfillment?

Concepts such as "you are ultimately alone," "only you can make yourself happy," "you have a right to the kind of life you want," "no one knows your dreams as well as you," "the right partner will share your interests, meet your needs, and grow at the same rate you grow," and in considering divorce, "what's best for you is best for the children," are not only inadequate to fulfill you when they are applied in the ways you will be urged to apply them; they will empty your heart and leave you at odds with all living things. The third verse of the *Isa Upanishad* reads,

> Those who misperceive their real natures are destined for worlds that are sunless and covered by a thick gloom.

You will be fulfilled by the gradual recognition that you are not alone, that you are capable of loving another as much as yourself, and that to give to those who are a part of your life is to receive immediately your own blessing.

This kind of fulfillment is difficult to describe because the ancient emphasis that has been placed on loving "thy neighbor as thyself" is now being misconstrued to mean that in the process of giving, we withhold from ourselves. But it does not follow that people who commit to loving another take inadequate care of themselves. Actually, they take better care, because now they value their body as the means or instrument that allows them to care for the other, as a mother in a distressed airplane breathes from her oxygen mask *so that* she can assist her child to breathe— even though she is more concerned for her child's life than for her own.

To those who are trying to make the transition from self-ness to one-ness, from ego to love, it can be said that whenever they extend love, they exercise their true nature and literally fulfill their identity. But of course those are just words. Until they *experience* what it's like to love another with all their heart and mind, the *descriptions* of what it's like may seem to be an insane call for self-immolation. But this is never the case. Without experience, however, it's difficult to grasp that in a real relationship—whether with your mate, child, parent, or friend—the experience of love is so important that not even the importance of your body can compare.

If we are going to quote the *Upanishads,* it's only right that we also quote Dave Barry.*

I can remember when there was nobody in my world as important to me as me. Oh, I loved other people—my wife, my family, my friends—and I would have been distraught if something had happened to them. But I knew I'd still be here. And that was the really important thing.

Rob changed that. Right at birth. . . . I can remember every detail of the time when, at 10 months, he got a bad fever, 106 degrees, his tiny body burning, and I carried him into the hospital, thinking . . . *please, give me this fever, take it out of this little boy and put it in me, please.*

---

* This is from a column that ran in our local paper, *The Arizona Daily Star,* July 5, 1993.

the ego's reaction to fear   The ideals of personal enhancement, personal definition, and personal empowerment are
merely a small part of a worldwide shift in attitudes. Perhaps at no
time in our history has humanity been more confused about the
actual nature of the self. Across the globe, instead of growing in
the awareness that we belong to a single world family, we are
identifying with ever smaller groupings and classifications. It's as
if we have come to believe that if we found our exact national,
racial, religious, or sexual niche, we would at last be real. The
bloody results of this ideal of exclusion demonstrate just how far
off the mark it is.

The great promise of our times, the savior to which so many
people now look to lessen fear and bring a little control back into
their lives, is selfishness. Naturally, it's not called "selfishness."
It's called "taking care of yourself"; "actualizing your potential"; "letting go of your need to give"; "doing what's best for
you"; "establishing your boundaries"; "nurturing—parenting—
protecting yourself"; "being yourself"; "not giving in"; "following your hopes—dreams—bliss—heart's desire"; and so on.
All of these concepts are good—*and* all of them are presently
being misused. So many of the couples we now work with express
their fear of giving as if it were a clear and present danger for
them personally. As a minister we know jokingly said, "I've never
actually met anyone who gave too much."

The ego's reaction to fear is always some form of withdrawal
into the smaller self. In marriage couples react by constricting
their giving, dividing their mind into "I am I and you are you,"
and placing their individual interests over the interests of their
partner. Thus the interests of the relationship are forgotten altogether. Looked at through the eyes of selfishness, there *is* no relationship, there is just me and not-me. Although the partnership
could benefit each partner enormously, it's not merely untried and
unexperienced, it's unseen. Only love can discern the bridge that
stretches between two hearts.

When the mind is afraid, it can't experience love, and this is why the present atmosphere is so disturbing to relationships. It's also why the solution, although difficult to achieve, is very direct. "There is no fear in love," wrote the apostle John. There can't be, "because fear involves punishment." The answer is therefore simple: "Perfect love casts out fear."

Love is not only our way out of fear, it is also our source of fulfillment. In this lovely passage John describes how we can reach that source:

Dear friends, let us love one another, because love is of God,
and everyone who loves is born of God, and knows God. But
the unloving know nothing of God, for God is love.

A real relationship, one in which two people love each other to fulfill themselves rather than withdraw from each other to fulfill themselves, is unquestionably a haven from fear—although it is not a protection from the world's dangers. It is a movable home, a place of peace, a true source of wholeness. Once it becomes the goal of any two people, it not only lasts but grows stronger and lovelier with every effort.

the mindset of betrayal

Each generation has sought control in different ways. For example, in the forties and fifties, it was generally believed that the way to make your life work was to "play by the rules"—in other words: stay married, work for the same company, attend your place of worship regularly, fight for your country when you were told to, and remain loyal to your alma mater and political party. The next generation tried to gain control by *not* playing by the rules. In the sixties and seventies it was widely believed that you could take possession of your life by freeing yourself from structure and making your own decisions. If your marriage wasn't satisfying, you got out of it; you didn't hesitate to change jobs; you felt free to question your country's political policies and moral values; and you made up your own mind about religion, what car to drive, how to dress, and what food and recreational drugs to put into your body.

No matter what time and place they live in, every couple is affected by the general mood of their country, the ideals in vogue, the social changes occurring worldwide, and the attitudes toward relationships most widely accepted. As we leave the twentieth century behind and begin the twenty-first, the atmosphere and conditions we find ourselves in are particularly hard on relationships.

Since the late sixties, the mindset of betrayal has been spreading through the industrialized world like an airborne virus. It has infected the relationships of singles and the marriages of all age groups. It will also have an effect on yours unless you take steps to protect it. If you are like most couples who get in trouble, you probably won't believe you are being influenced by the times. You will think that your urge to leave or to be unfaithful is based totally on your partner's personality and behavior and on your own unhampered free will. And if you act on it, perhaps only years later you may look back and ask, "What happened to us? Our problems weren't really that bad."

Many people who leave or are unfaithful experience the feeling that the divorce or affair took on a life of its own, while they stood by helplessly and watched the destruction of their relationship. It was as if all they had built were flattened by a road compacter that rolled out of nowhere. You don't want to reach that state of mind —and you don't have to.

We pick up the emotions and values that surround us and, to a greater or lesser degree, feel them as if they were our own. This is why it is crucial that we know ourselves deeply. In order to see through what is happening, a couple must either be centered in their own being, or they must have a shared approach that automatically protects them.

The essential first step is to say to each other, "I will never leave you. I will never threaten to leave you. And if even the thought of leaving takes root in my mind, I will use whatever means necessary to eradicate it. And no matter how often it recurs, I will return my mind to my single purpose in this relationship. The insanity of casting aside lives, breaking up homes, and betraying children will end with us.''

THE POWER OF CHOICE

As a boy who increasingly shuttled between parents and stepparents, Hugh was repeatedly beaten, and he saw his mother repeatedly beaten. In the early stages of our marriage, he would sometimes hit Gayle or swat one of the boys. This behavior would come on him suddenly. An instant before, he would not know that he was going to strike someone. It took several years and, what was for him, an extraordinary effort to change. But he did change. What he learned as a result was that anyone can make a decision so deeply that it becomes impossible for that individual to repeat the old behavior. We made a commitment never to leave each other that was as deep as Hugh's decision never to hurt his family again. Divorce or abuse has been unthinkable for us ever since. Any husband or wife has the freedom to make the same decision.

A close friend of ours made a similar commitment to her adopted son. He is one of those children presently being classified as having ''attachment disorder.'' His biological mother was an alcoholic, and he was sexually and physically abused by his father. At age three he was taken from his parents and placed in his first foster home. Our friend's was the fifth home he was moved to in three years.

During the adoption proceedings the judge asked our friend, ''Do you understand that adopting this child means that from this time on, he will be your son as if he were born to you?'' She said that she understood, and she swore to the judge and to the boy that she would never abandon him. She has kept her word, even though she now knows that the child may never be able to form a trusting relationship with anyone. She also knows that if there is any chance that he will, it must first be with her.

Why would anyone undertake such a task? Surely as a young girl this is not what our friend dreamed of spending her time doing someday. The boy was not related to her; he simply came to her attention. Knowing that she had previously adopted a child and therefore had an open mind to adoption, the boy's case worker called and told her his story.

Upon hearing it, our friend realized that what was happening to him had to be stopped. And she was there. Somebody had to commit to this boy. And she was there. She didn't take the phone call as a sign or as some mystical indicator of how she was to decide, but neither did she dismiss as mere coincidence that this child was brought to her attention. Likewise, we don't find ourselves where we are by accident, and declining to help those we can help should not be done lightly.

So far our friend's story doesn't have a fairy-tale ending. In fact, hers is a situation in which she has given much but has gotten little in return. Five years after he was adopted, not only does this child still not trust his new mother, he has done things that most other parents would find intolerable. He has punched holes in the walls, turned on the gas, broken windows, set fires, and threatened his mother with a knife. Our friend has had a long and successful career in teaching and counseling children in a variety of settings, but her firmness and love, as well as her considerable knowledge of childhood behavior, have so far brought about very little change. Even the experts in this field who have advised her have not yet been able to get a breakthrough. Friends and relatives have suggested that she "take the boy back," but this she will never do.

Perhaps you have seen or can imagine the deep strength that taking a stand such as this can bring. Our friend possesses the kind of integrity that comes only when one is deeply rooted in one's soul. Please compare this strength to the effects you have already seen on those you know who have discarded their spouse, or the children in their care, for far lesser cause.

There are no sinners here. We are speaking merely of whether it is good for you to resist or to be swept up in the present insanity. The simple fact is that it's not good for you to abandon your spouse. Each time you break a sacred commitment, the light in your soul dims. That is observable. Those who have discarded one relationship after another are usually a shell of what they once were. You can come back from this mistaken approach, but the effort required is greater than is imagined.

BEING LEFT

In most cases you can't stop someone from leaving you, but you don't have to participate in the mistake. This implies no particular behavior, such as court battles, pleading, threats, or frequent overtures. It doesn't even imply that you must resist the divorce. It means simply that in your heart you don't turn against this person. That much you can do. A divorce will not damage you permanently if you continue to bless this one in your mind. Blessing your partner does not require you to fulfill any particular picture. You don't have to *look* forgiving by having visits or phone conversations or agreeing to unreasonable demands. The essential action is unseen and in your heart.

Unfortunately, the usual pattern is for individuals to attempt to break the bond through blame and anger. They build a case against their former partner in order to justify what happened, and they try to wipe away their own misgivings through attack. This is a highly flawed approach. Not only does it split children's minds, if children are involved; it actually binds you to whatever mistakes you may have made, and it virtually assures that you will repeat them. Whenever you step away from someone physically, you must step forward mentally.

The loss that one feels from a divorce is very similar to the loss one feels from a death—so similar, in fact, that there was a period when we allowed people who had been left to sit in on our grief support group. To be left by someone who you believed loved you and would be with you always is deeply wounding. As with a severe physical wound, you may need to be very accepting of how long it takes your heart to heal and for the symptoms of loss you experience to fade away. If you do not turn to judgment and revenge as a way of lessening your pain, you *will* heal. But if you become bitter, you can easily carry the effects of what happened to you to your grave.

Almost fifty years after Hugh's father filed for divorce, Hugh's mother would still become upset and judgmental if his father came up in conversation. As well as being a running unhappiness, her anger also prevented her from forgiving herself for not having sought custody of Hugh. Censure simply can't heal the wounds of the past.

You don't have to understand why your partner betrayed you—in fact, it's best not to decide *anything* about your partner. But you do have to decide that all living things are in God's hands—or at least, not in yours—and free your mind from useless battles.

FEAR OF RELATIONSHIP

During the seventies and eighties, as crisis intervention counselors and as ministers, we married couples, ran groups for couples, counseled couples individually, and gave workshops on relationships throughout the country. Our children always traveled with us, but they eventually reached an age when they had lives of their own and wanted to stay at home. Traveling without them was difficult and dangerous, and so we suspended most of these activities, and we didn't resume them until a few years ago.

Immediately we were struck by the changes in attitudes that had occurred while we had been away. Not only were the types of fears people expressed different, but the degree of fear had dramatically increased. Although we were working with a good cross-section of couples, we decided to talk to other therapists to see if they were experiencing the same phenomenon. We questioned counselors, clergy, psychologists, and psychiatrists and discovered that their experience was surprisingly similar to our own. We decided to restructure our groups to accommodate this new mindset and began taking notes for this book.

If a real relationship is to be formed, it's necessary to move past fear—fear of psychoanalytical, therapeutic, or recovery-based classifications, fear of failure, fear of influences from the past, fear of loss of power, fear of having chosen the wrong mate, fear of falling back into old patterns, fear of losing your identity, fear of devotion and sacrifice—into the deep and empowering experience of union with another. A real relationship is an absolutely reliable source of happiness and comfort, but few couples have one. It can be attained by virtually any two who are willing to make a sustained effort, such as they might in getting back in shape, or completing an advanced degree, or regaining their health after an operation, or learning the fundamentals of a new profession. If the average golfer would spend the time, study, and concentration on his marriage that he does on perfecting his golf swing, success would be unavoidable.

Why aren't we willing to give a comparable effort to marriage? It's not that we lack courage. Nor do we lack endurance. We are capable of making enormous sacrifices for ourselves alone. Since the surgeon general's first warning in 1964, more than 30 million Americans have given up smoking, *most after repeated failures.* Nicotine is an addiction that many experts consider harder to break than heroin addiction. We undergo various extremely painful, expensive, and dangerous plastic surgeries. We spend years forcing ourselves into a new way of eating. We will endure fatigue and pain daily in weight rooms trying to change the shape of our bodies. We will deprive ourselves of almost anything—provided it's for our exclusive benefit. Yet to make even a small sacrifice for our partner can grate on us for years as a gross unfairness.

Many people speaking and writing on relationships today strongly encourage this whining and giving up, whining and giving up, over and over, until finally we have before us an entire generation of people who will go to their deaths loveless and alone, never having known what real commitment was and taking no comforting presence with them.

Don't allow fear to blur your purpose or dilute your efforts. Acknowledge the fear—whatever it may be—but continue to build the love between you, even if you are doing all the work yourself —which every spouse in every marriage will be called upon to do from time to time. It doesn't matter so much *what* you try as that you keep trying. If something doesn't work, wait and then try another approach. Your objective is not to receive good marks from those who think they know what is therapeutically correct. When Gayle stood by Hugh while he had one affair after another, many of her friends thought that she was weak and despicable. Hugh even looked down on her for loving him. But she was clear within herself that she did love him, that she had seen his potential, and that while she waited for him to come to his senses, she could use the time very effectively to work on her own strength and peace.

Happiness is not actually dependent on how other people behave.

Marriages go through stages; people shift gears and change; mistakes are a part of growth. Gayle understood all of this—at least well enough not to focus on Hugh's antics. Friends stand by friends. Friends stand by friends even when they are making mistakes. This is the key to both love and healing.

RELATIONSHIP: THE NEW REALITY

It is a long-cherished belief that love is more likely to lead you into a bad union—and to keep you there—than is anxiety. In other words, "love is blind," and fear is the friendly emotion that will protect you from it. In truth, the committed are better able to see a relationship, to evaluate its dynamics, and to know if the time has come to step away from it. Contrary to what is commonly believed, commitment does not cause one to remain doggedly in a mistake. Moreover, the mistake most people stay stuck in is not the relationship, but their attitude toward it.

This same principle applies to relationships of all kinds. It holds true even to one's body. It could never be a mistake that we have a relationship with our body, yet our attitude toward that relationship can and often is mistaken. Those who stand in judgment of their body usually do not, for example, understand the function of food: that it's there to nourish the body, not to reward, punish, or excite it, that it's one of many ways to express love and caring, just as sex is in a marriage. But since they don't love their body (and note that a body that is not considered beautiful, just like a child who is not, *can* be loved), they are always analyzing and comparing it—it never looks right, feels right, impresses others as it should, has the energy it should, or stays as healthy as it should. Because they disapprove of it, they can't *see* it. Their body is wonderful in many ways, yet they are literally unaware of its attributes. If their body becomes sick, they don't see clearly how to care for it and will often neglect doing the very thing that would help it most, because they unconsciously believe that it deserves what it gets. Whatever it may be—our car, our house, our child, our body, our spouse—unless we identify with it, we can't fully see it. Acknowledging our oneness, even our oneness with our questionable creations, increases vision. When a child identifies with a doll, the doll is better cared for.

Those who distance themselves from their partners are as blind as those who distance themselves from their bodies and are prone to do the things least conducive to their own happiness. If, for example, a couple is having an argument in front of a therapy group, many of the other participants will instantly spot the mistake in communication that the couple is making but is too blind to see. They may be so blind, in fact, that sometimes they still can't see it even after it has been pointed out by the other group members.

If the actual choice were between your needs and your partner's, the current approach to relationships would be reasonable. But since a relationship is a third reality that encompasses both of you, it has more power to make you happy than either your or your partner's reality alone. Whoever decides to give to it will receive a rich return, even if for a time the other person is unable to.

There is no private growth. It can't be targeted like an isolated set of muscles in one area of the body. What "grows" is not a single set of ego needs but our awareness of the spirit. And the spirits of all living things connect and are one. That can be felt if not seen. Growth simply can't occur on the level of separated individuals.

We have a friend whose life work is caring for people with multiple disabilities. For the past three years she has had the same six clients under her care. All of them would have to be institutionalized if it were not for the individual attention that she and the small staff she is a part of give. Most of them require "total care": They can't walk, bathe themselves, feed themselves, or carry on a conversation. One man has extreme scoliosis, cerebral palsy, and severe Down's syndrome. He laughed last week for the first time in his adult life. Another man has a progressive seizure disorder. He has had as many as ninety grand mal seizures a day and always has at least five to ten. He also has a bad temper.

Our friend, who has no other income, makes less than a starting schoolteacher, and yet she has found this work deeply rewarding.

It's not a status job, because very few people even know about her work. She receives no job security; her hours are difficult; and all her clients are dysfunctional, needy, uncommunicative, ungrateful, and physically unattractive. They are unable to further her political aims or express her religious beliefs. They are unable to participate in any of the sports or entertainments she loves. And obviously they could never be expected to fulfill her sexually. Today, any one of these privations, or any number of others, would be considered ample justification for leaving:

And yet she "gets her needs met." How? By devoting herself to the *relationship* she has with each of them. This job does not allow her much free time. As she told us, "I don't have a whole lot else going on in my life." Yet she remains unaffected by the popular calls to her ego: "What is your dream?" "What is it you have never done?" "You don't have to settle for this." "You can have it all!" Oddly, she doesn't want it all. She is content with her mute, deaf, twisted, incontinent clients. Admittedly, she is an extreme example, but she is mentally and physically healthy. She is a normal person. And although her work is not a marriage, the principle is the same for you and me.

Conversely, we also know a man who left his wife because she had a leg amputated. She was young, attractive, funny, intelligent, an exceptionally good mother to his two daughters from a previous marriage, and very much in love with him. He said, "All I have been dealing with for a year now is this leg thing. I need a life of my own." He had unthinkingly become part of the general picture, and most of his friends sympathized with his very common mistake in attitude.

A relationship exists independently of the egos or bodies involved. This is not a supernatural concept. It can be seen clearly in common, everyday life. For example, an infant cannot give—in the terms that the ego defines giving. It does not know that it has a relationship with its mother, in the terms that the ego defines knowing. It may not even *recognize* its mother. And yet there *is* a relationship, and the more the mother gives to it, the more the relationship embraces her in beauty. Those who care for the very old or the dying also know the benefits that can come to one who gives to a relationship in which the other party does not contribute —once again, in the terms that the ego defines contributing.

We live in Arizona, and in our house we have a large empty aquarium that our boys use to observe creatures from the desert before letting them go. When Jordan was eight, we retrieved a five-foot gopher snake from where it was sunning itself across our neighbors' front door stoop. Three days later, we told Jordan that the time had come to let it go. This was on a Thursday and he said that he wanted to keep it until the following Tuesday, the day kids could bring interesting things to class. We told him that the snake would have to be fed live rats, and we didn't want to do that. In fact, we said we *wouldn't* do that!

That afternoon, when we were at the pet store to buy "just one rat," Jordan saw how cute they were and said, "If we let the snake go, can I keep the rat?" At that time Jordan was allergic to anything with fur, but the store owner assured us that being small, it didn't have much fur. He also said he could guarantee that no feeder rat would live over three years. So we paid the two dollars and brought "Ratty" home. In the next few months we met a surprising number of rat lovers. Aside from the fact that they all seemed to have reached further into their minds for a name, their rats did not appear to be superior to ours.

Just like these people, Jordan loved his rat. Hardly a day went by that he didn't call us in to see some wonderful new expression on Ratty's face (ears up, ears down, eyes open, eyes closed) or some hilarious behavior (Ratty sleeping on his left side, Ratty sleeping on his right side, Ratty sleeping on his stomach, or— Jordan's favorite—Ratty looking up when the glass is tapped). Countless times he asked us which part of Ratty's body we liked the most. We couldn't just name one but had to make a case for it. ("I like his feet." "Why?" "Uh, because they're pink." "What about the nails?'' ''Yes, his feet have nails.'' ''They're pretty long.'' ''Yes.'' ''They're pretty sharp too.'' ''Yes, they are.'' ''What do you like best about his nails?'' ''They're clean.'' ''Look, you can see through them.'' ''I'll take your word for it.'')

If you let them crawl on you, feeder rats will chew holes in your clothes. If you let them sit beside you while you watch TV, they will chew holes in the couch—no matter how much it cost. They never put the toilet seat down; in fact, they never use the toilet. They are not loyal. They have no table manners. They will not meditate with you. They are not enthusiastic about your friends. They are classic enablers that demand you give to them but never give back. And if a feeder rat grows to love you, it will pee on you to mark its territory.

If people can love a feeder rat, you can love your spouse.

THREE
Beyond I, Me, and Mine

REACHING THE SELF
THAT CAN JOIN

our imaginary identity   To gain a little perspective, let's examine what the self is and what it is not. If we are going to define ourselves and withdraw into what we have described, we should at least be clear about the nature of what we are choosing. There was a time when a degree of uncertainty, and therefore openness, was generated by the questions: Who am I? What am I? Where am I going? Within separation psychology, the answers to these questions are often petty and temporal. Lip service is given to the spiritual, but the characteristics and limitations of the non-spiritual are applied to one's needs, and the terms spirit and soul are used mainly to indicate how deeply one can be wounded.

Surely all individuals have a moment in which they sense that there is something more to them than ego identity, and yet what but the ego feels the need of private fulfillment, of personal empowerment, of individuation, of separate rights? What but an ego could engage in domestic turf wars and cherish an opinion over goodwill? Naturally this does not mean that we put off healing our bodies and psyches. But healing ourselves is an act of generosity, not of selfishness. It was only when an alcoholic friend of ours was confronted by seven of his friends—who, in turn, each related instances of how his drinking had hurt them—that he turned his life around. If Hugh's mother could have foreseen the extreme suffering that her death would cause his stepfather, she probably would have given up the smoking that she knew was killing her. And if Hugh could have felt the pain and humiliation that his affairs were causing Gayle—something he did feel acutely later in life—he would not have thought of them as "my own business." **Healing is the recognition that we never suffer alone.**

As we have discussed in other books, the ego is an imaginary identity, very much like the imaginary friend that many people have in childhood. This playmate is entirely a projection of the child's mind, but to the child it is real and autonomous. It has a body, a name, a personality, and a history that is different from the child's. It says things that surprise the child, even though the child's mind is producing the words. It has needs and makes demands. And most important, once it has been established, it defends itself. For example, it might warn the child not to get too close to another child who is becoming friendly, because it knows that real companionship will dim its aura of reality.

Likewise, the ego is a false sense of identity, of something separate and apart from all other living things. It is formed primarily in childhood and has "a mind of its own"—its own thoughts, needs, emotions, and beliefs. It seems autonomous and real. It seems worth protecting. In fact, if we think there is nothing more to us, it feels like self-destruction *not* to be defensive. And yet it's composed entirely of the past. It is what the world, in a thousand conflicted ways, has instructed us to feel and think, and the current circumstances, whatever they may be, must be interpreted rather than seen in order to sustain what we have learned. **The ego is a body of lessons, none of which quite fits the present situation.** But it *is* an identity and operates as *our* identity —until we begin to sense something about ourselves that is deeper and more consistent. This is often a long process, and while it is under way, our ego needs must be dealt with. If the nature of a need has not been clearly seen, it will still seem to be desirable, and ignoring it merely builds up pressure. However, a need can be met in many ways and does not have to be satisfied in the old destructive way that we may be used to. For example, on one level, Hugh's affairs were a "need" to run from a barren inner life, but clearly there are less destructive ways to withdraw from the emotions caused by an impoverished attitude toward life.

During a meditation, after a near-death experience, while giving birth to a child, at the depths of severe suffering, or in the presence of love, we may notice a new set of feelings and thoughts, new in the sense that we discover them, yet ancient and familiar, and immediately recognizable as our own. These are the thoughts we think with God, the thoughts we all share in stillness, regardless of our religious beliefs. They are far, far more than an inner child or a former place of innocence. Once we experience our real feelings and think our real thoughts, we know, in that instant, that we no longer need to fear love.

And yet that instant can, and usually does, pass quickly. Our imaginary identity, like an imaginary friend, will defend its place in our mind, because it was set up by our mind to do so. However, to fight it back or become fearful of it is always a mistake. Children who fight their imagined playmates merely make them more real, more autonomous. When adults fight their egos, they push that part of their minds away from them, thereby making it less accessible to awareness and healing.

the key to recovery   For most people, giving is not a happy thought. It spells boredom, unfairness, sacrifice, loneliness, and loss of self. In the last few decades, the term *caregiver* has become synonymous in some people's minds with a person who is emotionally damaged and neurotically dependent. And yet for thousands of years it has been said that giving will heal you. This is a theme in almost every major religion and mystical philosophy. Why, then, do so few believe it?

One answer lies in the mental picture most people carry of what giving looks like. For example, when we speak in this book of devotion, many readers will think this a call for them to spend their lives on their knees in drudgery, or never to have an opinion, never to get angry, never to let their needs be known, never to give themselves a reward. But of course the giving that heals does not require *any* specific behavior. It is a deep inner healing, a healing of the soul, and not a rearrangement of external circumstances. To give is merely to be open and generous and to insist that your mind remember the seed of innocence within your mate whenever she or he forgets.

As we said earlier, to be happy, most people think they must focus on the small needy part of themselves—the part that knows only what it was not given, what it does not have, and what it must get now. Ironically, we often justify this narrow-mindedness as a key to improving our marriages and families: "A better me makes a better us." "If it's good for me, it can't be bad for you." "If it's best for us, it's best for the children." These statements are true, but not in the way they are usually meant.

What has not been clearly seen by many people who have looked at the dynamics of the recovery process—but who have not been through it themselves—is that joining, not separation, brings about healing. For example, it may be necessary for individuals trying to overcome alcohol or drug addiction to concentrate on that one problem—and to put themselves in a situation where they *can* concentrate. For a time, they may have to separate physically from their family and friends and enter a treatment center. But what happens at the treatment center? There they are required to relate to others in a healthy manner as an essential part of the healing process.

We had been married about ten years when Hugh's mother, after thirty years of alcoholism, entered treatment in Minnesota.

Until then, she had never before cleaned a toilet, made a bed, set a table, or mopped a floor—for a stranger. Yet when she got out, her belief was that doing these selfless chores had transformed her—and indeed, she remained free thereafter.

Not all treatment centers require the amount of menial labor this one did, but all the ones we are familiar with require some form of self-discipline and—more to the point—open, honest, and fair interaction with the other patients in recovery. They also require some form of acknowledgment of and cooperation with others.

Treatment centers are not "fun." They are not places of excess and self-indulgence. Rather, they are places of concentration, hard work, and triumph. It's true that people who put themselves into a recovery program are "taking care of themselves," but not in the insensitive and self-gratifying way that that phrase is presently being interpreted. Self-love is an oxymoron, unless the "self" is spiritual.

Every form of spiritual growth—which means realization of oneness—is brought about through an increased awareness of our effect on others. Addiction is not healed through pampering the bodily self. It may look that way, but it's not what happens. And likewise, a great love relationship is not built through "taking care of myself first." A relationship is in reality a child or creation of two people. Perhaps in your own life, if you look around at how children in other families are being treated, it may be obvious to you that those mothers or fathers who say, with considerable pretense, that they must put their own growth first, usually do not bless their child or their spouse in the process. Even those couples who put their interests over those of their children in selecting a place to live usually do not make either themselves or their children happier. Why? Because happiness is undivided, and any attempt to portion it out will always be distressing.

Thoughts such as "If I'm not any good to myself, how can I be any good to you?" or "I must love me before I can love you" or

"If I'm not growing in this relationship, you're not growing either" fail to grasp the true nature of strength, growth, and love. On one level, all of these statements are true—which shows how words of truth can be perverted. But in the way they are used today, they really mean, "If I always gratify my urges first, this will somehow end up blessing you."

releasing the imagined self   The experience of real companionship lessens a child's dependence on imaginary companionship, and repeated doses of love and sanity slowly lessen our fear of relinquishing a false sense of self. A child may feel a "need" for a fantasy relationship, but a real friendship begins to dissolve this form of fear. Familiarity with your self likewise dissolves the need to defend the ego and its many stances. Your ego can't join with your partner in a living relationship because it is a separate and separating set of opinions and reactions culled from your past. To the degree you are ego oriented, you will feel misunderstood and alone. A real relationship, however, will weaken the ego's overall grip on your mind.

Our received identity is not our real identity, and yet we cling desperately to this puny sense of self because we think it's all we have. What else can we believe but that it's also all our partner has? A thousand times a day, turn to the stillness of your heart and learn why you no longer need to be afraid. There is a part of you that is deeply connected to life and to each other. It always has been and always will be. It knows you well, so well that it never identifies you with your past. When it's only the smallness that you can see in each other, turn to stillness for another way of looking.

Never grow tired of the effort to know who your partner is, for in this knowledge you will come to know your self and attain true power. Anything that empowers you—for yourself and by yourself *alone*—can only make you lonely, and ultimately bitter. Although this will leave your ego intact, whatever sense of strength might accompany this victory is a fantasy that others will not share with any real joy.

No one can have the experience of being one with another merely by being told what to believe, however noble the beliefs. Beliefs are not experience and words are not God. The first line in the *Tao Te Ching* is "That which can be spoken is not the Tao." And Saint Paul wrote, "The letter kills, but the Spirit gives life." The part of us that touches God, we must touch, and this takes a deliberate and repeated effort. Never grow tired of this effort. Each day we have a thousand opportunities to choose a gentle vision, to be human rather than right, to understand rather than attack, to be strong rather than destructive. Every little event offers us a chance to decide with the better part of ourselves, and each decision we make draws the world closer or adds to its division. The family of man is trying to awaken to its oneness, but it has been in a nightmare of dissension for a very long time.

BECOMING A SEX—BECOMING A PERSON

two movements, one direction   An example of separation psychology's ego-enhancing effect—and its subsequent impact on relationships—is the retreat into the sexes that we have been witnessing since the sixties. We are now taught to think of ourselves first as a gender and second as a human being. On one hand we have biological attraction compelling people of opposite sexes to come together (and if it's *not* what brings them together, their relationship is described as flawed), and on the other hand we have an almost insurmountable set of gender differences keeping them from complete union once they do join. Within the new psychology, all Nature seems to be doing is forcing natural enemies into conflict.

Both the men's movement and especially the women's movement have made enormous contributions by uncovering destructive dynamics and bringing about needed social, economic, and political change. But no movement is immune to the philosophy of the times, and this can be seen in the distracting overemphasis in both movements on the need to attain positions of personal advantage.

Some authorities on women's issues seem to imply that because of the dynamics that must necessarily form between women and men, every woman is at risk of losing power and individuation in a caring relationship with a man. And some authorities on male issues appear to be saying that when a man becomes bonded with a woman, he is in danger of reestablishing maternal ties that manhood should have severed. There is very little difference between being kidded by the boys that you are "hen-pecked" or "pussy-whipped," or being told by a workshop leader that you have reestablished maternal ties. There is also scarcely more insight in being classified as an "obsessed caregiver" or a "compulsive rescuer" than as a menial, a doormat, or a drudge. All of these are shameful ways of thinking of oneself and are not inspired by love.

Obviously this does not mean that you should remain fearful or intimidated within a relationship or that you should join with your partner in activities or attitudes that are destructive to yourself or others. However, divorce is not the only solution to conflicts between the sexes. There are ways for us to solve our problems and still remain decent human beings. But the belief that withdrawal from a challenging relationship is virtuous self-affirmation has devastated our society.

In the latter half of the twentieth century, children have gone from an 80 percent chance of growing up in an intact family to less than a 50 percent chance. Think what this means. Now most kids born today watch their mom and dad fight until they turn against each other completely; see the divorce; live in a single-parent home; and witness ongoing struggles over visitation, child support, and other issues concerning them. And many of these kids live in a house with their single parent and his or her lover or series of lovers; see the lover, with whom they have become bonded, leave; witness the remarriage of one or both of their parents; live in a stepparent family or shuttle between two stepparent families; see their parents' affection and time divided between them and the new children; witness the breakup of one or both of their stepparent families—because divorce is now even more likely—and end up programmed to treat other people the way they have been treated.

Surely the major cause of this misery is not poor communication between the sexes.

is miscommunication a cause?*

A few days ago one of the boys was playing a computer quiz game and yelled out to Gayle,

"Flakes in hair!"

"Dandruff!" she yelled back.

"Are you sure? I've got to get this one to go to the next level."

"Positive!" she said.

He did not make it to the next level.

"You were wrong! The answer was 'blond'!"

Blond? Maybe the dandruff came from blonds overdyeing their hair.

No. He merely had been reading a term he was seeing for the first time: *flaxen hair.*

Of course differences in gender, background—and age—can result in occasional misunderstandings, but in our opinion this has very little to do with the causes of poor communication. If as a *people* we could focus our life purpose beyond our sexual identities and all the other small categories that we fit into, and begin to

---

* Also see "Are Disclosures Communication?" and "What Is Communication For?" in Chapter Seven, and "Is Confession Necessary Communication?" "Is Confession Honest Communication?" and "Is Confession Ever Appropriate?" in Chapter Nine.

"honor and preserve" what joins us rather than what makes us different, communication would no longer be the minefield of misunderstandings that we have come to believe it is. And we do believe this. We actually tell the people conducting surveys that the number-one cause of our divorces is that "we had problems communicating."

Those who have not been successful at relationships rarely understand why, and certainly "problems communicating" are not the cause, because they are always a symptom. Minds are joined, and if you want to understand what your partner just said, you can understand it.

During the honeymoon stage, partners have little trouble knowing what each other means. Once they begin to pull back into their separate interests, suddenly their sexual or religious or ethnic or family differences seem to make them miscommunicate. After helping couples talk things out for over a quarter of a century—couples of mixed race, mixed belief, mixed nationality, mixed sex, and same sex—there is no question in our minds about why partners don't understand each other. They don't *want* to. When they *do* want to, they understand. We have seen people who could neither hear nor speak understand each other. We have seen people who didn't know each other's language understand each other. We have seen humans understand animals. And certainly there are teachers and parents who understand children—and what a world of difference there *is* between them!

One danger in steeping yourself in sexual-differences theory is that you might identify your partner with his or her ego even more strongly than you do now. This is not automatic, but frequently it is the outcome. Your goal as a couple is to feel your oneness. Oneness will bring you everything you have ever really wanted. It will bring you home. But make no mistake, a purely analytical approach can get in the way of this process. Anything you use to stand back and look at this person as if she or he were a different species or life-form is not helpful. Your partner is a person, a spirit, a life, a being, a part of God. You have *everything* in common with what your partner actually is.

The spiritual healer Hugh went to as a boy, and who healed him of a broken leg on two occasions, with X-rays taken before and after in both instances, healed him while saying this prayer:

> *I am one with Thee,*
> *Oh Thou infinite One.*
> *I am where Thou art.*
> *I am what Thou art.*
> *I am because Thou art.*

Clearly those words reflected the experience of oneness the healer had when she closed her eyes. If someone can unite with *God,* obviously any individual can unite with another child of God.

The sixth verse of the *Isa Upanishad* reads:

> The one who sees the self in all living things, and all living
> things in the self, will not know how to withdraw.

Yet very few people, especially when they are depressed, unhappy, or angry, want any part of oneness. What they *think* they want is more separateness. And one sure way of getting it is to misunderstand. Even little misunderstandings will do:

> "Why did you put that new blue towel in with the yellow ones?"
> "I thought you said all the towels could be washed together."
> "No, that's not what I said."

> "I can't find the salad spinner."
> "How many times do I have to tell you where I put it?"

> "How do you work the plunger?"
> "We've been through this before. You just stick it in and push."

"But I thought you liked tuna casserole?"
"I've told you a thousand times I don't like it."

In each of these examples, the other partner didn't understand because he or she didn't want to. The husband didn't think he should have to be doing laundry, the wife didn't think she should be the one to unstop the toilet, and so forth. But even when the communication is crucial, if people don't want to understand, they won't. A husband having an affair doesn't want to understand his wife's pain—he wants the affair to continue—so of course he misunderstands what she is saying. But neither does she understand if she is the one having the affair.

separate but united?   Through the years, many factors have been blamed for the way married partners treat each other; now we are blaming our sexual differences. We aren't responsible for the home atmosphere our children are forced to grow up in; our sexual differences are responsible. The basic female and male personalities unquestionably differ, but the question then becomes in what ways you and your partner deviate from these types, and how every conversation can be worded to avoid not only the typical misunderstandings between the sexes but also the various ways you are each unlike your own sex. Many couples, after reading several conflicting books or articles on this subject, understandably throw up their hands and say that it's just too much to expect anyone to sort all of this out: "Life's too short. For years I've been trying to empathize with everyone else. Now they can just be a little understanding of me."

To be bound and powerless, not to mention getting a fuzzy identity, is supposedly the primary risk in forming a relationship. As the song says, "I could do anything I wanted to if I could stop loving you." One of the assumptions this reasoning is based on is that we are first a sex and second a person. Needless to say, some of the voices now being heard are adding to this confusion of identity by placing more importance on our male and female differences than on our basic humanity. If the dichotomy were as deep and absolute as these authorities are stating, true oneness would be not only an impractical goal but an impossibility. So extreme are the lines sometimes being drawn that the logical conclusion would be for everyone to have same-sex relationships.

We have counseled and performed marriage services for gay and lesbian couples and have counseled many we have not married. Like most families, we also have close relatives who are homosexual. We have yet to know any same-sex couples who could communicate more easily than opposite-sex couples. In fact, we have found that the *exact* same dynamics hinder homosexual couples that hinder straight couples, including even physical abuse, which exists in both gay and lesbian relationships.

Another interesting phenomenon, one we have also experienced ourselves, occurs when a man or woman differs from some aspect of the gender "norm." Frequently this person ends up with a partner who also differs in that same area. For instance, Gayle grew up with a passionate love of baseball and football. She is an avid reader of *Sports Illustrated* and the sports page of the local newspaper. She played baseball and touch football every chance she got, and she never complained when boyfriends wanted to watch some game on television, because she too was interested. And yet she felt that she had married the one Texas male who reached adulthood thinking that Minnie Minoso was a Disney character and who was sweetly philosophical after the Cowboys lost to the Steelers in the closing minutes of the 1979 Super Bowl.

In couples groups, one of the major complaints women have against their partners is the male's unwillingness to discuss the state of the relationship. However, it's not uncommon for a male to make this same complaint against his female partner. Yet inevitably he will think that he has managed to choose the one woman on earth who dislikes these discussions and has difficulty expressing her feelings. We have noticed that the same pattern of complementing opposites holds true in gay and lesbian relationships as well. The gender differences that men and women are now citing as grievances against each other are in reality no more than the natural balance that is discerned and chosen by two who belong together.

Danny, a gifted athlete who is a friend of Jordan's, does not have parents who exhibit this balance, especially in the area of competitive sports. He is an excellent pitcher and hitter for his Little League team and is an equally talented forward in basketball. Both his mother and father put tremendous pressure on him to excel in these sports and even though he greatly prefers basketball to baseball, they make him participate in both. Over the years, he has slowly lost his enjoyment of *playing* the *games* of baseball and basketball. He becomes angry when someone on his team makes a mistake; he argues with umpires and referees; he frequently fouls out in basketball; he throws his helmet when he strikes out in baseball; and above all, he cannot tolerate losing. Nor can his mother and father. We have seen both of them berate him for mistakes on the field and on the court. One parent does not provide a balance to the other, and Danny is the victim.

Any child may be unreasonably pressured by one parent to perform athletically, academically, or socially, but it's only when the other parent joins in that lasting damage can be done. Even if one parent is basically silent in his or her disagreement with the pressure, the child will still sense an alternative attitude and will benefit.

All egos are different. Male and female egos are not somehow more different. And contrary to present attitudes, female egos are not better than male egos, and their interests are not more spiritual. Two screamers are no better off than a screamer and a pouter. Be careful not to slip into the prevailing trap of using what you know about the opposite sex as ammunition against your partner. "You're just like all men—your truck is more important than I am.'' or "Why do women always want to turn everything into a major crisis?''

No teaching that makes you worry about the limits of your ability to communicate or that adds to your sense of isolation—no matter how stirring the call to autonomy—will lead you to the kind of relationship you want. If, however, the authority you are consulting is pointing out typical differences between men and women in order to give you a way of understanding and forgiving them, this can be very helpful.

If you can see that a given attitude—say, for example, the woman's willingness to ask for directions as opposed to the man's inclination to find the way by himself—is not a personal attack but an outcome of conditioning, you will not be as quick to become defensive. Studying female and male differences from this standpoint is useful, provided that you do not judge one sex superior to the other and that you keep in mind that no one shares all of the attitudes common to his or her sex and that some people share very few. This type of study should be approached with the same gentleness that one would use in learning about what a four-year-old or a nine-year-old or a teenager is going through. Loving parents do not see, for example, the "righteousness" of a nine-year-old as a wall that splits their oneness with their own child. They wish to understand this aspect of the child's growth so that they can support the process.

If the differences between women and men went to the heart, the best you could hope for would be an alliance—and alliances are always broken when a new alliance seems more in one's interests. Surely we want something deeper than a passing compatibility. And yet the ever-changing ego exists only on the surface, and this is all it can offer. Fortunately, it is a mask that your mind can gently lift from your partner's face.

listen to the emotion behind the words   A few weeks ago our friend Stacy and her eight-year-old boy, Sean, traveled

here from northern California to stay with us for a few days. One afternoon, about an hour after Sean, Jordan, and Jordan's older brother, John, came in from playing basketball in the 106° Arizona sun, Sean suddenly became weak and started running a temperature. We tried giving him Advil and later Tylenol, but the only thing that brought it down was having him lie quietly in a cool spot on the floor. His temperature rose two more times, but by bedtime he seemed fine.

During the night his temperature rose dramatically, and this time the only thing that brought it down was putting him in a cold bath. The next morning, from studying *The Merck Manual* and other medical books, we were all convinced that he had suffered a mild sun stroke. When his temperature suddenly began rising once again, Gayle and Stacy took him to the emergency room of a local hospital, while Hugh stayed home with Jordan.

Shortly after they arrived, a young doctor began interviewing them about what had happened. Even though their thoughts were unusually well organized because of how carefully they had monitored Sean's symptoms, and even though he read several times a detailed chronology that Stacy had written out that included the exact fluctuations in temperature and when they occurred, the doctor seemed incapable of understanding what the two of them were saying.

Aside from this, his behavior was nearly perfect. He listened very attentively, tried to repeat back everything Stacy and Gayle said, asked Sean sympathetic questions, and took notes, but he kept having to go over and over the same material, each time getting some aspect of it wrong. Finally he said, "I can't understand what you women are saying. I'm going to have to get another doctor," and left the room.

The second doctor was much older; he and his wife had reared a family; and he indicated in several ways that he had a deep respect for what mothers have to say about their children. He had no trouble understanding Stacy and Gayle—even though he repeated back nothing they said and asked no sympathetic questions of Sean. He immediately came to the same conclusion they had—that this was a heat sickness—and his instructions on how to deal with it were precise and compassionate.

No matter what communication techniques you use, if you have a grievance, a prejudice, or a judgmental feeling toward each other, you may listen, but you won't hear each other. Critical thoughts must be suspended, if only for an instant, in order for you to receive the information you need from each other. The following is an example of how even a strong criticism of your partner can be momentarily set aside.

When her husband, Greg, switched jobs a few years ago, Diana began having terrible arguments with him almost every day when he came home from work. They both attended a church that taught its members never to be "idly critical" of another person, and yet each day Greg would be filled with new complaints about the behavior of the people at the company. Diana would react to this with mild reprimands, and although he would halfheartedly agree that it was against their religion for him to talk this way, Greg would soon be furious with her over some other issue, and she would end up being drawn into still another fight.

Diana told us that what helped her get out of this pattern was something she reread that Hugh had written in *Notes to Myself* in 1970:

> I don't want to listen to just what you say. I want to feel what you mean.
> I won't hold you to your words. Deep emotions are often expressed in irrational words.
> I want you to be able to say anything.
> Even what you don't mean.

She said that she made the decision to listen less to what her husband said and more to his emotions—and to be supportive of them. The first day she did this, she quickly saw that Greg was not so much critical of the other employees as he was upset about how he was being treated by management, even though that was not exactly what he was saying. In her sincere desire to be understanding of what he was feeling, Diana said things like, "That must really be upsetting. It would sure upset me." After only a few minutes of this, it was as if a floodgate opened and all of Greg's unhappiness with the job poured out. For the first time in their marriage he cried in front of her.

Because the job paid considerably more than he had ever made, Greg had not allowed himself to even consider quitting it. Now, feeling Diana's support, he was able to admit that he was conflicted about staying. She told him that there was no question in her mind that he should quit, and after a long talk he finally agreed—and with tremendous relief.

There is no formula here. The results came not from what Diana *said* to her husband but from her deep desire to understand what he was going through, a desire that she was able to feel only when she set aside her insistence that he outwardly conform to a religious ideal. As it turned out, on the deepest level Greg wasn't being critical of other workers, yet as long as she merely analyzed his words, she was not able to sense what he was feeling. **Understanding is a function of the heart, not of the intellect.**

relationships based on mutual interests   Our core of self exists in the present, whereas our ego is the accumulated effect of past influences. The past generates interests and disinterests, and the self generates love. To the ego, you either believe in Santa Claus or you don't. Love doesn't take either position—it becomes Santa Claus. Those who seek partners whose most important qualification is that their interests are the same as their own are making a mistake, because their primary motivation is not love. No matter what they believe they have in their new partner, they will soon run up against the fact that all egos are to some degree different—even in their areas of similarity—and on that level there are no well-matched couples.

Common interests are a foundation of sand. For example, just one injury can wipe out a lifetime of athletic and outdoor interests. Whatever degree of ego similarity is present at the start of the relationship will fade as soon as the partners' interests change —and egos always change. Then, to the degree that the original motivation was not love, the partners think, "There's nothing between us anymore."

Many people who advertise in the personals "seek" someone who will "like" not them but their "interests." They define themselves *as* a set of interests and define love as getting a good match with those interests. So that there will be no mistake about this, the interests are enumerated: "DWM who likes to bowl, party, hang-glide, and listen to Joe Cocker music seeks slim passionate SWF with same interests for permanent relationship. No kids please."

At your core you and your partner are the same. Learning to love is essentially the process of moving past the smaller likes and dislikes into a vast preexisting ocean of rapport. The deeper interests, the ones that will reward you most quickly and satisfyingly, take both partners into consideration. Naturally this does not mean that a couple must do everything together or that they can't have separate activities they enjoy. Rather, these should always be pursuits that are within the goodwill of both partners.

An unusual example of how this principle operates can be found in our own relationship. As we have mentioned, in the early years of our marriage Hugh had a strong interest in other sexual partners. In those days most of our friends believed in open marriage, and although Gayle initially gave Hugh the freedom to do whatever he wished in this regard, she eventually saw that promiscuity is very destructive and began to oppose it. Hugh's interest was no longer inclusive of Gayle's feelings once she changed her position. Now his interest clearly did not represent the relationship as a whole, if in fact it ever had.

One day, during the period when Hugh was working to become

physically and especially emotionally monogamous, Gayle bought three pornographic movies and a projector and gave them to him as a present. It was out of love, good humor, and her intuition of what would be most helpful to Hugh that she did this. Of course, what is funny and loving in one relationship is not in another. Hugh was very touched by this offbeat gift and delighted in telling other people about it.

The ways that men relate to their male friends and women relate to their female friends can create conflict in a relationship—if it is singled out for ridicule. A woman may make disparaging remarks about her husband's need to get together with the boys, drink beer, and watch "the game" on television. A man may ridicule his wife's desire to talk "for hours" on the phone with her buddies. Whenever we try to contrast ourselves, we also tend to become judgmental of the differences we are pointing out. From there it's easy to slip into a warlike state in which we try to make our partner feel inferior. Disparities between the sexes exist within the thin ego layer of each partner's personality and are not worth an instant of discord.

We have demonstrated in hundreds of workshops that any two who relax into their true feelings will arrive at a common understanding, no matter what the issue. There is no male and female answer—there is only the answer that brings peace, and it can take many acceptable forms. At the conclusion of a successful argument (which we will describe within the section "Norming and Performing" in Chapter Eight), you will usually have a number of solutions to choose from that are equally pleasing to you both. The heart of your oneness, of your *relationship,* is very generous, and the path it points to is very wide. It can easily accommodate all your differences if you fall back into a broader self. Never be afraid to broaden the definition of who you are.

As your relationship progresses, you will find that classifying each other or yourself as needy, abusive, frigid, narcissistic, codependent, rageaholic, or using any other separating description, is no longer useful, because you now *want* to share whatever burdens the one you love. Two can solve a problem more easily than one. This is one of the great benefits of having a relationship. Thus, to withdraw into a smaller self by labeling your partner or yourself works against your personal interests.

FOUR

The Part of You That Chose Your Partner

REPEATING THE SAME MISTAKE

our ability to choose   Why do people keep getting themselves into the same sick relationships? They don't. The myth that
a dysfunctional syndrome, which was set up in childhood, plays
itself out again and again in a person's choice of a partner is
actually the reverse of what ordinarily happens. If you fear that
there is within you an unconscious tendency to pick the wrong
person, you can now erase this from your list of problems. There
is simply no real evidence to support it. *Please* don't burden yourself with this nonsense.

If, as has been said, 90 percent of all adults grew up in families
that were dysfunctional—which may be true—it does not follow
that these people's instincts for choosing a good partner have been
obstructed or perverted by the experience. Consider for a moment
all of the urges, instincts, and drives that still function strongly
and naturally. What logic is there in singling this one out as universally thwarted? No one says, "If I hadn't come from a dysfunctional family, I wouldn't keep buying Chevies." There's no
deep pain and guilt from abandoning a Chevrolet, and therefore
no need for a theory to justify it.

People who believe they have disconnected from their ability to choose a good marriage partner do not think this about their ability to choose a good business partner, a good religion, a good profession, or a good school for their child to attend. Who would think of going into therapy before trusting herself to form simple friendships? Who would rely more on a checklist found in a book than on his own good judgment? Most people, no matter how neurotic their mother and father were, will tell you that they have good friends and that they know what a good friend is. And yet after they have left their latest mate, they will say that their ability to pick their *best* friend—their partner for life, the mother or father of their children—was warped during their formative years, and in this one area their psyche is so damaged that they are self-destructive.

The thought that our mating instinct has been dysfunctionalized is a recently constituted belief. It rode in on the tide of selfishness of the seventies and eighties and did not arise out of any real evidence to support it. It came as part of the assumption that we have a right to a life free of adversity—including a partner who is just like us and a sex life that always runs smoothly.

the life we have a "right" to   We have shifted from coping and relating to blaming and leaving. We no longer allow each other any margin of error. The sharp increase in the number of complaints filed, job-jumpings, lawsuits, firings, abandoned pets, abandoned children, adoptions that "disrupt," divorces, and breakups are only a few of the ways that we are presently acting out our belief that nothing bad should happen in our lives.

We have a right to many things, but a world without accidents, mistakes, and human frailties is not one of them.

If we take the assumption that we deserve freedom from hardship into our primary relationship, when our partner is verbally abusive, has an affair, loses a job, becomes impotent, sinks into a long depression, obsesses on a career, or enters a hundred other difficult stages that human beings go through, the only conclusion we are left with is that we have made a mistake in choosing this person and must undo it, or that we must remake ourselves into an entity so strong and independent that we will never again feel pain.

Several years ago, an unmarried couple, an accountant and a potter, began going through a difficult time, precipitated primarily by the question of whether they should get married. Eventually the woman, not wanting to make this commitment, moved out, leaving her daughter and son by a previous marriage in the man's care. She made it clear that she was finished with the relationship and that, as soon as she was on her feet, she would collect her children and be out of the man's life forever.

They had been with each other for many years and had planned to spend their lives together. He had bonded deeply with the children, and her leaving was such an unexpected blow that he became depressed. Frequently he could not go to his office in the mornings. He cried often and seemed very near to a breakdown. After a month by herself, the woman returned and said that she now realized how deeply she loved him and that she was willing to get married and to commit in any other way that the man wished. She had evidently spent the time away thinking deeply about what they had together and how much their relationship meant to her children.

Although the man agreed to resume the relationship and even to get married, he began attending one of the many groups that are an outgrowth of separation psychology. There he learned that his pain had been caused by his own codependence. He was told that he did not need anyone in order to be whole, that he could think and feel for himself, and that what he must do now was to nurture his wounded inner child, actualize his potential, and release his natural self-esteem, all of which would be possible through an understanding of the childhood origins of his programmed dependency and through surrender to his Higher Power.

The more meetings he attended, the more independent and separate he became. Gradually his commitment to the group grew stronger than his commitment to his new wife. This became clear, for example, whenever there was a conflict between anything she wanted the family to do together and one of his scheduled meetings, or whenever she expressed an idea that was at odds with the philosophy of the group.

One day the woman called us and said that if this continued much further, there would be very little on which to base a family relationship, and could we meet with the two of them and make some suggestions? She also said something that we have heard from several husbands and wives in similar situations. She told us that it was as if her husband were "having an affair with the group," and that meeting night after meeting night she was left at home like a rejected wife, only to have her husband return each time more distant than before.

After several sessions with them it became obvious to us that the man's primary fear was that something could happen between the two of them that would again throw him back into the suffering he had gone through before. Above all, he was determined never again to experience pain like that, and through the group he felt that he was slowly strengthening himself to the point where he would no longer be vulnerable.

Having spent years helping parents who had a child die, we had seen suffering before—suffering that for the most part was far more devastating than what he had been through. Although they were definitely in the minority, we had also seen several parents try to armor themselves against ever having to suffer again. In every case, they had eventually divorced their spouse and become estranged from their remaining children. Perhaps they became less vulnerable, but they also lost touch with their humanness.

We asked the man to consider the amount of suffering in the world. We gave him many examples, most of which he was familiar with but had not thought about recently. We said to him,

"Given the condition of most humans living on this planet and given the history of our species, do you think that suffering is a normal or an abnormal part of life?" He of course saw the point, but he went on to express a very common sentiment: that most pain is caused by the stupidity of others, and that fully actualized individuals can either eliminate or greatly lessen their reliance on those who can hurt them, especially if they are willing to turn to their Higher Power.

misapplying the term *higher power*   Here we have the main assumptions behind separation psychology's approach to suffering: First, suffering always involves someone else, and if it were not for this other person or people, it would probably not have occurred. Second, one suffers because of an unhealthy dependence on others. Third, one can grow beyond this dependence. And fourth, God, or one's "Higher Power," comes to one as a separate empowering force—in other words, one can have a private relationship with God that does not necessarily include one's spouse or family.

This last belief is perhaps the most pernicious because it cloaks a loveless concept in holiness and devotion that no one dare question. In our opinion, the founders of Alcoholics Anonymous, as indicated by "The Big Book" and other sources, did not have separate empowerment in mind when they coined the term *Higher Power*. In "Bill's Story," the co-founder of AA writes, "Never was I to pray for myself, except as my requests bore on my usefulness to others." "A price had to be paid," he goes on to say. "It meant destruction of self-centeredness. I must turn in all things to the Father of Light who presides over us all."

Today, as addicts and alcoholics enter twelve-step-based treatment centers, many are told that if they truly "work the program," they should prepare themselves for the fact that their marriage will probably not survive, and they are given the latest statistics as confirmation. A friend of ours who recently returned

from one of the better-known centers said that she was also told
that if it came down to a choice between her marriage and her
recovery, she would have to choose her recovery. Obviously in an
extreme case this might be true, but to routinely give this kind of
advice to all married addicts is irresponsible and overlooks the
effect on the *addict* of a marriage breaking up. This friend had
recently married, and she and her husband had a very caring relationship. He had given up social drinking as a way of supporting
her, yet she came back with the general impression that their relationship would soon break up. She was filled with considerable
anxiety over this.

This unfortunate emphasis on the part of some treatment centers and within some AA groups was clearly not the attitude of the
founders of AA. In his book *Twelve Steps and Twelve Traditions,*
Bill Wilson observes that "permanent marriage breakups and separations . . . are unusual in A.A." He states that "most married
folks in A.A. have very happy homes. To a surprising extent, A.A.
has offset the damage to family life brought about by years of
alcoholism." As he indicated on several occasions, he saw the
twelve steps as a powerful aid to marriage. In the same book he
writes: "The alcoholic, realizing what his wife has endured, and
now fully understanding how much he himself did to damage her
and his children, nearly always takes up his marriage responsibili-
ties with a willingness to repair what he can and to accept what he
can't. He persistently tries all of A.A.'s Twelve Steps in his home,
often with fine results. At this point he firmly but lovingly com-
mences to behave like a partner instead of like a bad boy. And
above all he is finally convinced that reckless romancing is not a
way of life for him."

All of this is very far from some of the twelve-step rhetoric
heard today, especially in many AA spin-off groups and in books
generated by separation psychology. Perhaps our interpretation of
the original twelve-step philosophy can be argued, but there
should be no doubt that a loving Father-Mother God would not

injure one of its children in order to heal another. Unquestionably, some forms of codependence exist, but the remedy is not found in the litter of damaged lives strewn across the final decades of the twentieth century. Surely Love does not want the sacred trust of bringing up a little child to be thrown aside by one of its parents in the name of personal healing. Surely Love does not want a woman or a man to be deserted late in life—or any other time—so that a private dream of self-actualization can be pursued by the other partner.

Turning to our Higher Power does not raise us above the difficulties of forming relationships or of domestic life. Nor are we released from commitments, obligations, or ordinary destiny. It should be recalled that Jesus' life did not proceed without considerable suffering. Nor did Martin Luther King, Jr.'s, or Gandhi's. And it could certainly be said that none of their lives ended well. Countless other souls who were very close to their Higher Power had far-from-ideal lives. Closeness to God does not guarantee a life free of suffering; it guarantees closeness to God.

After the accountant had made his comments about suffering and his Higher Power, we were able to be quite open about the qualities in him we loved most, because, as well as someone seeking our help, he was also an old and good friend. We told him that it was precisely because he *had* suffered so acutely that we knew how deeply human he was. We would have expected no less a reaction from him. It's natural to be devastated when the one you love deserts you, for this is what the woman appeared to have done. His suffering was not a flaw that he must now eradicate, but an indication of spiritual strength—the same kind of strength that, for example, caused Jesus to weep on more than one occasion.

We also pointed out that his suffering was not the fault of his partner. Although "trial separations" are often a mistake, in this case if she had not gone off by herself, she might never have realized how good they were for each other. She had needed to face ending the relationship in order to look deeply at that alternative. If she had known in advance what conclusion her leaving would lead her to, she could have been gentler in her approach, but the fact was she did not know; she really had thought she was leaving, and it was pointless now to go back and assign blame.

Our friend admitted that if he could, he would not change what she had done, but he was still fearful of quitting the group, even though he had no history of substance abuse and there was no danger to his health or safety in quitting. We assured him that there was no reason to quit—if he was certain that the effect of going was to strengthen his devotion to his family. The group was fairly large, and we asked him if anyone in it had a permanent relationship or if any author of any book the group was reading had a permanent relationship. After considering this for a moment, he said, "I can only think of one person, a man who's been married for three months." He of course was talking about himself.

your box of missing parts   There is simply no mistake to be made in picking a mate, or at least the chances are very small that you will choose someone who is truly dangerous. You *will* end up with someone who has far more flaws than you originally thought. And obviously it's true that people who have multiple relationships tend to carry the same problems into each one. When they do this, new dynamics form that look very much like the old ones. This is not because they are choosing the wrong person, but because they are not yet healed. Dynamics form over and over for the uncomplicated reason that we pick a partner with the characteristics that could most facilitate our growth and then turn around and do battle with those characteristics.

Ego oneness is you thinking and acting like me. Yet many couples feel a deep oneness with each other and still have "very little in common." Parents share almost none of the interests of their infant and yet feel their oneness with the child deeply. They would not want to eat infant food, make infant sounds, sleep as much as an infant, be burped, or have crying as their major form of communication. This afternoon, Gayle (forty-eight) was in the driveway shooting baskets with Jordan (nine). Periodically the ball would go into the neighbor's cactus, and she would have to pull out the needles. Left to herself, she probably would have chosen to work on her mystery, which Jordan has no interest in helping her write. Yesterday afternoon, Hugh (fifty-five) was running up and down a full soccer field trying to compete with Jordan and his soccer-wizard friend Jonathan. They stopped frequently to ask why he couldn't beat two third-graders, especially after they had spotted him five points. Left to himself, he would have preferred to do *anything* else. And yet, because of the oneness he feels with his son, Jordan's happiness was in large measure his own.

The yearning for oneness is the source of the love instinct. The ego's resistance to oneness turns love into war. If love is given merely a little time and a little willingness, it can easily move past all separate interests. Most couples can look back in old age and see a rightness, almost a perfection, to all they went through together.

Your partner knows your ego better than you do and is a rich source of insight, but to hear what would be most helpful for you to hear, you must do two things: Recognize that you do not want to be ego driven. And question your assumption that every suggestion your partner makes is an attack.

Any two people *could* love each other, and in cultures in which one's mate is chosen by others, a deep affection sometimes develops despite the arbitrary nature of the beginning. In the West, the inner wisdom that draws two people together can be seen more clearly, at least by someone outside the relationship.

In counseling, our repeated experience has been that not just any two end up together. The strengths that one partner has almost invariably complement the other's weaknesses. This coincidence is so striking that it seems mystical. And perhaps it is. However negative a couple *thought* were the reasons that brought them together, it is usually clear that a part of their mind knew what it was doing. It's as if God sent you the box of your missing parts.

To the friends who are onlookers, the majority of divorces seem inappropriate, and they are saddened by them. Ask most people how many couples they know who have gotten divorced, and of those how many they believe were necessary, and it becomes obvious that despite the fact that we are being told from all sides that we don't have the relationship we deserve, most people already see the wastefulness of this attitude within their own circle of friends. It's usually much more obvious to others than to themselves that two people balance each other nicely. This is why a couple can begin a relationship highly incompatible, as we did, and a far greater force begins its healing work. The differences in strengths contain the potential for healing.

There is of course nothing wrong with having a comparatively easy time in the early stages of a relationship. And perhaps testing can inform two people of some of the difficulties they will need to work on at the outset. What these tests and checklists cannot calculate are the problems that will arise after the partners change, as they will begin to do quite quickly. In a sense, the egos involved go through a series of marriages in the course of one permanent relationship. People's tastes, interests, goals, and even physical characteristics are so radically different five, ten, or twenty years into a marriage that most couples look back and laugh at what they once thought were the reasons they first got together.

Contrary to the notion that you can't trust your mating instinct if your family was dysfunctional, the simple truth is that your own quiet knowing is the one thing you possess that can be trusted as to whether you should form a partnership with this individual, who will go through as many changes as you have, and whose core will remain as changeless. For an engaged couple to decide against marriage on the basis of a test may discount the deep knowing of their hearts about the unseen potential. A test can't tell you what you will have if you walk beside this person for a lifetime, but the peace of your heart can inform you whether to begin.

WHEN DO WE NO LONGER NEED OUR PARTNER?

Another widely held theory in separation psychology states that people do in fact choose "exactly the kind of partner they need at the time," but that when their needs change, they instinctively discard that person. Or to put it in the jargon, "When they can no longer maximize each other's growth, they choose to make a change." It sounds almost as simple as changing a set of tires. The appeal of this philosophy is that it makes choosing your partner "exactly right" and discarding your partner "exactly right."

If you are about to act out this theory, please consider for a moment what you will throw away. You have already put in a lot of work. You have made some progress, perhaps more than you realize. Once you leave, you will no longer have a friendship with the palpable depth that comes only from long-term effort. And now you will have set for yourself a course of short-term relationships, each ending when you determine that your growth has been served—although you can think of many times when something benefited you that at the time you believed was of no benefit.

Do you really want to end your life completely alone, or at best in a relationship that has only a temporary purpose, like some one-night stand? Don't you want to feel another person's soul inside you and their blessing covering you? And to know, with a knowing that the world cannot give, that this happiness will not die, even with the passing of your bodies? Don't you want to know love? If so, then you must shepherd this relationship through its difficult periods. The growth that comes from staying with a friend far outweighs the benefits of the temporary break in the storm you get from leaving.

If we accept this premise—that our personal assessment of our growth supersedes our spouse—then we are also free to discard many other people: Our parents—we have certainly outgrown needing parents. Our friends—aren't we much different now than when we first met them? And our children—clearly we are not that starry-eyed youth who once needed to have a baby.

Unfortunately, all of these things are in fact happening. Parents are not being visited in nursing homes. Friends are being discarded because they are no longer "convenient." And children are stuck in day care and left there even after the parents come home.

Our needs have become our God, and meeting them has become our religion.

We now live in a culture in which if someone needs to shoot a gun, he shoots it. If someone needs to rape, he rapes. Hugh recently took John and Jordan to a movie about gangs. Halfway through it, he realized that the boy sitting in front of them had a .357 strapped to his hip. Hugh phoned the police department and was told that as long as he had his parents' permission, a child of any age could carry a loaded weapon. The officer added, "I know it's not common sense, sir, but it's the city ordinance." Later, when we asked some other parents about this, we were informed that some children "need to feel safe." Well, of course. If they *need* to feel safe, what other consideration could rank higher?

We marry to get our needs met. We have children to get our needs met. We leave all of it behind to get our needs met. But what set of needs are we speaking of? In an interview, one psychologist, when asked to explain why many people say they are not better off since their divorce and report having feelings of anger, grief, loss, and a sense of worthlessness for years afterward, answered that these people don't understand that they needed to divorce in order to grow. They were looking only at the change and not at the need for growth that caused it.

The one great need is the need for eternal love, and we have lost sight of it as we struggle through the underbrush of lesser needs. If Gayle can finally have this with a man who for fifteen years not only fell short of "meeting her needs"—a period longer than most marriages—but also tortured her emotionally on several occasions with his affairs, then *any* two who put their relationship first can have it also. But it means getting past the "plateaus," and the "stress points," and the "acute periods," and the crises. Every relationship has times of great unhappiness as well as times of great happiness. Ours was no different. Even during those fifteen years, in many respects we had a typical relationship, and there were numerous aspects of it that were healthy and fun. The only thing we did differently was that we didn't break up during our times of crisis. But more than just staying together, we also began actively working to forgive each other and experimenting with ways of living together in peace and oneness. That's when we began to discover the *permanent* blessings a real relationship brings. The world is a place of unhappiness. A real relationship doesn't eliminate the world. It climbs out of it.

FINDING YOUR ''PERFECT MATCH''

There is an amazing pretense in pronouncements made on TV and in much of the current literature on relationships about the beauty and wonder of being separate but equal. If two people are "equal," they don't *need* a relationship. And if they're separate, they don't have one.

We know from our own marriage that in the areas where our egos are most equal, we have also been most dysfunctional. For example, we both tend to let things slide and be late on our timing; we both tend to overindulge in sugar (we're talking here of serious chocolate abuse); we both tend to acquire pets too quickly and to be too quick to find other homes for them; we both tend to make major purchases impulsively. These areas of "equal interests'' have been much harder to remedy than the areas where we were supposedly incompatible. We were not able to deal effectively with them until we first established a loving basis for combining our individual talents. If we had been alike in more than these four or five areas—that is, if we had been what is presently held up as "right for each other"—our progress would have been slower and more difficult.

Very rarely do we find couples in our groups or in individual couples' counseling who are a "perfect match," but when we do, their problems are sometimes particularly resistant. One couple we worked with had everything. They both were very good looking, very successful, very well off, and very well known. They liked the same restaurants, the same movies, the same cars. They agreed instantly on what house to buy and on what considerable improvements to make. They both had a passion for exercise and even pursued the same novel recreation (dog racing). Neither wanted children, and yet they both loved their one macaw. They took the same stands on diet and religion, and they shared a belief in an unusual disaster and world-conspiracy theory. Being right was the driving force of their personalities, and money was their greatest passion.

After five years, their marriage began to unravel over how to split the profits from one of their many stock accounts, an issue they never resolved. They didn't clash over this; they just began drifting further and further apart. Their appointments and errands were increasingly timed to keep away from each other, and finally, for seemingly very understandable reasons of scheduling, they began taking separate vacations.

It was quite difficult for us to demonstrate to either of them why they needed the other, and they eventually divorced. That was several years ago, and if we had that counseling to do over, we would probably approach it differently. They had both been in good marriages when they met each other, but the allure of finding someone who was so easy to be with was too great, and even though they each had children, they had gotten divorces in order to be together. In working with them, it became obvious that there was an unusually deep spiritual longing within both of them. We might have had greater success if we had focused less on solving the money issue between them and more on helping them understand the spiritual wound that people carry when they abandon those with whom they are presently committed, regardless of how that commitment began, and the spiritual benefits that come from persisting in deepening the bond between them.

A POTENTIAL FOR HEALING CAN LOOK LIKE WAR

If you will hold your partner quietly in your mind, you will see a unique set of strengths, regardless of whether they have been used well or misused up to this point. Although it's more difficult, it is also possible for you to assess your own. Notice that in almost every area where you tend to be strong, your partner tends to have less ability, competence, or potential. And—once again, harder to see—you tend to be lacking where she or he is not. Unless your relationship is very unusual, the dynamic that has formed between you is that you each use your strengths to attack the other's weaknesses. This can usually be seen most clearly during a fight, but it operates on some level much of the time.

In our own relationship, Gayle's strengths are that she is creative, happy, unselfish, and highly intuitive about people, places, and what needs to be done. Hugh's strengths are that he is steady, fearless, devout, peaceful, and easygoing. On a spiritual level, Hugh sees the direction our lives need to go, and Gayle sees how to get there.

Although these have lessened over the years, some of Gayle's weaknesses have been that she was anxious, volatile, fearful, had feelings of inadequacy, and had trouble saying no. Hugh, especially in the early years of our marriage, was selfish, superior, absentminded, and frequently inept. Needless to say, we still have some measure of these same weaknesses.

Like most couples, soon after we met we began building the habit of looking down on each other's lacks and mistakes—because they were not our own. This unhappy practice continued for about fifteen years before we seriously got down to reversing it, but by then we had uncovered a mountain of issues to use against each other. For example, Gayle has always found it difficult to answer the phone, deal with strangers, decline invitations, or give instructions to employees. Hugh has never liked reading the mail, answering letters, buying and mailing presents, or shopping for clothes. Gayle doesn't like repairing things; Hugh doesn't like assembling them. Gayle doesn't like feeding and cleaning up after pets; Hugh doesn't like taking them to the vet. Gayle finds it much more difficult than Hugh to get up during the night with the kids, but it's hard for Hugh to arise earlier than usual in the morning. The list goes on and on and, as in other relationships, our weaknesses permeate virtually all aspects of our life together.

If partners use their abilities to attack each other's disabilities, a relationship can become a nightmare, and for us, by the end of the fifteen years, if it wasn't a nightmare, it was at least a very nasty dream much of the time. Every event had a small measure of built-in pain that we often triggered. Because Gayle was unable to remove bugs or mice from the house or the occasional dead bird from the lawn, Hugh would perform this task—but not without silent contempt, plus frequent lectures on why certain (live) creatures were good to have around. Gayle's father was a banker, and she looked down on Hugh's difficulty with balancing the checkbook and his philosophy of never paying a bill until after the third notice. In disgust, she eventually took over these tasks. Likewise, Hugh's absentmindedness and problems with directionality made driving with him a very, very long thrill, and so she took this task over also—but not without joking about it to their friends at Hugh's expense. Hugh took advantage of Gayle's fear of saying no by continuing to practice an open marriage long past the point when she had stopped believing in it.

To heal these and numerous other conflicts, we first had to identify each pattern and actively seek out ways for our abilities to complement each other. This required a degree of honesty that we were not in the habit of practicing.

For example, Hugh initially felt that because he was the one who was earning our income, he was also the one who should control how it was used. It took him several years to admit that Gayle had better instincts for handling money, but when he did (and when we both got our spending under control), we began eliminating the periodic financial crises we had always had.

Because of her upbringing, Gayle's tendency was to buy our children anything they wanted. Hugh, who as a child was never allowed more toys than would fit in a two-foot-by-one-foot chest, tended to resist any purchases at all. One of us saw the value of generosity; the other, the value of self-sufficiency. When we finally allowed these insights to complement each other, even though the boys got a little less for holidays and birthdays, they obviously began enjoying themselves more. Hugh spent more time playing games and doing projects with them, and Gayle was happier, in part because she felt less guilty about the amount of money these occasions were now costing.

Hugh bought the lot and, with help, physically built much of the first house we owned. Because of this he insisted on controlling the design. The results were an artistic triumph but a functional disaster. There was almost no closet or storage space, and the kitchen was largely unusable—a sore point for as long as we lived there. We have since learned to defer to Gayle's instinct on the kind of house we should live in and Hugh's ability to negotiate the purchase and execute the needed structural changes.

A real relationship is the decision to unite spiritually, to pool all strengths and abilities, to become each other's caretaker, and thus to be a single body. A body understands that the right hand can reach things on the right side more easily than the left hand—and that there is no humiliation in this. It understands that legs are better for walking than arms. If it didn't, and arms and legs were to fight over the right to this function, the body would be immobilized. In a real relationship competition between the two halves is equally unnecessary and insane.

No harm will come to you from sharing a single heart.

FIVE

Prime Thoughts—Core Dynamics

THE VOICE OF OUR IMAGINARY IDENTITY

Any couple who wishes to develop a deep peace between them must begin the work of dissolving the walls their separate egos have built. The primary indicator of an area of separation is a feeling of censure (irritation, defensiveness, estrangement, disapproval, disgust, dislike, anger). Whenever either of you feels any degree of this kind of distancing emotion, you are identifying with your ego. Your ego's nature can't be helped, but it is possible to become progressively uninterested in its offerings and to reach a point when they are no longer a factor in your relationship.

Only by becoming aware of one's ego, by acknowledging it in all its aspects, can it be relinquished without being repressed. It does little good to merely act calm when one feels angry, to act sympathetic when one feels bitter. A clear recognition of what one's ego emotions are, and what the feelings of the heart are, is essential to making a choice between the two. Thus two steps are needed: A way to increase awareness of ego activity, and a way to touch one's heart or core.

Many means for accomplishing these goals have been taught and written about. Most spiritual paths and a number of therapies

offer excellent procedures. Here are a few that we have worked
out for ourselves.

ego watching   You must first have a simple, pleasant way
of monitoring your idle thoughts and feelings. Thoughts precede
emotions, and it's always possible to take any mood you find
yourself in and, with a little practice, trace it back to an earlier
thought. Thoughts are to the mind as food is to the stomach. Once
a particular thought is "swallowed"—that is, believed and accepted—it predisposes the mind to a particular emotion, just as
eating certain foods predisposes the stomach to a certain reaction.
If either of us has caffeine late at night, the first thing we eat the
next morning "causes" indigestion, whereas the same food on
another morning would not.

The ego never stops chattering. Many of its ideas we dismiss.
"I don't swallow that," one person might say to another, and
likewise we pass over many of our own idle thoughts. But periodically some idea, some characterization of reality, catches our attention and we take it to heart. Now we are primed for an ego
reaction. When Gayle was a girl, her father would always say to
her mother, "Well, what did you accomplish today?" when he
walked in the door from work. Some days she enjoyed the opportunity to list the amazing number of things she had done, but one
day she was holding a stack of dishes in her arms when he asked
the question. She glared at him, threw the dishes against the wall,
and said, "Not a goddamn thing."

We never react negatively for the reason we think. We do or say
something separating because of how we are presently disposed to
react. The question did not cause Gayle's mother to throw the
dishes, or else it would have always caused that. And likewise,
**what your partner does or does not do can't control you, but
your state of mind can.**

How something strikes you is only in your control if you are
aware of what is behind your attitude. Your idle thoughts may

seem unimportant—until you make the connection between them and how you react to the present. Gayle's mother impulsively threw the dishes, but people can also have sex impulsively, get married impulsively, even murder impulsively, and certainly they can file for divorce impulsively. At another time, in another mood, the individual would not have made the same choice.

There is a country song about a husband who suddenly confesses all of his affairs to his wife. She immediately takes their child and leaves, which of course the song applauds and goes on to advise every woman similarly treated to do also. Overlooked in this ideal is the obvious fact that **abandonment is a greater betrayal than affairs.**

The last affair that Hugh had was when John, our first child, was only a few months old. Because there was no one to leave him with, Gayle was carrying John in her arms when she walked in on Hugh in a hotel room. That was fifteen years ago, and by anyone's measure, Hugh has been a wonderful husband and father ever since. No one could be more loyal and family oriented than he has become. If Gayle had impulsively left him, John would have grown up in a single-parent or stepparent family; neither of us would have experienced the delight of Jordan, our second boy; the two of them would not have had each other as brothers; we would not have formed a writing team, and certainly this and our last six books wouldn't have been written; we would never have started The Dispensable Church* and begun helping couples; and, perhaps most important, we would not have had each other's companionship and support in our walk home to God.

---

* We began working on a crisis hotline in 1978. This led to our personally counseling battered women, rape victims, and people who were suicidal. We then started the Santa Fe Grief Support Group for parents who had had a child die, and a separate group for others in crisis (mugging victims, etc.). In 1981 we founded The Dispensable Church in order to teach an approach to everyday life that would cut across all forms of crisis. (*Notes on How to Live in the World . . . and Still Be Happy* is our summary of those teachings.) As ministers we began counseling couples, and this and our work with families and children (including our own) has occupied most of our time to the present.

Not only can the habit of taking ego thoughts to heart predispose a person to dramatically separating and life-changing actions, but it also peppers the day with bits of inappropriate behavior that can turn a long-term relationship into a running hell. So first we need to become deeply aware of the ongoing *stream* of ego thinking.

FOUR SENSITIZING TECHNIQUES

1. Schedule one or more short periods into your day in which you do nothing but watch your mind. Write down any thought that you notice. Or say your thoughts out loud. Or within the mind itself, emphasize the thoughts; for example, see them in italics, or hear the appropriate mood music behind them, or picture a speaker attached to your head broadcasting them.

2. Set your watch, or the timer on your stove, to go off at some convenient interval (for example, every five or ten minutes). Go about your day as usual, and when the alarm sounds, stop and freeze the contents of your mind and see how many of the thoughts you were just thinking you can describe to yourself. Try hard to catch any thought that contains elements of attack. This technique gets around the problem of a watched mind becoming increasingly still. In fact, if your mind starts anticipating the end of the time period, you can vary the intervals or make them longer.

3. A variation on this, and one that will often grow out of it, is to check up on your mind whenever you think of it. This type of awareness will gradually become second nature, and you will no longer have extended periods during the day in which you are thinking attack thoughts unconsciously.

the god bag   The fourth exercise adds another level of awareness. We will be discussing shortly the basic generating thoughts—what we call **prime thoughts**—that underlie all ego reactions, but before we come to that, if one does no more than identify the **justifying thoughts** (also to be discussed later) that are part of the current upset, and deal with them quite specifically, this alone can sometimes restore a conflicted mind to peace.

This exercise comes from our earlier work with people who were suicidal. Individuals who find themselves in a suicidal state because of something that has recently happened in their lives (as opposed to people who are chronically depressed from a chemical imbalance, for example) are tortured by their minds. They believe that what happened to them is depressing them, whereas what they discover when they monitor their feelings is that the intensity of the depression fluctuates according to what scene, fantasy, or circumstance they are dwelling on. These thoughts accompany and justify their mood, and without them the mood dissipates.

There is of course a great deal more to helping someone get past a suicidal period than the following exercise, but we want to describe it here because of how well it illustrates the connection between thought and emotion, a connection many people don't believe until they have seen it for themselves.

One night we were called to go over to the house of a man who, in quick succession, had lost his wife, his children, and his job. After an hour or two of listening to him describe the divorce, the custody fight, and his firing, it was clear which scenes, recalled or projected into the future, and what revenge fantasies were preoccupying him most. After taking several steps to insure his safety (calling one of his friends to come stay with him, destroying the dangerous drugs in the house, and so forth) we asked him to follow only one instruction: an exercise we called The God Bag.

First, we reassured him that his reactions were similar to those of many other people we had worked with and in that sense were normal and reasonable and, most important, could definitely be controlled. We told him that we understood that his calling us for help meant that he no longer wanted to travel down the dark road he had been on, and thus it was important that he not condemn himself for the revenge fantasies he had, for the humiliation he felt, or for how he believed he had participated in what had happened. *Above all, it was essential that he not get into a battle with his mind,* or add still another guilt—the guilt of thinking the wrong thoughts—to what he already felt.

We were able to help him write out a list of the thoughts that were directly involved in his present suicidal feelings—which, in his case, was a one-time crisis. One of these was the memory of a confrontation he had with his wife just after the divorce, while his two children watched from her car. Another was a fantasy of her phoning, and what he would say. Another was a fantasy of her being killed in an accident. In all we identified nine recurring thoughts that were deeply upsetting to him. He had a copy machine, and we made four copies of the original and cut each of the five lists into strips, with one thought per strip. We asked him for five small plastic trash bags and put one set of nine thoughts into each.

We told him that by putting the thoughts into the bags, he was turning his thoughts over to God.*

One bag was for his kitchen, one for his bedroom, one for his living room, one for his car, and one was to carry with him to other places. The rules of the exercise were that he could think any of these thoughts any time he wanted to (in religious terms, he could take them back from God whenever he wished), but when he noticed that he had begun, he had to fish out the strip with that thought on it from one of the bags and hold it in his hand until he had finished. Then he had to put the thought back into the bag (give it back to God). That was all.

Three months after we saw him, although he was still dealing

---

* Naturally we would have omitted this religious language if he had not been religious. Others we have worked with have pictured turning their thoughts over to their Guide, their Higher Power, their Higher Self, their Sanity, or to the Greater Good.

with his losses, the man told us he had not had a single suicidal urge since that night, and he attributed this entirely to The God Bag. The results we get from this exercise are not always so dramatic, and as we said earlier, far more than a single exercise is needed if one is going to work with people who are suicidal. Nevertheless, awareness and mental discipline are always fundamental to individual happiness, as well as to a healthy relationship.

how you will benefit from these exercises   When you first begin these exercises, the difficulty you will have remembering what your thoughts have been, for example just in the last few seconds since the alarm went off, will demonstrate how unconscious idle thinking is. The mind *is* conscious of an idea while it is being thought, but it forgets it almost instantly, and this is how a single recurring thought (prime thought) can once again come into your awareness, be deeply accepted, and set up a predisposing mood, the origins of which you have soon forgotten.

Another outgrowth of these exercises is that you will repeatedly see the cause-and-effect relationship between the part of your mind that thinks in words and the part of your mind that has emotions. This is a very important link to establish, because until you do, you will think that you are a victim of almost everything your partner does and that your only remedy is either for your partner to change or for you to leave.

You will also discover that the ego part of you has critical thoughts about everything—every person, place, and event. These judgments isolate you and leave you alone in the world.

predisposing expectations   Perhaps the most common predisposing thought is an almost unconscious decision of how the day should go. These expectations are always an outgrowth of our prime thoughts, but it's not necessary to be aware of a prime thought in order to catch and eliminate expectations.

An expectation literally prejudges what is a good day and what is not. Notice that you begin this type of mental activity soon after rising; notice also that the day almost never goes the way you want. At times it will seem as if the day has a mind of its own and quite perversely sets out to thwart your expectations. However, once you have accepted your ego's idea of what will make you happy, it's very difficult not to feel the emotion that seems justified when things don't go your way. This is why awareness of your thoughts is especially helpful in the mornings and why the lack of it can allow an entire day to get away from you.

Whenever you find that you have formed a picture of how some upcoming event should go or how some time slot would best be filled, ask yourself if this is a plan worth keeping. If after a moment's stillness you believe that it is, instruct your mind to remember that love comes first and that all plans are tentative and secondary to it. **Organization and goals are useful and needed, but all plans must yield to the well-being of your relationship.** Often it's helpful to follow with a brief fantasy of some ways your plan might be thwarted and from what part of you you will respond if that happens. Picture yourself remembering the importance of your relationship and how that will feel. In other words, put in place an alternative attitude to disappointment, irritation, frustration, or distance to which you can quickly turn.

coming home from work   Most people coming home are looking forward to seeing their partner, and the one who is home is looking forward to that person's return—and yet within a few minutes after she or he walks in the door, the couple is fighting or at least withdrawing. There can be several reasons for this. One is merely the ego's desire for a change in emotion. Perhaps the work day was frustrating, the returning partner is still feeling this impotence, and anger seems an easy way of breaking out of that mindset. But an even more consistent factor is the hidden thought of "You left me—you should never have left—if you really loved me you would never go," as well as "You should have come with me; you should be like Ruth of the Bible and always be by my side."

If you will watch your mind carefully, you can see this quite irrational but very common thought. It has to be seen before it will be believed, because since it is absurd to expect your partner never to leave your side, you might think that it's unlikely that your ego could be reacting in this way.

To counteract this little feeling of abandonment, we used to routinely sit down together when one of us would come back after an absence of more than a few hours. Before asking each other questions ("What happened at work? Is dinner ready? Did you mail the letter to Scott?") we would first "take a moment to join," which in our case meant closing our eyes and surrounding our relationship in light. Naturally, if the person coming home can pause before entering the house, much of what was hatching in the mind during the day won't make it into the home. We know other couples who have worked out their own rituals for releasing unhelpful attitudes. One woman immediately takes a shower and changes clothes when she arrives home, in order to "shed the vibes."

gaining access to real feelings   The ability to distinguish between ego feelings and real feelings is also rooted in a disciplined mind. To touch one's core, one must become physically peaceful and mentally still. This can be accomplished in many ways, and it has been our experience that there are *not* some methods vastly superior to others. However, it's good to find a few that you are comfortable with and simply to let those be your approach, rather than spending a lifetime trying to discover the perfect way to begin. Often these will be very personal to you. Gayle sometimes repeats to herself Jesus' words, "I and my father are one." Hugh has a particular CD of Gregorian chants that he finds quieting. On many occasions we have meditated together on a passage from *A Course in Miracles* that we have either selected at random or taken in order. We have joined together countless times to consider silently the questions "What kind of person do I want to be? What kind of life do I want to live?" We have also used approaches such as watching our breathing, listening to the sounds around us, counting each thing we are aware of, or quietly acknowledging each sensation we feel in our body.

Once in a sermon Hugh gave at The Dispensable Church, he told how all week he had been silently chanting, "Gayle is everything I want. Gayle is everything I need. God is everything I want. God is everything I need." The next week a woman came up to him after the service and said, "I've had the most peaceful week. I've been chanting the only thing I could remember from your talk." "What's that?" he asked. " 'Gayle is everything I want,' " she said. Then she added, "I guess the words aren't really important."

Of course, sometimes the words are very important, but what this woman experienced was the power of pure intention, which rises above words. It is the effort that does the work, and that is why an endless search for the perfect technique, the perfect words, the perfect setting in which to begin, misses the point. All you ever need do is to start, to try, to do your best—using whatever tools you have.

It's impossible to decide how effective a meditation has been. Your ego will always compare today's meditation with yesterday's and try to choose between the two. That conclusion, whatever it may be, is worthless to you. A daily practice of prayer and meditation has a cumulative effect that goes far beyond what one could have imagined and definitely brings into consciousness one's true feelings.

PRIME THOUGHTS

distinguishing characteristics As you practice the thought-awareness exercises we described earlier, you will keep bumping into one or more deep recurring thoughts, which you will eventually recognize as entirely negative in their effect on your relationship. These are the thoughts that trigger your and your partner's core dynamics. They are quiet, underlying thoughts, and at first they may be difficult to sense. Often, as with one of Hugh's prime thoughts, they are even difficult to believe. Still, if you persist in practicing the awareness exercises, you will run across them so many times that you will have no doubt about their grip on your general attitude toward your partner. Here are examples of some typical prime thoughts:

"Nothing ever works out."

"Marriage ruins relationships."

"Sooner or later they always leave."

"I'm being held back in this relationship."

"Women are emotionally unstable and the root of all trouble."

"There will never be an end to this."

"Men are no damn good, and you can't rely on them."

"Nothing I do will ever be good enough."

"If I weren't married I could get someone I've always fantasized about. Someone who's (rich, spiritual, more open to sex, more intellectual, less demanding, more athletic, young and beautiful)."

"I will always be alone."

"If you would only change, I could love you."

"I will never have the life I want. I will never do the things I've dreamed of."

"I'm being (driven crazy, damaged, slowly killed)."

"I will never be loved."

"If I could just be on my own, if I could just be free."

"I will always have to do all the work in this relationship."

"God has pets, and I'm not one of them."

There are of course many other such thoughts, and the ones that you have may be very different from those listed above. They may also be difficult to identify because of the slight absurdity of their logic and especially because of the quietness with which they are "spoken."

Every prime thought has these basic attributes:

1. It comes before the dynamic and "primes" the pump for the dynamic to begin.
2. It is a characterization of reality that you deeply buy into.
3. It comes from your ego and therefore your past.
4. It has little to do with your partner, although it can be made to fit.
5. It is very resistant.
6. It is largely unconscious and is usually experienced as an impression rather than as a precisely worded thought.
7. It takes a form appropriate to the occasion.

the part of your mind that speaks in sentences

There is a *layer* of thoughts that mask the prime thought, which we refer to in this book as **justifying thoughts.** If you have not already, you will eventually discover that you are not upset for the reason you are telling yourself. You are upset because of a previously accepted prime thought. However, it's necessary to become aware of your immediate justifying thoughts so that you can step back from them and see your upset with more perspective. Otherwise, you will mindlessly persist in your attack.

Justifying thoughts are always about the issue at hand. ("He never closes the milk carton." "She would argue all night." "He doesn't know how to earn money." "She never picks up anything." "He plays too rough with the baby." "She's letting the children manipulate her.") They are the things you tell yourself are the issue. But the real issue is the prime thought, which is below this layer.

Prime thoughts can definitely destroy a sound relationship. A young couple, Leane and Steve, volunteered to participate in our

"How to Argue in Peace" demonstration for a workshop of ours they were attending. They had been married only five months and were deeply in love. They had come to the workshop not because of any problems they were currently having, but to learn a process for resolving issues that might arise later. It took them a long time to think of a conflict between them and when they did, it seemed pretty lame to the rest of the group. Leane said that sometimes Steve didn't take out the trash as soon as she would like. And Steve said that sometimes Leane nagged him about this. The group laughed because they were looking at each other with such love while they described this so-called problem.

We then had them take the next step (see the heading "How to Have a Real Argument" on page 208), which was to close their eyes and get in touch with the fears that they could sense behind this conflict. From the way that they looked at each other when they opened their eyes to share their fears, it was clear to everyone that there was more to this lightweight difficulty than first appeared. Leane was abandoned by her father when she was seven and her prime thought was "You can't trust men," and Steve had grown up with a mother he could never please. His prime thought was, naturally, "You can never please women." They were obviously in a unique position to help each other heal.

Therefore, it was not surprising that Leane voiced the fear that since she had mentioned to Steve several times in the past that he tended to let the garbage accumulate—and he had not subsequently altered this behavior—that maybe Steve didn't really respect her and love her and that some day he would leave. Steve on the other hand felt pressured. He thought that Leane was being unreasonably critical of the way he did things. If how he handled the garbage was important to her, what was in store for him as she got to know him even better?

In discussing his fears, Steve realized that he wasn't resisting complying with Leane's wishes about the *garbage* so much as he was trying to keep her from starting down the road of total nonacceptance of him. Now he saw that his behavior was not the way to make her more accepting, and on the spot he committed to a specific schedule of garbage takeout. Leane realized that the garbage had only become important to her when Steve didn't immediately respond the first time she mentioned it. She had taken this as a lack of commitment to her. Now she saw that Steve did love her, that he had no intention of leaving her, and that the garbage itself wasn't that important. As her way of helping resolve the issue she said that she would take it out herself if ever it bothered her again.

A letter that we received from them about a year later indicated that they were very much on top of this budding dynamic and had begun to assume the role of each other's healers rather than each other's attackers. If they had continued approaching new issues in the old way, their prime thoughts would have increasingly dominated their attitudes toward each other. Soon there would have been many areas in which Steve resisted Leane's wishes, and Leane could easily have become as nagging as Steve's mother had been.

You were unhappy *before* you met your partner, and your prime thoughts were the source—whether you were single, in transition, or in other relationships. The present relationship may be amplifying your unhappiness, so that now there seems more of it, but it's not what is causing it.

You wish to become more familiar with your mind so that it can be a comfort instead of an affliction. Especially, you want to be aware of the part of your mind that speaks in sentences. Here, rather than within your emotions, you will find both the justifying thoughts and one or two prime thoughts. If you are unaware, the way your mind proceeds is that **a prime thought generates justifying thoughts, justifying thoughts generate an emotion, and emotions generate some form of your relationship's core dynamic.**

About an hour and a half ago, Gayle went to the money machine and discovered that we had a zero balance. After John graduated from junior high last month, Hugh took him to Lake Havasu as a graduation present, then when they got home, the four of us went to Knott's Berry Farm and Disneyland. We knew these trips would be expensive, but we had not expected them to drain our account completely.

Only a few minutes ago, Hugh asked Gayle if she was going to have time to fix us our usual blender drink. She bridled and said, "Of course!" and stormed off. As she walked away, she began to ask herself what was wrong with Hugh's question. It didn't matter that she is the one who makes this particular health drink—Hugh could learn how to make it himself. Hugh also hadn't given her much of a hello kiss before he asked the question.

Then Gayle caught herself, and instead of continuing to blame Hugh, she started looking for the prime thought. Naturally it had to do with our zero balance. The thought she had accepted was her usual fear that we are going to run out of money, a thought that was always in the air during her childhood and that was a part of her mother's and father's driving fear that "one's life is always on the verge of catastrophe."

The prime thought is a very quietly spoken description of what seems to be fundamental reality. Almost anything can trigger it. It takes an appropriate form. (Running out of money is a form of catastrophe.) It is so deeply believed that very little supporting evidence is needed; even a memory will do. It often presents itself in the morning, within the first hour or two after you awake, or in the afternoon, between lunch and dinner. But it can come anytime.

If you are in a particularly unhappy period, you may "hear" it within seconds after you awake, but you will always be free of it the *instant* you awake, and that is the best time to start watching your mind. Having a notebook by your bed where you can write down what you notice is an excellent way of speeding up the identifying process.

CORE DYNAMICS

You probably carry with you only one or two prime thoughts, and these interact with your partner's to produce only one or two core dynamics. Most individuals have a single prime thought and most relationships have just one dominating dynamic, but there are so many exceptions to this that it's not helpful to make a decision about the number of factors you have to deal with. By far the best approach is to **stay away from all labels** and concentrate on an ever-expanding awareness of your ego and your self. You may find that your principal dynamic is one that has been described by others, but don't at that point stop noticing and turn instead to someone else's characterization of this pattern as your source of information about your relationship. Remember that your dynamic will always be more or less unique; that is why your continued awareness is essential.

Most couples, perhaps all, soon begin to realize that their upsets have a pattern. They have seen this little dance so many times that they can even sense when it is about to begin. And yet they seem helpless to stop it once it starts. They know how the argument or clash of wills will invariably end, but no matter what they try to do differently, it never seems to make any real difference.

These are often your first awarenesses that a central pattern dominates much of your relating. It is essential to understand that all relationships begin with one or two dynamics and that no matter who your partner was, this would still hold true. A new relationship would merely bring a new dynamic, or a new version of the old one, but the need to achieve oneness would remain the same.

All dynamics are caused by prime thoughts. This is one reason you can sometimes sense when one of your relationship's more destructive patterns is about to be played out—you are sensing that something has "primed" you to participate.

Dynamics are simply patterns of interreactions that you and

your partner keep repeating. They are referred to as "dynamics" because they contain the forces of change, and this is very important to keep in mind. At first they may seem to work well, may even appear to be the glue that holds you together, but because you are each forced to play a role—and must maintain that role for the dynamic to continue working—as you change, the barriers of the dynamic must hold in ever-increasing tensions. Thus all dynamics eventually become destructive to the relationship.

Many authors and workshop leaders describe their favorite dynamics in detail and provide tests and checklists for you to use. Please note that in most cases all you need is a *percentage* of confirming answers in order to know that you have a fit. Yet the answers that did *not* fit indicate that **something is going on within you or your partner that is an exception to everything that will be said about the dynamic.**

We have yet to deal with any couple who did not deviate in some major way from the general pattern their relationship appeared to fall into, and most relationships deviate in numerous ways. If a couple tries to decide in what ways they vary, and how these variations operate, the task becomes needlessly complex, and the simple goal of healing is usually forgotten.

Those who wish you to put your relationship into their favorite classification, may also offer you a course of action to take, which, because the classification doesn't quite fit, will not quite work. Sorting all of this out is an unnecessary burden on your affection. You can see for yourself what is going on today, and today draw your remedy from your own calm wisdom.

Aside from a few examples we will give, the reason we won't go into more detail about the various forms that dynamics can take is that not only are they too numerous to describe, but in our opinion it is unnecessary for a couple to use them as anything but indicators that there is a dynamic operating in their relationship. To give all that you have together a single label can be very disheartening, and furthermore, it is unnecessary. It's sufficient that you realize that all relationships begin with certain ego patterns and that the work cut out for you is no greater than for other couples. There are, however, time savers, and identifying the prime thoughts that trigger your dynamics, and observing for yourselves how your dynamics operate, can be enormously helpful.

FOUR EXAMPLES OF CORE DYNAMICS

feminine female—macho male   One dynamic that has been much written about—and generally overapplied—is based on the sexes of the partners. Usually this takes the form of a very macho man and a very feminine woman. It is a good illustration of how the central dynamic of a relationship can appear to be what makes it work. Each partner seems to be appreciated for his or her personality type, and as long as they don't want to express more of themselves, the relationship is stable. When, however, the man wishes to bring forth more of his feminine side, or the woman more of her male side, conflict ensues. "I want a real man, not a wimp," the woman may think. Or as one male relative of ours has said many times, "Only a foreign woman, preferably a Latin or Oriental, knows how to be a wife." He has already discarded a string of American women, who he always perceived as wanting to "make him into someone else."

Even though both partners initially like their respective roles, neither of them can truly benefit in the ways they believe they can. The woman may see her husband as the one who will take care of her and defend her, thus relieving her of many of the anxieties of simple survival. The man may think of his wife as the devoted admirer and supporter who gives him the strength to carry on. This is a dynamic in which there can seem to be great closeness and mutual admiration while it lasts, yet when it begins to fail, it

can suddenly turn very cold, the wife perhaps becoming the nag-
ger and manipulator and the husband becoming rigid, arbitrary,
and closed-minded. But like all dynamics, it actually never delivered on its promise from the beginning.

To put oneself into another's protection is as tenuous and uncertain as human fate and frailty. No man is a rock. And this fact
must slowly or quickly become apparent to the woman, as well as
the self-imposed weakness that living up to the ideal her dependence has imposed. Eventually she comes to want to express her
masculine strengths. Nor is it truly an inspiration for a man to
have a wife who believes he can do anything. He is made more
painfully aware of his inadequacies, knowing that he can never
show them. Eventually he will want to express his feminine
strengths.

In any dynamic, change is inevitable, and every relationship has
one or more dynamics in place that outline the area of greatest
potential growth. If a relationship is to become real, both partners
must allow for change—and not seek it with another person of a
different personality type. The macho man must allow his wife to
become more assertive, if this is the direction she begins to go,
and the feminine female must support her husband in expressing
his vulnerability and sensitivity, if that is what he chooses. However, change within a dynamic never comes without some disrup-
tion and period of adjustment. To make this all worthwhile is
within your power.

The ego has no home and no companion. It lives in anxiety and
misunderstanding. It can't connect because it is not present. It
looks on everyone and everything through the attitudes it has accumulated. This does not mean that you forever chant a mantra
against the world. Nor does knowing the truth entail some kind of
tricky Pollyannish thinking. You want to become more honest, not
less. You want to look past a single dimension and see your partner. Peace is the house of God, and here is where you wish to
dwell.

one who runs—one who chases   Another common dynamic is the one that develops between an ego that wants to keep its distance and an ego that wants the appearance of closeness. Variations of this are one who chases and one who runs away. And one who engulfs or smothers and one who denies or withholds.

The roles of this dynamic can be played by either sex. The woman may play the part of untouchable royalty and the man that of needy commoner. Or the man may think he is too mature for childish displays of affection, and the woman may think she must have a steady stream of outward proofs that her partner loves her.

Although the role of the person who needs closeness was once looked on with more favor than the role of the person who needs space, this attitude began to reverse under the ever-broadening definition of codependence and other categories of "loving too much." Now many view those who require distance as more self-actualized, whereas before, it was those who sought the picture of affection, closeness, and sharing who were so classified. Within this dynamic, however, both positions are void of either love or strength.

Real closeness is not actually being sought. If I try to pressure you into demonstrating your love for me—knowing that you don't like such demonstrations—I am driving a wedge between us. **The ego tries to force the appearance of closeness in order to create separateness,** and the ego's valuing of separateness is the driving force of all dynamics.

Likewise, those who keep their distance, thinking that they are thereby made stronger and more complete, are equally deceived. Having to be the one who is superior, or the one who never makes affectionate overtures, or whatever variant of this dynamic individuals may find themselves acting out, is to cut oneself off from help, and who is ever capable of doing more by refusing help? Who has greater insight by not listening? Who has greater peace by not feeling loved?

This dynamic is solved in the same manner as all unhappy patterns. First it must be seen. Then a deeper reaction must be put in place and practiced until it becomes natural. This of course requires great patience with yourself, as well as your partner. Remember that all dynamics are walls that you will eventually press up against as you begin to change. They also include familiar roles that are frightening to depart from. But you will change and you will depart. That is why dynamics cannot act as the foundation of a real relationship. Instead of seeing every change your partner undergoes as still another example of his or her perversity, your new reaction must be to look past the behavior to the spirit. You have already seen your partner's spirit, and you can trust what you know.

one who judges—one who reacts   This dynamic appears to be triggered by those individuals who become judgmental about almost everything. Their partners chafe under that attitude and periodically react in irritation or anger. If residual rage is high in either person, this dynamic can sometimes result in physical abuse. But that only happens in a minority of cases, and even in these the early stages of the relationship may mask the rage for a time. When it does come out, it can be shocking to *both* partners.

Traditionally, the judgmental partners have been the ones who were blamed for the dynamic. But this interpretation has also changed somewhat in the last couple of decades. Now chronically judgmental people (the "emotionally abusive") are often dismissed as lost souls, whereas their partners, because they remain in the relationship, are singled out as being in a position to take responsibility for themselves and weakly choosing not to. In other words, the greater blame falls on them because they don't leave.

Once again, neither partner is more to blame. In relationships in which no partner carries an air of criticism, naturally the dynamic doesn't form. In relationships in which the less judgmental person does not rise to the bait, the dynamic also never forms.

There are many people who are thrown in with someone every day who is gruff, ill-tempered, or sullen but who don't take it to heart. In some rare cases they find it part of that person's charm—although admittedly this is not easy to do.

Both our grandmothers were critical of everything, and both of them lived with our parents. Gayle's grandmother's attitude was annoying and disruptive to Gayle's parents and therefore damaging to Gayle, whereas Hugh's mother and stepfather usually found his grandmother's attitude amusing, but even when they didn't, they never took it personally. Visitors to the house often had the feeling that she had come to like her role of being critical and blunt on all occasions and secretly delighted in the laughter it caused—although she was by no means a humorous person.

As is true of all dynamics, neither party benefits from their role. In the world, anger often has a powerful effect. The angriest part of a speech is reported most widely; in a close fight the angriest boxer usually wins; the angriest complaint is dealt with first; the angriest criticism is remembered longest; and so forth. It would also appear that the angrier partner gets his or her way more often. And so to be always on the verge of anger would seem to be a key to staying in control—except that because of this attitude there is no real relationship and the person is in control of nothing worth having.

Those partners whose role it is to react also don't receive the benefit they think. They believe that they must stand up for themselves, that there has to be a limit and it has just been reached, and so they turn to the same mistaken source of power that their partner turns to. It's interesting that self-esteem is now tied to assertiveness; that "standing up for yourself" is synonymous with getting angry; and that taking up a cause means doing battle with others. The assumption that anger is power is definitely a subtext of separation psychology, even though the opposite sentiment is often given lip service.

Ultimately, anger never works. It's the ego in total charge of the mind, and there is no love in it. Parents who are always getting angry on behalf of their children, supposedly out of love for them, find they can't switch this emotion off at will. Shortly after being irritated with one of their child's tormentors, they find that they have also become irritated with their own child. The same of course applies to adult relationships. For example, it's very difficult to be angry at a politician or commentator on television and then turn in peace to one's spouse. To value attack is to become an attacker. The value itself must be questioned.

At present it's often assumed that this dynamic is essentially tied to sexual differences: the male being the disapproving one, the female reacting to his moods. In our experience these roles do not divide along sexual lines and gender is not the controlling factor. It's interesting, however, the number of people, women and men alike, who don't realize that they have taken on the role of disapproving parent in their relationship. Sometimes these individuals can appear very open, sensitive, even enlightened. They may be very well versed in holistic health, animal testing, civil liberties, metaphysics, and any number of other "correct" subjects that would seem to indicate a caring, understanding person. Their judgments and attacks, sounding like enlightened insights, can be particularly negative, and their mindset can be quite resistant, given the fact that they almost never think of themselves as judgmental or, as if often true, hostile to the opposite sex.

Whether this is recognized by the more critical partner or not, freeing the mind of censure is not only practical, energy boosting, happiness enhancing, and simplifying, but it is the one step required to dissolve this particular dynamic. However you may interpret your partner's actions, and no matter what you decide to do about them, practice affirming this person's basic innocence, and you will be increasingly free. Once again, dishonest mental gymnastics are not required. If you see something as wrong, then that is simply the way you see it. Do not try to reinterpret. Merely ask yourself if there is something more to a person than guilt.

the destructive alliance   There is of course the special
dynamic in which two people reinforce very destructive behavior
in each other. This has been taken out of context and applied so
broadly to the human condition that it seems to be misused by
almost every couple who studies it. Unless one or both of you is
doing something that is detrimental to your or other people's
health or safety, you simply don't need to concern yourself with
the mountain of literature on this subject, most of which is now
too generalized to be of any real help and much of which will
definitely poison you against each other. Obviously we all could
do a better job of helping one another get past mistaken approaches, but that is why two people come together—to find a way
to join strengths instead of weaknesses. Naturally we start out
doing this all wrong. But let us have a little faith in what brought
us together. **Pathology is not the driving force of the universe.**
Each partnership has its own path to walk, and we need not be so
quick to question it. A lot more is going on than the body's eyes
can see or the ego mind can imagine. There are worse approaches
than to trust.

HEALING A HURTFUL PATTERN— SOME PERSONAL EXAMPLES

For a pattern of interaction to be disturbing to both partners, both
must contribute. If one partner were able to stop participating, the
dynamic would either dissolve or cease to be a problem. We recently had an opportunity to work with a couple who behave similarly to us in at least two ways but who, because of how their
dynamic causes them to participate emotionally, create problems
for themselves that we don't have. In the following example
please note that behavior in itself does not create the dynamic, and
yet most couples direct all their attention to changing each other's
behavior. The prime thought and the emotions it generates is all
that ever needs to change, even though partners usually do modify

their behavior in order to make it easier on each other to step back from the problem.

Jody and George each have variations of commonly held prime thoughts. These interact to form a dynamic that many couples would recognize but, as is true within most marriages, does not fit precisely into a standard category. George's thought is "Everyone but me is incompetent, especially women." He has no trouble tracing back this attitude to his father. Jody's thought, to use her words, is "I'm the one who always has to do all the work, especially when men are around." This she can see was also her mother's dominant attitude.

These prime thoughts interact to form a dynamic in which George plays the role of one who is decisive yet abrupt, one who acts yet doesn't listen. Jody's role is to be generous yet resentful, patient yet "longsuffering." The dynamic plays itself out in many daily patterns, although they have already eliminated some of these during the first few months of their marriage by becoming more fully conscious of their thoughts. One pattern is for George to wait *impatiently* in the car while Jody makes them late by locking doors, turning out lights and doing other tasks that she *resentfully* thinks George should have helped with.

When we called them this afternoon for permission to write about their dynamic, they laughed because they said they had just discovered another way that it takes form. That morning George had finished cleaning his truck, a task he had started the day before. He knew when he did this that Jody had wanted him to seal some wood siding that the Arizona sun was beginning to get to. Because of an appointment they had, it was not possible for him to do both, but as he jokingly told us, "It's more competent to finish the job that you've started." If they hadn't interrupted their argument and turned instead to searching out what was behind it, Jody might have played out her usual role by attempting to seal the siding herself, thus proving that she always ends up having to do most of the work.

We don't have George and Jody's particular dynamic, and although Hugh frequently causes Gayle to wait in the car while he locks up the house, turns out the lights, and so forth, no issue is made of this. And when Hugh does some task that appears to benefit him instead of doing a task that is more of a mutual benefit, Gayle does not get angry. Thus an unhappy pattern cannot form in either instance.

As you begin dealing with some of your relationship's hurtful patterns, you might bear in mind the following stages we have noticed in our own patterns. To begin with, here are two simple techniques that we have found useful:

1. In order to stop participating in the pattern that has developed between you, it's very helpful to become aware of the thought that sets up the part you personally play. As soon as you sense that a pattern is beginning, stop and freeze the contents of your mind and begin tracing back every thought you are aware of. In order to do this, you must learn to break with the situation you are in. Very briefly, by yourself or with your partner, put your body where you can concentrate. You only need a minute or two. Go into the bathroom, step outside, pull the car off the road, put the phone down, excuse yourself from the dinner table. If you had diarrhea you wouldn't think twice about doing any of these things. Please recognize that your relationship is as important as diarrhea.

Although the preconditioning thought may have been forgotten, it has not left your mind and can usually be remembered. Simply *try* to remember it. What you are looking for is the idea that changed your mood prior to the unhappy exchange you and your partner are starting to have.

2. Another simple technique, and one we have used ourselves for many years whenever some vestige of a dynamic begins to recur, is to carry a small notebook in which we record every thought that is even mildly critical of each other. We find that if we will do this for several days, we once again become sensitized to the deep beliefs that set up the misery. The contents of these notebooks are for your personal use only and should not be shown

to each other. To do so can lead to further misunderstandings and will definitely influence what you record.

When Hugh first started doing these two exercises, he was very surprised at the prime thought behind his hostility toward Gayle. At first he couldn't believe that he was capable of having accepted such an unreasonable idea. He was also shocked at how many years he had been controlled by it, simply because it had remained unconscious:

He discovered that he believed that women, and especially one's wife, are the cause of all the trouble in a man's life. Reinforcing this was another prime thought: that women will always desert you. The source of the latter was easy to trace. Through a series of events that she felt powerless to control, his mother had in fact abandoned Hugh, and his father reminded him of this throughout Hugh's childhood. When he didn't behave, his father would imply that his mother had left because Hugh was not worth loving.

In trying to trace the first prime thought, Hugh was fortunate that his dad was still alive, and the next time he visited him, he listened very carefully to his father's conversation. In the course of one evening meal his father used the phrase "these damned women" three times. He was a real estate broker and in those years the entire nation was in a recession, but he blamed the depressed residential market in his hometown on "these women who have driven up the prices to a point where no one will buy. They get listings by telling owners that they can get them some ridiculous price."

Hugh's father's sexual prejudice was not unusual, and most parents pass their attitudes toward the opposite sex along to their children. It is tempting for divorced mothers and fathers to mistakenly undermine their child's appreciation of the other parent and thus of the other parent's gender, not realizing what long-term problems they are creating for the child.

It was good that Hugh could see where his attitude had come

from, but seeing it didn't do all the work. Recognizing the origins
of a prime thought can be immensely helpful, and therefore tracing it as far back as one can is definitely worth the effort, but the
memory of where it came from is not essential to healing. There
are one or two prime thoughts that we have gotten beyond that we
have no solid insights as to how they developed.

Hugh recognized that the way his part in our dynamic operated
was truly insane. Whenever anything was going on in our lives
that he didn't like, he would *first* blame Gayle and *then* look for
the reason it was her fault. If one of our boys got sick, it was
Gayle's fault—because she was less rigid about their diet than
Hugh was. If the battery went dead in the car because Hugh left
the lights on—this was an inconvenience only because Gayle
didn't offer to take care of it. If Gayle suggested that our family
take a trip, anything that went wrong was her fault—because she
was the one who had initiated the plan (even though Hugh had
agreed to it). And so on.

His attitude was all pervasive and led to our primary dynamic
of the sullen husband and the reactionary wife. As he became
increasingly aware of what he was doing and his critical moods
became shorter, Gayle, to Hugh's surprise, became *more* sensitive
to these moods. Her angry reactions did not lessen at what he
thought should be a fair and comparable rate, and for a long time
he believed he was being mistreated. Recognizing this she started
trying very hard to respond in a more helpful way, and she was
remarkably successful.

Anyone reading this who has a similar problem to Hugh's
should understand that someone who has suffered from some mistake of yours over a long period, as Gayle had with Hugh's silent
judgments, will eventually become very sensitive to the mistake,
just as the body becomes sensitive to even a minor chafing in an
area of previous injury. Eventually Hugh realized that Gayle's
reactions could be useful to him—if he truly wanted to rid himself
of every vestige of the problem.

When he first became conscious of these two prime thoughts, he decided to question his ego whenever he found himself dwelling on any version of them. For example, if his thought was, "Once again Gayle put dishes in the sink without running water over them (e.g., all my burdens are caused by my wife)," he would stop and quiz himself as to what he believed and what he wanted to do about it. He would always feel a resistance to doing this, because, of course, the ego doesn't want to be brought into awareness.

For example, he would say, "Yes, it's true that she did this, but what do I want it to mean? Do I believe she's stupid? Do I believe she is my sworn enemy and is plotting to drive me insane? Do I believe she has lost all respect for me and won't even honor this simple request? After all, I'm the one who does the dishes. And what do I want to do about it? Do I want to kill her? Do I want to yell at her? Do I want to make her use paper plates for the rest of her life? Do I want to refuse to do this little chore—even though she does most of the unpleasant tasks in our relationship?"

Hugh would pause after each question and try to discover what were his ego's feelings, and then what were *his* feelings.

Please remember that this is a discovery process only. It does not, for example, make an assumption about the ego and then look for supporting evidence. You question your mind for the sole purpose of broadening your awareness, not to make the ego into a devil figure.

The ego is made and sustained wholly by our own mind. Since we control it, fearing it would be a mistake of ignorance. It is like a bad habit that continues only because we are not aware of doing it. Therefore, if you strongly question your ego—and we urge you to form this habit—please don't be concerned if you discover that at times it's quite vicious in its motivations. This imaginary identity is an attacker, an opposer, and it feels especially hostile toward someone you love. But remember that you are only uncovering thoughts and feelings that are already there. It can never hurt you to become more conscious. You are not adding negativity, merely acknowledging it, so that you can make a choice.

Your ego is background noise, like a TV you can hear from another room. It's the CNN of your life. It's composed of many voices and many conflicting opinions, all from the past, and as you have already seen if you have tried the awareness exercises we have been suggesting, you in fact let most of it wash over you. Every few moments, though, something catches your interest and becomes important. Among the sound bites that grab you are woven your prime thoughts, and you want a little warning to go off inside you whenever you catch yourself taking them seriously. Otherwise, you remain unconsciously controlled by your past.

When you notice yourself buying into one of these thoughts, all you need to do is first examine it in the ways we have been discussing, then once again become bored and disinterested, once again let it sink back into the drone of words that pour forever from your ego.

PART II

The Eight Mindsets of a Real Relationship

THE PROBLEMS THAT THE VAST MAJORITY OF COUPLES HAVE ARE surprisingly unoriginal, and yet each couple is likely to believe they live in a hell all their own. Within their circle of acquaintances, they may not be aware of any other couple similarly afflicted, but if they were able to stand at the center of these other relationships, in all likelihood they would see one or more versions of their own, surrounded merely by different circumstances.

Awareness of the eight mindsets that most relationships pass through should, if nothing else, give you and your partner cause for hope. They are not merely levels of problem solving; they are also the natural levels of increasing fulfillment.

These mindsets are not rigid or required, nor must they last for a prescribed length of time. In fact, a couple can pass through several of them in a day and reverse the process the following day. But generally speaking, one mindset will tend to dominate the couple's manner of relating for a period of weeks, months, or years before they move on to the next. Most relationships go through the mindsets as stages or levels of growth and do so in this order: **falling in love; the honeymoon mindset; period of adjustment; "something's missing"; crisis; forgiveness; "norming and performing"; attainment.**

Our purpose in describing the common mindsets or stages is, first, to give you a solid basis for hope that if you work hard at understanding each other, you can be assured of reaching new levels of fulfillment. And, second, to provide you with a realistic picture of what other relationships are going through. Our descriptions are based on our own counseling sessions with couples and on supplementary interviews with couples we have not counseled, as well as on interviews with other therapists and counselors, some of whom drew up their own list of mindsets for us. Of course there may be other exceptions, but the only couples we and those we consulted have seen who have not gone through the usual stages are those in which one or both partners have a history of multiple relationships. These people often have merely a brief courtship and honeymoon period (stages 1 and 2), then go straight to "something's missing" or crisis (stages 4 or 5), then break up. Their task is more difficult, but they too can achieve a real relationship if they commit to staying. Once they make that decision, they usually go through all of the stages we will describe.

The dominant mindsets that couples pass through are quite easy to identify; what is missing is a general awareness that we all have a remarkably similar road to travel. Most people think they are in circumstances they should not have to put up with, or that they are incapable of handling, whereas they are merely going through a version of what all couples go through—and will have to go through again if they break up and start over with someone new. This is not usually apparent, because the conditions and events surrounding each couple differ and the manner in which they play out their mindset will be personal to them. For example, many couples (but certainly not all) pass through a stage that includes intense sexual attraction, and yet one couple may act this out in a very private way and therefore give the appearance that they are not physically attracted to each other.

As you read our descriptions of the eight stages, and especially if you discuss them with each other, it is vital that you never use them to assess the value of what you have together. Also, be especially careful not to compare your level of growth with that of your friends'. Despite how open they may appear to be, it's a safe bet they are not broadcasting every issue they are presently dealing with. They may not even be *aware* of every issue. What you can be assured of is that no couple's path to a real relationship is shorter than yours. The distance to love is the same for everyone.

As a couple's friendship grows, it's unlikely that they will proceed from mindset to mindset in a completely orderly manner. Some couples will skip a stage altogether; some will slip back for a time to a level they thought they were beyond; many will shift between two or more stages before moving on. There can also be precipitating events such as being fired, overcoming an addiction, moving, a sudden increase in income, the death of a parent, an affair, pregnancy, illness, and so forth, which may temporarily throw a couple back into an earlier stage. These come in some form to every relationship and are the storms we all must weather. Often they catch the couple off guard, because many of them are not perceived as difficulties.

Sometimes it's not easy to appreciate fully the advances your relationship has made because of the great show of normalcy you are probably seeing all around you. Most couples are quite aware of the image they wish to project, even though they may not talk openly to each other about it. The role they adopt can continue even during therapy, because they believe their real patterns are too shamefully different to reveal. When they finally begin to describe what they think is a unique problem, an experienced therapist can complete almost every sentence they begin, so often has the therapist heard it before.

Any article, book, or workshop that gives you a sense of not being alone can be helpful—provided that the authors or group leaders are in a permanent relationship themselves and have reached one of the later stages of this type of growth. Unless individuals working in this field are themselves experiencing the benefits they are attempting to lead others toward, it's very difficult for them to communicate the type of happiness that is available and the steps needed to reach it. Add to this the deeply rooted tendency we all have to pull others into the same problems that we ourselves are experiencing, and it becomes clearer why so many of these "authorities" are presently hastening the end of the relationships they touch.

If you find yourself starting to put your spouse into some negative category and believe that it's not good for you to be in partnership with this type of person, or even if you find yourself becoming a little more suspicious of your partner, close the book, walk out of the workshop, end the counseling session, hang up the phone. Do it gently—in an unmemorable and undisturbing way—but do it. You must protect your mind. Anything that poisons you against the one you have chosen to live with for life should be avoided.

Recently we worked with a couple who were deeply confused over the conflict they were having after the wife had freed herself from multiple addictions (cocaine, Demerol, and alcohol). For the first time in her adult life, she had been dry for over a year. They had both quite naturally assumed that this freedom would bring an end to most of the issues between them, just as other couples mistakenly assume that finally getting married, or having a child, or getting a house, or receiving the inheritance, or attaining professional status, or having the surgery, will, of itself, increase their happiness.

Whatever you seek in the world will hurt you. This is a state-ment that is very easy to misinterpret. Nevertheless, it contains a truth that can be freeing to your relationship. Naturally, it does not mean that people are better off unmarried, childless, poor, or un-healthy, or that planning, organization, and practicality are to be avoided. It points to the fact that a purely external pursuit will always take you out of your relationship and therefore remove you from your source of peace. The only way an outward goal can be harmless is if it is undertaken *in order* to increase your experience of oneness. For example, there are people who see clearly that greater income would be beneficial to their family. It is possible for them to work very hard toward this goal, to achieve it, and for the extra money to smooth out certain difficulties—provided that a new set of expectations, ones that are essentially loveless, don't take the place of the original purpose. But it's very difficult to keep this from happening. This is especially true in the case of money, sex, position, power, and other externals that our culture considers its greatest prizes. Practice not getting caught up in the world, and if you do, you will eventually learn how to protect your relationship from the effects of victories as well as defeats.

To show how subtly purposes can change, let's return to the wife who had overcome substance abuse. Before they married, her husband had taken her in and cared for her off and on for seven years. During this time he would not agree to marriage until she had been dry for one year. They came to us for help nine months after the wedding, and by then they were barely hanging on.

Through guided fantasy we took them back to a point just be-fore the woman had made the decision to free herself, and we had them both relive their expectations. It was clear that they had loved each other deeply and had seen that the elimination of the addictions would make life easier on each other. Yet when the work of drying out actually began, other expectations were gener-ated.

Those who have been as severely addicted for as long as this person had—in her case, eleven years—quite reasonably think that all their problems flow from this one mistake. They have forgotten how difficult life is for nonaddicted people. In addition to the expectation that their troubles will be swept away, their minds usually begin amplifying an unconscious belief that life rewards those who do what is right. For thousands of years this has been a widespread, although quite superficial, interpretation of many of the world's religions and metaphysical teachings. The thought is that God or Principle or Law or even the power of your own mind will produce a pleasing effect in the external world if only you do your part. And of course the act of giving up an addiction requires a great deal on one's part. An entire lifestyle must be given up, as well as a heavy reliance on one's principal means of escaping pain.

In the throes of her enormous effort, these thoughts of private reward gradually took the place of the woman's original purpose, and the man also had a subtle change of heart. He remembered all the years he had put aside other pursuits, all the money and time he had sacrificed, just to care for this woman, and an expectation began to grow of how grateful she would be and how much of their mutual burden she would be able to take over once she was free.

As the months went by and the woman realized that she was indeed free, each new difficulty that she encountered came as a blow. Life was now supposed to go smoothly. But of course, life was no different for her than it is for anyone. In addition, her partner, instead of rewarding her with increased love and attention for her achievement, was more demanding and critical than before, because now he had his own expectations.

The result of this dramatically *good* event—the overcoming of multiple addictions—was that their relationship was thrown back to an earlier, more conflicted mindset. We can't yet report that they survived this storm, because we are still working with them, but they have made progress and their prospects seem good.

No couple need stay stuck at a single level of growth, and the efforts of just one partner can be sufficient to advance the relationship. At any given time, one of you will be stronger than the other and more able to carry the weight of the marriage. Normally, this shifting of the burden occurs frequently, sometimes moment by moment. But longer periods of willingness will be demanded of you. It may not seem so to you at the time, but the responsibility for the relationship will eventually be shared, and a moment always comes when you are able to look back and see that you each have been equally blessed by the other. This fundamental law of balance means that there is no need for you to keep score.

SIX

Early Stages

FALLING IN LOVE
(ALSO CALLED COURTSHIP;
DATING; THE ATTRACTION STAGE;
CONQUEST AND SURRENDER)

doubt is not evidence of a mistake   This stage marks
the beginnings of infatuation and many of the other preoccupations that come to bloom during the honeymoon period. Because
at least one of the partners is in the process of making a final
decision, the primary difference between the courtship and honeymoon mindsets is that hesitancy and inner conflict, and therefore a
seeming need to influence the other person's mind, are often
stronger factors than they will be later. Naturally, questions and
conflicts can continue indefinitely or can strongly resurface later,
but during the honeymoon stage that will follow, the minds of
both partners are comparatively at rest about their decision to be
life partners.

In contrast, "falling in love" is sometimes a battle of wills in
which one first identifies "a good catch," then makes "advances" or "hits on" the intended, "pursues," and finally
"wins" that person's affections, who is then referred to by some
as a "conquest." This pattern is not unfair or dangerous, especially if it's recognized how much a part of human nature it is and
not later reinterpreted as coercion.

However, many people, when casting about for justifications for leaving their partner, will go back to this time and say that they were forced or tricked into the relationship. This is of course inaccurate, because they were aware of what was happening and were free to decline. **Our mind always contains some conflict, and we can look back at any period of our lives and recall the uncertainty we felt.** The courtship, being a period of decision, contains more inner debate than some other stages and is therefore an especially easy target for reappraisal. But to reappraise this period will not prove that "I never really loved her," or "I was young, and he charmed me into thinking he was someone he wasn't." Something besides hormones and animal magnetism is at work during courtship.

At the onset of any relationship that is not a betrayal of a third person, there is at least one deep recognition of the innocence and purity of one's partner. There can also be an accompanying intuition or moment of knowing that this is the person with whom you could find love—not the *only* person of whom that is true, but one who, if you can stay committed, would be an ideal learning partner. Most relationships do not begin with such an intuition, and those that don't are not inferior to those that do. However, you will *always* have at least one instance in which you recognize your partner's goodness. This may not be fully conscious at the time, or it may be heavily layered over with excitement, euphoria, and titillation, but the memory of what was once seen can usually be retrieved with little effort. Sometimes this recognition comes late in a relationship, but in all likelihood it provided the impulse—for both individuals—to pursue the partnership. Although it may recur from time to time, it is usually quickly forgotten. In the later stages of the relationship, this recognition gradually becomes a constant.

The purity and clarity of this vision—which is actually a glimpse into your partner's soul—is similar to what many of those who are at the end of their lives experience shortly before their deaths. For a moment the clouds of doubt part, and they see that they have nothing to fear; they are at peace; and they relax into this new stage of their journey. Then doubt and confusion may return—often unwittingly fostered by those around the dying who don't want them to go and believe that they have "given up"—and so, influenced by these strong opinions, their final days are sometimes more conflicted. Likewise, the falling-in-love period often begins with a very pure insight but later is clouded over by the swirl of ego thoughts and feelings that are stirred up by a couple's struggle to know oneness.

falling in love outside the relationship   Although essentially harmless at the start of a permanent relationship, falling in love can be ruinous when directed at someone other than one's partner. We will go into more detail on this, and what can be done about it, in Chapters Seven and Eight, but it should be noted here that *some people do not develop the capacity to fall in love until later in life,* and because they suddenly feel these sensations for the first time, they assume that they didn't really love their present partner but do love this new person. Falling in love is not love; it's merely the ego's version of love and is therefore without roots. However, it would appear that these symptoms can strike almost anyone at any time. It therefore poses one of the primary threats to a permanent relationship. Today, people of both sexes think nothing of throwing away their home, the security and self-confidence of their children, and the friendship of a lifetime, all for the possibility of a new romance.

With all the promise and glamour in which media of all types wrap new relationships, the thought can very well be present in both partners that with a new person they could once again have "the greatest thing in the world." From all sides, the call is to trade in a chance at reality for still another fantasy. Many people are presently jumping from one relationship to another in an attempt to keep themselves within this state of euphoria, leaving a trail of broken lives and broken commitments and an ever-deepening sorrow they cast upon the world and eventually upon themselves.

Many groups and books based on separation psychology imply that falling in love is a form of addiction, and used merely as a periodic fix it is indeed an addiction and a very destructive one. However, the conclusion should not be drawn that falling in love is therefore destructive *whenever* it occurs and invalidates all relationships of which it was a part. If this were true, most marriages would have to be discarded, because at least one partner, and usually both, had these feelings initially.

Falling in love is only destructive when it's sought for its own sake. A similar pattern can develop around the experience of having a baby. (Interestingly, both falling in love and becoming a mother have their accompanying flow of "happiness hormones.") These parents love giving attention to an infant, but as soon as the child is old enough to develop a personality, the parents lose interest or, worse, turn against the child. The parents' solution to this feeling of void is to have another baby and neglect the older child. Likewise, people for whom falling in love is truly an addiction lose interest as soon as they begin to see their partner clearly. They don't want a real partner, they want a doll they can pick up and put down at will. This pattern can be eliminated if they will simply stay committed—outwardly, if that is the best they can do at the time—and work hard at being kind. Once they begin experiencing real love with a real person, recovery has begun.

Those who discover that their spouse has become attracted to someone else can make a mistake that is equally destructive. They may overreact, not realizing the superficial and temporary nature of infatuation. We live at a time in which sex is pictured as both the greatest good and the greatest evil. It is difficult for anyone in this atmosphere not to be preoccupied with it in one way or another. Our culture's reaction to anything sexual sometimes approaches the psychotic. For example, movies with a hint of sex or sexual language are restricted, whereas ones with graphic violence and extreme cruelty often are not.

Frequently, if the uninvolved partner can weather the storm, the relationship will return to normal. Many older couples can look back at such a period in their marriage and laugh gently at it. Falling in love may seem to replace real love, but it cannot do so; yet many relationships break up over a failure to understand what is happening.

not "enough" in love   Driving home yesterday, Gayle found herself singing along with a country tune about (what else) love. The lyrics said that if it knocks you off your feet, makes your life complete, turns you upside down, and so forth, "then it's love." How many people are in that kind of relationship? If everyone was, the world couldn't possibly function! And yet, still singing along, she realized that across the country there were probably thousands of women who at that very instant were doing the same thing she was, and if not with this song, then with a similar one. We've been hearing these all our lives, as well as getting the same message in poetry, movies, interviews, books—you name it.

Many people, seeing this giddy, wondrous, all-fulfilling picture of "true love" almost everywhere they look, secretly wonder whether they are sufficiently in love or whether their partner loves them enough. Plagued by this question, they may try to act more like the popular ideal or to get their partners to act more like it. If on top of this they hear or read the current line on this subject—that "passionless marriages" are doomed—they may develop a deep suspicion about the rightness of this relationship before it even begins to develop.

Almost never do partners have a truly "symmetrical relationship," matching passion with passion, sexual desire with sexual desire, friendship with friendship, spiritual growth with spiritual growth. And yet this is the impossible ideal of our times. Many people who love their partner and children deeply have never fallen in love (become infatuated) and never will. These are by no means passionless people, nor are their marriages "passionless relationships," if by that is meant that these individuals feel less strongly or act less enthusiastically. Gayle, who has never fallen in love, even during adolescence, is very passionate and fiercely loyal, far more than Hugh used to be, who would become infatuated with every woman who passed before his eyes.

Although many relationships are intensely romantic at the start, many others are not. We have seen very successful marriages begin in a variety of ways. Some partners start theirs with almost nonstop sex; some have a gently growing companionship and derive their pleasure merely in doing life's little chores together; some couples begin tempestuously and feel all things strongly; some found their marriages entirely on their love of children and family; some are very businesslike, taking satisfaction in good planning, superior organization, cooperation, and mature decision-making.

Provided there is commitment and devotion, none of these beginnings imposes a limit on future growth, pleasure, and fulfillment. What you are seeking is something far beyond matched or mismatched passion, far beyond infatuation or a mutual lack of it. Allow your relationship to begin at its own pace, think peacefully about it, and row it "gently down the stream." Remember, you are in the boat together, and you will be rewarded with four *merrilys* for every three times you row gently.

THE HONEYMOON MINDSET (ALSO CALLED BEING IN LOVE; THE PERIOD OF IDEALIZATION; MISTAKEN IDENTITY; EXPANSIVE STAGE; MAKE-BELIEVE; INFATUATION; ROMANCE)

other honeymoon-type periods It's curious that as much as this stage has been discussed through the years, surprisingly few couples recognize when they are in it, or if they do, understand that almost every aspect of it will end. By its very nature, it *must* end. And yet when it does, nothing real has been destroyed.

Most new objects or events that we think of as positive, we appreciate most at the start, while anticipation and fantasy are at their strongest. We often experience a kind of honeymoon period after beginning a new job, buying a new car, moving into a new residence, getting a new pet, even having a new baby. Yet whatever is external that we believe is going to delight us, satisfy us, complete us, serve us, or pleasure us, sooner or later begins to disappoint. Happiness flows from kindness, which exists only in the present, and anything that can exist outside of kindness—for example, a new car or a new body—is not a substance that *of itself* can feed the spirit.

A relationship can definitely feed the spirit, but many people mistake the body for the relationship, as for example when a wealthy man runs off with his young secretary or a famous woman runs off with her bodyguard. The physical body of an infant, a boss, a friend, or a lover is just a physical body and does not guarantee a relationship of any kind. Yet many now believe that having a special body in their lives will make them feel special, or that having a new body will renew them. This is an innocent and very common mistake, but it is one that has begun to cause widespread damage to existing relationships since the sixties.

Preoccupation with *anything* external leads to disappointment. This includes one's new partner—or more accurately, the partner's bodily appearance, bodily age, bodily behavior, bodily possessions, and so on. In many ways the intensity and brevity of the modern honeymoon period is a product of false hopes. When one reads the diaries of early Americans, for example, it's clear that they took marriage much more in stride. If one's spouse was uncommonly cruel, the marriage could indeed be unhappy—but it was seldom looked to as a panacea. Once this changed, the honeymoon period became an emotional time bomb that could burst into disappointment acute enough to wreck many marriages. This will not happen to you if you realize that the high you are feeling now will end, and yet this will not be evidence that your choice of a partner was a mistake.

what does the honeymoon stage look like?   It's essentially the only description of love to be found in songs, books, movies and on TV. Even most interviews center on couples who are still in this stage, and those couples who are well past it often tailor their descriptions to make it appear more like this favored picture. Unfortunately, it's also the essence of what many "serious" articles and books use as their model of true love, essentially because the authors—in many cases—are not experiencing anything profoundly deeper. **Beware of relationship books written by those who are still in the honeymoon period!**

Many couples who have attained a permanent relationship have learned to be quiet about it because of the frequent encounters they have had with the general disbelief in lasting love. Those who don't believe in a reality that endures can be cruel in their attacks on those who do. And those who think that sex is love can be quick to label a real relationship as lacking in vitality.

We have heard hundreds of couples describe their feelings while in the honeymoon state, and it's interesting that on the surface many of the words are similar to what couples say who have reached the level of enduring love. It's as if a part of their minds can sense the potential of what they can be together, and they merely make the very understandable mistake of believing they are already there. Thus the honeymoon period is basically a period of make-believe. The difference between it and real love is that specialness underpins one and oneness underpins the other. Couples who are in a relationship's honeymoon stage are aware of how different they are from other people, whereas couples who have built a deep bond are aware of how alike they are. Being around two people who are ''in love'' can be uncomfortable, because often they have withdrawn into their own emotions and, unconsciously at least, feel separate from ordinary mortals, whereas partners who are secure in their love tend to be more outreaching and embracing.

Excitement and euphoria play along the edges of romance, as well as an underlying anxiety over whether all of this will end. For example, one partner may be afraid to let the other partner out of sight for fear that person might die, but usually the anxiety is more generalized and is often accompanied by the somewhat guilty feeling of ''I don't deserve this'' or ''This is too good to last.'' Partners who have attained a permanent union are no longer preoccupied with losing each other, because they sense that their love binds them with something greater than what their body's eyes can see.

Once two people have worked through the first six stages, their times together are essentially free of fear, and although they can have periods of distress, they no longer experience the misery and anger that marred many of their earlier efforts. They have now touched something that is more real than the events that swirl around them. Occasionally the world witnesses a striking demonstration of this, as for example on the *Titanic*, when some women chose to drown with their husbands rather than escape on the lifeboats. It is unlikely that fear of loneliness or wifely duty were the motivating force. It is far more likely that these couples knew on some level that no real loss would occur. Once you have felt genuine love, even death begins to lose its terror. Compare what these women did to what is presently passing as adequate justification for deserting one's mate, and the depth of what *could* be attained by any couple can begin to be appreciated.

If you are reading this and suspect that you are still in a honeymoon mindset, it's important that you not begin worrying about which of your emotions are real and which are make-believe, or which of the characteristics you see in your partner are there and which are mere projection. It's always best to enjoy whatever stage you are in and merely be alert to certain easily recognizable symptoms of trouble. There is nothing to do to get through this stage more easily, or rather, there is always the same thing to do: stay in the present; treat each other gently; love and laugh together.

Perhaps more than any other, the honeymoon mindset seems to have a life of its own, and if you will just stay together, remaining as relaxed and flexible as possible, the relationship itself will take you to the next level. Simply by making the decision to join and see each other's innocence, you have put yourselves into the care of a powerful and benevolent force. This is your time to trust.

body love   The most written and sung about characteristic of the honeymoon stage is physical attraction. Love is often defined entirely by this mental preoccupation and the bodily sensations it produces. Listen to the lyrics of almost any song about being in love, and it's obvious that the allure of the other person's body, if not the most important consideration, is at least foundational to all that follows. The older songs talk about there being "something in the way she moves," something about his eyes, something about her hair: "I like the way you walk. I like the way you talk." Whereas the newer songs just come out and say it: "I want to see you naked." "I want to sex you up."

Among the more important physical attributes constituting this attraction is the fact that the person is a little different. They are taller, or better endowed, or more athletic-looking, or have bigger eyes, or a different color hair, or a younger body—something that sets them apart from the body type one is used to thinking of. This "difference" not only makes this person a special prize, but seems to be evidence that this time the relationship itself will be different.

The problem with all of this is that by defining love physically, many potentially excellent partners are eliminated from consideration because they are overweight *(slim* is one of the most frequently used words in personal ads), or because they are past thirty, forty, or whatever the magic cut-off date is for the person who is looking. The assumption is that only a very narrow range of body types can be arousing, and unless there is arousal, there can be no love. The overlooked fact is that one's spouse will age fairly quickly, and that as humans age, they gain weight. There are very few people who do not weigh more than they did even a few years ago, and there is no one who is younger.

Those who begin their relationships heavily attached to the physical allure of their partner's body think that they are no longer in love once physical attraction lessens. The average period of infatuation or hormonal high lasts two to three years, which corresponds to the divorce peak. Just as "we have great sex" is supposed to mean that the couple is in love, little or no sex means that they are not. These couples make the mistake of believing that when their sexual desires taper off, their partner's *respect* for them has also diminished. They may feel ugly, inadequate, old, unlovable, worthless, "half a man," or "incomplete as a woman."

The equating of love and sex is subtly and overtly expressed in all types of media, and it is completely off the mark. We know numerous couples, young and old alike, who have "below normal" or nonexistent sex lives but who are deeply in love, very respectful of each other, and unconcerned with how they compare with the latest media fantasy.

Another mistake that confusing sex with love causes is periodic attempts to force renewed sexual interest. One partner becomes anxious about the frequency, variety, or intensity of their love-making and tries to coax new interest out of the other partner. This often has a dampening effect on that partner's desires, and if the pressure persists, it can even lead to a rupture in the marriage.

Our culture emphasizes individual sexual encounters and not the development of a sex life. The richness, the thoughtfulness, the planning, the caring that a couple brings to this one thread of their relationship is what blesses them, rather than how each time in bed compares with another. The habit of comparing ("How was it for you this time?") is deadly. So often couples will begin a session with us by saying, "The sex hasn't been good lately." By this, they expect us to realize just how bad things really are.

Whatever is new, different, and forbidden can't remain new, different, and forbidden once it's yours. The initial feelings of excitement and euphoria *must* change. They may be replaced with something more satisfying and consistent, but since these feelings are based on scarcity, only if a couple would deprive each other of all physical contact could the feelings be made to last longer, and even then, they would probably give way to resentment or depression.

There are of course ways to restimulate sexual feelings, and many books and articles have been written on this subject. What is not acknowledged is that in most relationships one partner wants to change things and the other is lukewarm or resistant. So some degree of coercion is often needed to attempt the restimulation, and this strains the relationship.

Much of what is written promises you high-level sexual intensity no matter how long you have been married, which the authors pretentiously claim to have achieved for themselves. Most of these articles and books also imply that sexual intimacy is the basis of all successful marriages, which is wholly erroneous. To keep this "vital fire burning," they might suggest, for example, that if you have been married for twenty years or more, you should try having "teen sex" (in the back of a car), try having sex in public places, try rolling around naked on the floor, refuse to turn off the lights or hide your thighs, and so forth. Some of these approaches might produce temporary results for some couples, but the danger is that many others—especially the longer-married couples to whom these writings are often addressed—might find them disturbing or even damaging to their relationship. This is not because the techniques are bad to try—certainly many of them are not—but because the philosophy that usually accompanies them does not allow for failure and thus reconfirms the couple's suspicion that something is wrong with their relationship.

Most of the strategies suggested (wearing something unusual, watching a pornographic video together, creating an exotic atmosphere in which a mutual fantasy can be played out, having detailed private fantasies, and so forth) trick the mind into believing that one's sexual partner is different or someone new. These approaches are not truly a revitalization of the old relationship. Although there is nothing sinister about them, you should not expect to attain the permanent change promised. Once again, these approaches can work temporarily, and if they are fun for both of you, there is no harm in experimenting with them. Some authors recommend inviting other people to participate, but this is a serious mistake, and we strongly recommend that you protect your relationship against any version of this—even "innocent" adult party games with strong sexual overtones.

Eventually you will want to look to your love life for something deeper than passion and titillation—if you wish to preserve it. Lovemaking can become a lovely and gratifying form of sharing, and while this is desirable, the absence of sex is not an indication that "something is wrong." Your relationship will do more for you than sex will.

Generally speaking, couples are happy and satisfied with each other during the honeymoon period. When there are conflicts, they often arise over a difference in sexual needs or in feelings of being smothered from too much togetherness. Usually a gentle honesty about what you want and don't want will help lessen these conflicts. Coupled with this must be an equal willingness to listen. Don't make the mistake of believing that if your partner truly loved you, he or she would always know what you want in bed. No one, no matter how much in love the person may be, is that intuitive.

Often one partner will like more experimentation, while the other will, perhaps, like more "soulful" or slower-paced sex; one partner may want more conversation, the other may not want any; and so forth. None of these positions is better or higher than any other. They are just ego differences. Rather than read some ominous meaning into them or jump to the conclusion that you are permanently incompatible, be open-minded in your approach to possible accommodations and try to remember that you *want* to make life easy on each other.

If your partner is not in the mood for sex, you should give no more thought to this than you would if your partner weren't in the mood for a movie or Chinese food or going over to the Smiths'. One of you will always want Chinese food more; one of you will always want sex more. There is no deep meaning in this, and certainly these differences are not indications of greater or lesser commitment. You can train yourself not to have hurt feelings at being turned down, and likewise, you can go ahead and have sex even when you don't particularly want to. These two facts allow ample room for dealing with this very common problem.

Today many people feel they are not being honest, or not "honoring themselves," if they have sex when they don't feel like it, even though they will go to work, floss their teeth, pay bills, and engage in countless other activities when they don't feel like it— and concepts of integrity and honor never cross their minds. For many people sex is their way of relieving physical tension, and having sex regularly and cheerfully is a kindness you may wish to show your partner.

Like most parents whose children are still fairly young, 80 to 90 percent of our free time is spent doing things with John and Jordan that our egos would not otherwise choose to do. For example, this year, when Hugh realized that skiing was one of the few activities we could do as a family, he learned to ski, even though he's fifty-five, has a strong fear of falling, and can't stand to be cold. Gayle kindly stayed by his side for the four days it took him to graduate past the bunny slope.

After years of "sacrificing" in this way, we have learned that *any* activity is inherently interesting—if one is willing to look for ways to enjoy it. Certainly sex need not be an exception. Naturally, this task is made easier if both partners will work on it patiently and creatively together.

infatuation*   This characteristic is almost as commonly a part of the general definition of being in love as physical attraction. Unless an individual is exceptionally intuitive and miraculously honest, some degree of this initial form of self-deception is unavoidable during the honeymoon stage. We simply can't see all aspects of this other person and must therefore fill in the blanks, which we do, quite naturally, in line with the favorable impressions we have already formed. The danger comes as we begin to get a fuller and more accurate idea of our mate's personality during the "period of adjustment" and realize that we were mistaken in a number of our assumptions.

Before this happens, and as the blanks are initially filled in, an aura of great familiarity can develop around the new-found lover. During the early stage of a relationship, you will often hear people says things such as: "It's as if we've always known each other." "We respect each other as we are." "We like the same things."

---

* See Chapter Ten, "How Not to Fall in Love."

"We can tell what the other is thinking." "We'll say the very thing the other person was about to say." "We are always running into each other; we show up at the same places; it's the strangest thing." "We never try to change each other; we leave each other alone." "I think we knew each other in a past life." And so forth. All of this is very innocent and not the least bit profound. The two are simply doing nothing to disturb each other's projections. As long as a person is largely imagined, that individual can be anything we want.

Later, when you discover some characteristics you do not like very much, it's vital to see that your partner was not trying to deceive you. When people are "in love," they naturally present themselves in the best possible light, and in their desire to do so, often many of their more unpleasant attributes will temporarily disappear. Your lover may say, "I'm a changed man" or "You make me feel like a natural woman." It all seems quite sincere at the time. And of course you are similarly modifying yourself. You may find that you suddenly develop a taste for foods that are good for you—especially if your lover likes those same foods. Or that you are more open to opinions on certain subjects—especially if your lover holds those opinions. Or that you are more playful, or need less sleep, or laugh more easily, or smoke less.

For many people, one common symptom of being in love is that their appetite lessens and they begin to lose weight. This is quite different from deciding to go on a diet. You simply find yourself wanting less food—hardly a sinister calculation. Interestingly, this may occur only in affluent countries, where being thin is considered attractive. A friend of ours who has lived extensively in Guatemala, India, and other countries in which plump women are thought to be more beautiful, told us that there, thin women who are in love—if they have the food to do so—will sometimes begin *gaining* weight when they are in love. This is an excellent example of how our unconscious makes those changes that will help us be successful in a courtship.

Because a spiritual awakening has not actually occurred, real change must await a later effort. At that time, perhaps we will recall how easily we once were able to alter our behavior just to please our partner—especially now that we believe that everything we think and do is untouchable and that it is unconscionable that our mate would ask us to change.

Both partners play another important part in forming this shared picture of an ideal relationship: They suspend their judgments and overlook behaviors—and even physical characteristics—that they would ordinarily find objectionable.

If the mind is carefully watched, this process can be easily detected. Little warnings go off, and we dismiss them as unimportant—which they probably are, but we have not actually seen this, only delayed dealing with it. For example, we may sense that our lover is prejudiced with regard to race or sex, but instead of feeling him or her out on this, we dismiss it as a false fear. We want so badly for the relationship to work that we don't allow ourselves to see or hear anything that could cause us to stop and reconsider. This is not as dangerous a form of denial as it has been made out to be, because we are usually dealing with ordinary human failings and not a hidden insanity or a murderous violence. The only mistake we are really making is believing that we are going to end up with a better partner than the average person has to put up with.

ego peace   A common emotion during the honeymoon stage is a sense of contentment. In our heart we say to this person, "Make the world go away," and our lover works this magic. The gnawing anxieties, the depression, the worries, the need to compete, all are swept away. We find we are comfortable around this one we love, needing to say little, seldom having to explain ourselves, never feeling inadequate or judged.

The difference between ego peace and the peace of God is that the first is based on specialness and the second on love. Ego peace is similar to the sensation of humility that politicians feel just after winning an election, or the euphoria athletes feel just after vanquishing an opponent. In the honeymoon stage people feel temporarily satisfied because of the great prize they appear to have won after the struggle of courtship. Naturally there would be a sense of satisfaction or "peace" after such concentrated effort. Again, there is nothing wrong with this emotion, but it will tend to come and go, and eventually vanish altogether—until it is replaced with a permanent recognition of oneness. Ego peace is a harmless counterfeit of real peace and should not be feared, but don't allow this pleasing emotion to set you up for disappointment later, when real effort will be required of you.

The honeymoon period can also be characterized by the peace of God, which flows quite naturally from the partners' many attempts to put each other's happiness first. Unselfishness comes more easily at this time because the ego is comparatively satisfied and is not putting up as much resistance as it will later. If one or both partners chooses to be generous, the "giving is receiving" example this stage provides will be unmistakable. One has a clear sense of joy in the *effort* to please one's partner and unequivocal proof that it's possible to make another person happy. This can be very helpful to remember when later you are tempted to think that your unhappiness is caused by what you are not getting.

love of intensity and the reversed infatuation   Ego peace is merely one of a feast of emotions that can characterize the honeymoon period. One typically feels everything that one ordinarily does not feel, and this new experience somehow validates the love. "I've never felt this way before," the person will say, as if that were proof the love is real. Unless it's built on the ashes of a third person's pain, the love of course *is* real, but not for the reason that one feels different.

For some, the honeymoon period turns into an emotional high that must be kept at all costs, and so whenever feelings begin to lag, the flames of a new issue or crisis will be fanned. Thus some couples go from crisis to crisis, never allowing themselves to settle into the humdrum routine of ordinary life. This intensity becomes a habit, a familiar way of relating they can fall back on whenever they are confused. Even though this is actually a pattern of pain, each has a role to play in these crises and knows it well, understands the boundaries, and feels safe that at least things won't get any worse than this.

The danger in living within this highly charged pattern is that one or both partners can suddenly feel burned out and withdraw. This can even happen during the honeymoon period, quickly bringing an end to it. A sudden reversal of infatuation occurs in which a negative case against one's partner is built as quickly as the positive case was before. Now the mind fills in all the blanks with the *worst* of characteristics. This is a major crisis unconsciously designed to end all smaller ones by terminating the relationship itself. It *will* end the one-crisis-after-another pattern, but it also cuts off a friendship during its early growth.

In the present climate in which most relationship books and articles encourage readers to think the worst of any behavior they don't like, the phenomenon of reversed infatuation is on the increase. The approach of analyzing relationship behavior pathologically has ended up branding so many of the common interactions between couples as symptoms of a dysfunctional, abusive, or failed relationship that the absurdity of this approach is becoming apparent. We recently heard a psychologist on television reply to a question about what are some of the signs that your husband no longer loves you. The only two she gave were "If he's stopped performing oral sex" and "If he no longer chats with your mother when she calls to talk to you." Another psychologist said that a husband's unwillingness to argue is a form of verbal abuse, and that if this is a part of your relationship, you should get out.

"express everything"　　　The ego side of us thinks that feelings of closeness should be translated into physical symbols of closeness. This comes from the belief that appearances are everything. Thus a new couple is likely to believe that all forms of sharing that can be thought of should be expressed. They think they must go everywhere together and reveal every thought and feeling they have, even though this is impossible. However, after a lengthy attempt to practice all varieties of outward togetherness, one partner may begin to feel "engulfed" by the other. Your mate has become a "clinging vine" that, if allowed to continue unchecked, will strangle you.

A gentle honesty about your feelings may help bring a more acceptable balance, but your openness should also include the recognition that there is nothing weak or unhealthy about your partner's desire to be with you. Only a few years ago, your desire to have less contact might have been characterized as "anal" or "repressed." Unless one of you is truly out of control, then all you have here is an ego difference, and nothing more than this should be imputed.

The notion that the negativity of the ego should be outwardly expressed ("continually vented") comes from the assumption that if you "get it out," it's no longer in. Just the opposite is usually true. When you allow your words to express your decision to attack, your feelings will seem more real, not less, and you will stir up your partner as well. Now the problem will appear to be out of your control. Once you have seen that it's not how you truly feel, it's always best to look closely at any negative urge and take steps to dismiss it completely rather than "honoring" it by laying it on the heart of your partner.

Unless what you do together increases the peace between you, it serves no real purpose and may cause unnecessary burdens. For example, it's not necessary to confess every last sexual indiscretion from your pasts, and it's certainly not helpful to confess sexual feelings or fantasies you are currently having about other people. Of course your ego has these. Your ego has everything any other ego has, and almost every bizarre thought imaginable can pass through your mind at one time or another. You don't have to be "honest" about these idle thoughts. In fact, they are so random and contradictory that it would be impossible to voice all of them without sounding like a babbling idiot. To hurt your partner's feelings or to plant the suspicion that you are not fully committed is not truthfulness.*

---

* See also "Are Disclosures Communication?" in Chapter Seven.

SEVEN
Middle Stages

PERIOD OF ADJUSTMENT (ALSO CALLED WAKING FROM THE DREAM; CONTRACTION; BEGINNING OF CONFLICT; POWER STRUGGLE; PERIOD OF DISCOVERY)

With very few exceptions, couples in a new relationship quickly discover that no matter how alike they first thought they were, on an ego level they are in fact quite different. As we discussed earlier, these differences are not accidental, and they work to the couple's advantage. Each has chosen well a person who can bring forth the dynamics that most need healing, but they can only heal them by seeing that the role they play in each other's lives is a benefit, not a curse.

During the courtship and honeymoon periods, couples are willing, even eager, to embrace each other's separate interests. Their willingness, however, is based on their goal of winning each other's affections and, later, the euphoria of having accomplished this. It doesn't yet spring from a genuine experience of oneness and therefore is temporary. The period of adjustment is the time in the relationship in which it begins to end. It's also the first real opportunity the couple has to begin deepening their relationship.

We performed the marriage service for Beth and Kim five years ago. They were very much in love. Kim was an artist and Beth worked in a shop that sold Native American artifacts. For almost three years we heard very little from them, but a mutual friend described them as "solid" and very happy. Kim worked long hours at her painting and Beth enjoyed cooking gourmet meals and keeping their little house surrounded by beautiful plants and flowers.

In the fourth year of their marriage Kim called to tell us that Beth was leaving. She seemed confused by this, stated that she didn't understand what was happening, and asked for our help. We told her to have Beth call. A few days later Beth did so and said, "Kim is incredibly selfish and doesn't care about anyone but herself. I'm sick of having to do everything around here. I'm leaving because she's never going to change."

According to Beth, Kim spent every day and often many nights working "obsessively" in her studio, which was the extra bedroom in their house. Since taking over the duty of feeding the dogs and cats, Kim had let them go hungry for days. Beth said she was actually afraid to leave town because she couldn't trust Kim to care for the animals. On top of this Beth had to do all the cooking and most of the cleaning, shopping, and laundry.

We had to do our counseling by phone because Kim and Beth don't live in Tucson, and since Beth wouldn't agree to a conference call, we next phoned Kim to discuss what Beth had said. Kim had heard it all before. Beth demanded that the animals be fed at exactly six every night, Kim said. "If I'm an hour or so late, Beth considers them unfed for the day and rushes in to do it." She said that she had come to realize that "Beth is an uptight control freak with a neurotic need for cleanliness." And she added, "My painting is the only thing Beth can't control and she just can't stand it."

We finally got Beth to agree to a conference call, although at first Beth would not speak directly to Kim. We started off by mentioning the mutual friend who only a few months before had said they were very happy. Had this report been untrue? No, they said, they were happy then. We asked Beth if Kim had been putting in her long hours painting at that time? Yes, she's always done that, Beth said resentfully, but recently it had gotten even worse. We asked Kim if Beth had been keeping everything as clean as usual at that time? Kim said, "Of course." We asked Beth if Kim had helped more with the animals, shopping, and housework? No, Beth admitted, Kim was actually a little better about that now, "but only slightly."

So what had changed? Behavior that was once acceptable, or at least overlooked, had now become intolerable.

We asked them to list one or two other things about each other that they no longer liked. Kim mentioned being irritated at the "short rolling strides" Beth took when she walked, and Beth talked about the way Kim ate: "She mixes up her food when she eats and can't really taste anything I've fixed." But they both admitted that none of this had bothered either of them deeply for the first three years of their marriage. Their explanation was that they had been blind to each other's real nature: Beth's generosity was really a need to control and Kim's devotion to her work was really selfishness.

In fact, they were still not seeing each other as a whole. They had simply moved from glamorizing to vilifying—first, by concentrating only on positive characteristics and later by seeing only negative ones. Beth is by nature very generous but does like to control the way the household is run, and Kim is creative and devoted but does become preoccupied and insensitive to the people around her when she paints. However, when Beth first met Kim, one of the things she most admired was Kim's total devotion to her art. In a town of writers and artists, Beth had always felt vaguely self-conscious about not doing something "creative" and Kim not only had an abundance of creativity, she also had the discipline to work hard. Even back then, Beth had noticed that when Kim was at work on a painting she became absentminded. For example, she sometimes wouldn't hear Beth when she spoke to her; she forgot things from the store she was supposed to pick up; she would be late for appointments, and so forth. This kind of withdrawal had quite naturally become worse in the last couple of months because Kim was less happy since the relationship had begun to sour. Yet at the start of their relationship, Beth had found Kim's total concentration on her work charming and exotic.

When they first met, Kim had noticed Beth's attention to detail and at that time had admired it. For example, it was Beth's excellent credit rating that allowed them to buy their home. Beth could cook, garden, maintain a balanced checkbook, and do many other things that Kim found difficult. During the first years of their marriage, Kim didn't particularly mind that Beth wasn't as easygoing as she was.

As long as the honeymoon stage lasted, Beth and Kim were a near perfect balance, but after three years—when the hormones began to leave their systems and the infatuation began to evaporate from their minds—they saw each other more realistically and it began to dawn on them that their partner was as flawed as any other human. The mistake they made was that they became fixated on the flaws they were now seeing and did nothing to correct their limited perceptions. A relationship between two imperfect people is like any mechanism with working parts, it will need adjustments and corrections from time to time. The time had come for some of Beth's responsibility to rub off on Kim and some of Kim's easygoingness to rub off on Beth. The time had not come for them to go to war.

Two years have passed since this crisis and Kim and Beth have maintained a schedule of regular "checkups" with us. As Beth says, "Even our Volvo needs regular service, so why not give regular care to the one thing in life that is most important to us both?"

when you withdraw, what do you withdraw into? Accompanying the lessening of willingness that characterizes the period of adjustment is an increase in the couple's resolve no longer to accept each other totally. In part, this is an ego reaction against the more genuine and uniting elements that were experienced during the honeymoon stage. The ego will always attempt to regain the ground it has lost, and so quite naturally the partners will eventually begin reasserting their differences. This of course leads to problems in cooperation and compromise. How to resolve these difficulties while maintaining complete autonomy is the focus of many relationship books, and if keeping your egos intact is what you think you want, much of what we write may seem threatening. We can only assure you that you lose nothing worth having when you lose your ego-centeredness.

We have never known a relationship that didn't go through some "period of adjustment," a misnomer because the two are not really trying to adjust, but to win. It's a battle of wills that can last for weeks, months, or years. This is up to the couple. And again, their efforts to unite are made more difficult by the atmosphere of the times, which supports as laudable any endeavor to define and contrast oneself.

On a spiritual level, the couple is attempting to carry out the practical details of their decision to unite, and despite the difficulties, they continue to try. Great strength can come from this effort, and there is much that can be learned about the rewards of merely persisting. This knowledge and strength will be carried into the next stages of growth—if only the couple will stay together.

Because the relationship begins to settle into its main patterns, it can seem as if this stage will last forever. This may be the first time you are tempted to break up. Before, infatuation was still strong enough to mask the work that lay ahead. Now it seems as if all these endless squabbles and petty difficulties, the bad moods and feelings of estrangement, the anger and hatred, could so easily be swept away if you merely found a new body to live with—or at least rid yourself of the unreasonable one that you are now saddled with.

Trafficking in bodies is not a rewarding approach to life. When people base their happiness on what their body can get them or what another body can do for them, they are destined for increasing disappointment. Like all other bodies, theirs will become sick. It will sustain injuries. It will grow old. It will wither. And eventually it will die. If you look to a younger body to renew you, or if you look to your own body as the source of your fulfillment, your descent into misery is assured.

On the ego level, the emotion behind the jockeying for power that characterizes this period can be surprisingly deadly. If we look closely, we can see that we feel we will no longer be given the love and respect we need, or that we will lose our independence and freedom—even our identity—if we don't get our own way about who tells the story, who picks out the refrigerator, whether farting should be allowed, whether the dishes should be washed immediately, whether the toilet seat should be left up, or whether issues should be brought up during the game, when it's time to go to bed, in front of the children, during sex, or at all.

If you are still in that pattern, what you may have lost sight of is the truth that your partner did *not* enter this relationship with the intention of victimizing you. Any more than you did. There is no malice here, no desire to destroy. For either of you to be defensive at the beginning of a relationship, or at any other period of change, is inappropriate, although it's indeed common. And it can establish a pattern that becomes very difficult to leave behind. Naturally, this does not mean that you shouldn't take time to work out your separate roles and duties, or that you should disregard your deeper fears, but this does not require hard-driving negotiations, contracts, deadly quiet battles of will, or any other form of loveless rigidity. It can be done gently and happily if you will trust each other at least a little and ask yourself often whether the issue is truly worth taking a stand.

If you really believe you have married someone evil, then get out. But do you believe that? Remember, you live during times in which people feel obliged to be right and to have their way about almost everything, a time in which every last and least detail is more important than an opportunity to unite. You already know what it's like to be separate and alone, so let yourself experience the pleasure of lowering your defenses, relaxing the boundaries of your personality, releasing a few of your more cherished opinions, and making the admittedly time-consuming effort to unite with another soul.

As a couple, all you are really doing in these little skirmishes is protecting yourselves against an *illusion* of danger. Unless your relationship is one of the potentially violent exceptions mentioned earlier, you are both responding to each other's fear—fear of what *might* happen, of what you think happened before, of what a thousand books, tapes, articles, and interviews are saying *could* be happening. Undoubtedly some people are more selfish than others, but regardless of how selfish your partner is, this person's aim in life is not your destruction. Don't be afraid to look at that gentle truth.

"now it's my turn"   Most people come into a relationship feeling that they have already been betrayed, especially by one of their parents but also by many others. If they are divorced, this has only added to the sense of unfair treatment and damage they carry with them. In addition, many feel betrayed by their country, their destiny, or by God.

We all reach a time in life when we see that things have not turned out as we had secretly believed in our youth they would. We become afraid to hope, and yet we enter a new relationship in which someone appears to want—more than anything else—to love and care for us. Naturally a part of us is skeptical and holds back. We feel that protecting ourselves is more important than loving another person.

Having been used, we want to turn the tables next time and assume the position of power. Even in a relationship that seems new and special, we may not have an *overwhelming* reason to believe it will turn out differently than previous ones. All people are slightly suspect, including our new partner. We wonder if we are about to be betrayed again, and are we just going to stand before an oncoming avalanche and take it? the way we did as a child, before an unfair and selfish parent? the way we did as a student, before a despotic teacher? the way we did on the playground, before a bully no adult would control? the way we did in our first job, before an unappreciative boss? the way we did in our first marriage, before the one who had pledged to stand by us forever? These feelings are often buried deeply in the mind, but they can definitely be uncovered if we care to look.

Thinking that the betrayer is more powerful than the betrayed, we begin jockeying for position, trying to stake out our boundaries, trying to establish areas where it seems only right that we should be deferred to. In other words, thinking that the betrayer is more powerful than the betrayed, we position *ourselves* to betray. After all these years of taking care of everyone else, this new relationship is finally our chance to get a little caring back.

Thus a new relationship becomes an opportunity to receive, not an opportunity to give, and there are now many shopping guides for finding such a person. And yet if you look closely, all these guides really tell you is who to reject. And if you read enough of them, you will eventually reject everyone.

checklists, inventories, quizzes   It's time to stop ana-lyzing your partner's behavior—and your own—according to some checklist you've read in a magazine or book. Instead, look quietly into your heart and ask if you really think your partner is damaged beyond hope. How is building a case against the very one you have chosen to walk through life with going to help your relationship? These pop-psych questions and lists could be helpful if a couple used them as a way of joining together to focus on a problem and resolve it, but most couples use them to stand back from each other in judgment. At present they are generating more doubt than learning. Anything that creates in you a new suspicion about your mate is not helpful—regardless of the author's intention.

The human behaviors that are being made much of today are quite innocent when you look back on them after many years of marriage. For example, we don't know *any* couple who has not had some history of what is presently being defined as verbal abuse.

Gayle grew up hearing stories about her Uncle Zeke and Aunt Clara who were prominent citizens of the small east Texas town where they lived. Aunt Clara ruled the local Baptist church and was the primary arbiter of the town's social life. Uncle Zeke ran a successful hardware store. They had a strong marriage. Once every year or two, however, Zeke would go off to a neighboring "wet" county and buy whiskey, come home and get roaring drunk. Aunt Clara would pick up her Bible and confront him with the fact that his soul was in imminent danger of going to hell. He would reply with something like, "Any man who had to look at you over the kitchen table for thirty years would welcome hell." While he ranted, she would follow him from room to room praying loudly for him to see the error of his ways, all the while thumping her Bible against whatever piece of furniture happened to be handy. He would eventually break something, grab the Bible out of her hand and throw it down, storm out of the house, and for some reason would then proceed to saddle his horse and ride it up and down the boardwalks of Main Street, following too closely behind whatever citizens happen to be walking there, until he got arrested and thrown in jail.

The women of the town sympathized with Aunt Clara while their husbands muttered about not blaming a man for needing to let off a little steam now and then. No one accused either of them of abusing the other. Nor did they accuse each other of abuse. No one suggested Aunt Clara was codependent for not leaving this man who periodically humiliated her in such a public way. No one implied that Uncle Zeke's behavior was the result of Aunt Clara's verbal emasculation of his inner savage. When he was released from jail, he would come home and Aunt Clara wouldn't speak to him for two weeks. Then they would resume their lives. He passed on when he was ninety-two and she was eighty-five. It was the first time anyone could remember seeing her cry. She died two months later.

Very few people who write and lecture about forming long-term relationships are in a permanent relationship themselves or know the amount of work required. They quit before ever completing the work, and they teach that quitting solves problems. In our experience very few counselors truly believe in oneness, and they are unconsciously antagonistic to what they themselves have not experienced.

We buy many of our books at Bookman's, a huge used bookstore in Tucson, and it's interesting how many authors who were writing on making marriage work one year are writing on how to cope with a divorce a few years later. These are sometimes side by side on the shelf! One couple wrote a book on how to stay married, and while the manuscript was being edited, the wife fell in love with their publisher. When we met her, the book had only been out a short while, and she was already divorced and remarried.

The popular "disease" and its list of symptoms that supposedly afflict relationships changes every few years, sometimes every few months. In the fifties, relationship checklists were supposed to help you determine if your spouse was still romantically attracted to you. A few years later, they focused on whether he or she was having an affair. In the late sixties and seventies came the widespread concern over husbands exhibiting signs of male chauvinism. In the eighties and early nineties the lists classified ways relationships were dysfunctional. As we write today, the new sets of questions are designed to provide you with guidance on whether you should terminate the relationship you are presently in, or even form a relationship at all with the person you are considering. These latest "tests" are designed to highlight the relationship's potential problem areas and predict its chances of failure.

Discovering a deeper basis for union than ego compatibility is essential to your happiness, because the one unalterable characteristic of all egos is that they change. They don't remain the same, no matter how accurately they are classified at the start of a relationship. Within a few years if not months, you will be living with someone noticeably different, and this will happen more than once in the course of the relationship. The same process of change will be occurring in you.

A half century of self-analysis has transformed lovers into skeptics and cynics. Today, most of the couples we work with mistrust their instincts to choose and are suspicious of the one they have chosen. They carry a deep debilitating reservation that their mate is not the best of all possible partners. This leaves their minds filled with wariness rather than devotion.

The person you are looking for doesn't exist.

"Could I be happier with another person?" is an unanswerable question, but it is not harmless. If we are hungry and food is set before us, we must do more than just analyze it if we are to discover whether it is satisfying. To sit before a feast and starve—because we can't answer the question of whether it is the *right* feast—would be insane. Is it not equally insane to question an opportunity to love?

Do you have the right person? There is no right person out there. There never has been. People are not right or wrong. No divorced mother thinks she has the wrong child. In fact, in her heart, no mother even *believes* in the concept of a wrong child.

And yet she is very likely to think that she wrongly chose the child's father.

Your present relationship is a sufficient path. It will get you Home. You can't make a mistake in trying to find the place where your partner's soul touches God.

"SOMETHING'S MISSING" (ALSO CALLED PERIOD OF DISILLUSIONMENT; BEING TAKEN FOR GRANTED; RESTLESSNESS; COASTING; THREE-YEAR, FIVE-YEAR, OR SEVEN-YEAR ITCH; MIDLIFE CRISIS)

During the period of adjustment there is often sufficient struggle, confusion, anger, scheming, and other expenditures of energy to distract the couple from seeing each other dispassionately. However, a time eventually comes when the basic dynamics of the relationship are firmly in place and become apparent to one or both partners. The usual method of trying to get past them—by either passive or active attack—has not worked, and now there seems to be nothing to do but to live with the status quo. Feelings of boredom, resignation, or even hopelessness can begin to surface, unless one of the partners becomes so caught up in the business of daily life (earning a living, parenting, housekeeping, moving, and the like) that these are not yet fully acknowledged.

It's always possible for one partner to enter or leave any stage before the other partner, or to skip one altogether. For example, some people never experience the sensation of falling in love, even though their actual love may be quite strong. And the "something's missing" mindset is frequently experienced by one person before the other. This is often because the other is too busy to notice, but it can also be because that individual sees the potential of the relationship more clearly and is content to wait for it to develop. Gayle, for example, always saw Hugh's potential as a husband and father more clearly than Hugh did, and she merely worked on herself until Hugh came to his senses. Hugh, on the other hand, always denied that *anything* was wrong. Thus, in a sense, we both missed this stage. In most relationships, however, one of the partners feels discontent before the other, but eventually the other will feel it.

sexual passages   The "something's missing" mindset can be triggered by many factors, usually several in combination, but perhaps the most common is that the sex between the two partners becomes familiar. Surveys indicate that this usually occurs within three years of the start of the relationship, but it can also happen within weeks or months.

Like all other dominant attitudes, "something's missing" can come and go. Often it follows the sexual intensity of the honeymoon period, but it can also recur after later periods of renewed sexual activity, especially if sex is contrived or forced. It may also occur after a time of danger, crisis, or triumph. Or a relationship may sink very gradually into these doldrums over a long period of time, until something—a conversation, an article, a book—brings these feelings more fully into consciousness. However, an interpretation that is harmful to the relationship may accompany the heightened awareness. For example, many people incorrectly see sexual passion as a goal rather than a stage. Intimacy is comfort, passion is longing. You simply don't reach comfort through longing. And yet comfort is denigrated within the media's picture of the kind of sex every person has a right to.

If you cling to the notion that an exciting sexual encounter is the very core of your bond, when the novel fires of the honeymoon period cool, all other aspects of your relationship may seem to go flat. "What's the point in being married?" the disgruntled partner will ask, not realizing that a misguided disappointment about sex does not *of itself* spread throughout a marriage. Depression, for example, can make food taste flat, and elation can make it taste wonderful. The food remains the same. So too can all the nonsexual ways a couple has of relating, even though they may be undergoing a transition in their sex life.

During this transition, your relationship *can* be quite happy—if you don't become preoccupied with this one very small way of communicating. Intercourse can never remain the mainstay of a permanent relationship, and you do want a permanent relationship. Remind yourselves that you live at a time in which sex has been taken out of context and made into an almost supernatural activity, invested with meanings and potentials that are humanly impossible. We repeat:

- Sex is not the weathervane of the health of your relationship.
- Sex cannot continue indefinitely at the level of excitement, titillation, and intensity at which it began.
- Sex is not love, understanding, intimacy, or friendship.
- Sex is merely one way of communicating.

And it *can* be a very lovely and fulfilling way—but if injury or medication or tragedy or age or illness or religious conversion or any of a hundred other unforeseen factors changes this part of your physical relating or brings it to an end altogether, you are not doomed to unhappiness. In fact, you are not even on an unequal footing with other couples. Happiness is not dependent on sex; it is dependent on oneness; and the experience of oneness is dependent on your willingness to continue trying.

The sex life of the relationship can be acceptable to both partners, and yet the feeling of "something's missing" can still come over one or both of them. Although many factors (the discovery that one's partner does not have as much money as thought, meeting someone at work who appears much more interesting, the seemingly never-ending chores of domestic life, the emotional drain of child care, the monotony of earning a living) can trigger this mindset, they do not *cause* it. Something *is* missing, but not in the relationship, which still remains basically untried. Your reliance on some circumstance or condition that surrounds the relationship has been disappointed, but that is the fault of expectation, not of love.

Instead of remaining fixed on how sex should be or once was, many couples discover that they can relax into this new course that their sex life has taken. They come to savor the comfort and familiarity of the pattern that has evolved. It becomes a beloved ritual that brings reassurance and warmth. This attitude only develops, however, if the couple has a deep affection for each other, that is, if the sex is a part of the relationship and the relationship not a part of the sex.

Sex in itself, whether exciting or familiar, holds no *power* that can transform a relationship. Nor does income, family size, age, in-laws, or place of residence. Of course, this is not the assumption of our times, as can be heard in sentiments such as "What you need is to get laid" or "What you need is a job that will fulfill you" or "What you need is a red Corvette." All couples really need is to deepen their friendship, because friendship is the experience that blankets all others.

loneliness   One emotion that consistently appears during the "something's missing" period is a feeling of loneliness and estrangement. This is a natural result of the termination of the honeymoon stage and the settling into the present reality of the relationship. It is compounded by the alienation many people presently feel within our culture. Loneliness can be especially pronounced in those who saw their parents divorce and grew up feeling forgotten or abandoned. Even for those who came from intact families, wise, long-married relatives who can counsel them are usually scarce or live too far away.

Developing and maintaining intimate, caring relationships has become more and more difficult. Alienation and loneliness are now basic emotions for most people, and one of the benefits of the courting and honeymoon period is that the couple has, possibly for the first time, a sense of belonging, of importance, of being cared for by someone who needs them and wants to be with them. They are rarely lonely during this early stage. But when it comes to an end, the blow can be enormous.

We cannot stress too strongly the importance of not allowing the feeling of loneliness to push you into giving up on your marriage. We realize you may feel cut off and depressed in the presence of your partner, yet the closeness you felt before was merely the precursor to the splendor of oneness that waits at the end of your willingness to commit to this relationship. Even if you can't believe in that possibility, surely you can see that the answer to alienation is not a still greater act of alienation.

mood is all your ego has   The "something's missing" feeling can be expressed in many ways. Here are just a few that we have heard numerous times: "I feel alone even when we're together." "There's nothing between us anymore." "We have no more love life." "Where are the bells?" "The feeling's just not there." "We haven't made love in weeks (months, years)." "The magic's gone." "I feel like I'm going to miss something in life if I stay in this relationship." "There's no growth taking place here." "I've learned what I needed to know from this person." "I have no energy left; maybe we have too many issues." "Sometimes there's too much past to deal with." "Sometimes love isn't enough."

Our egos are always feeling something; there is always a prevailing emotion. In meditation we sink below these surface sensations into the ocean of stillness that is our base, our core. Or as we have described it in another book, we "drown in God and breathe in peace." But even then, if we were to check up on it, we would see that our ego has not stopped reacting.

As mood is all it has, the ego part of us naturally believes that a change in mood is very significant and immediately casts about to divine the meaning. Thus people who suddenly feel a little sad can spend hours trying to figure out what has happened and what should be done about it. The "something's missing" stage is basically a mood swing. The relationship is going through a normal growth period—even though it may feel just the opposite—and everything is still on track. Couples overreact because they don't see what is really happening. It's much the same as inexperienced parents misinterpreting the developmental stages of their first child. These behavioral changes can seem like personality disorders because the parents don't realize that other children of the same age have these identical patterns.

We have a relative who since her early twenties has been a member of a rigid religious community and consequently has had very little normal contact with children. When her first boy reached the "terrible twos," she interpreted the child's assertiveness as a deep disrespect of her and her values. Every time he showed the least symptom of "willfulness" or was in any way disobedient, she would beat him. (This, she said, was more lenient than the advice given in Deuteronomy, which was to have a "stubborn and rebellious son" stoned to death.) The boy developed chronic anxiety, asthma, and a number of other problems— but his mother said, "It's far better that he's sickly than go to hell."

If she had spent time around many two-year-olds, this relative would have learned that what appears to adults as willful defiance (because if an adult behaved that way, it would be) is really the exercise of a newly discovered option, as when a child discovers that the bumper car he has just been plopped into has a steering wheel, and he doesn't have to go in the direction everyone else is traveling! Two-year-olds are not attempting to insult, humiliate, or maim their parents—concepts they aren't even capable of grasping; nor is their "defiance" a "loss of faith," as that word originally meant. It is actually a broadening of faith or confidence.

Likewise, the very natural feeling of "something's missing" should not be interpreted as a loss of love. After all that the couple has been through, they are now pausing, taking a second look, trying to determine the new limits they are under, and through processing the considerable amount they have already learned, readying themselves for the long haul. Now the time approaches for the couple to begin working toward a more consistent and reliable sense of friendship.

are disclosures communication?*   Instead of showing a couple how to gently and gradually develop their friendship, today the official line is that if something's missing, if a couple seems blocked, if the relationship has gone flat, it needs a few shots of intense self-disclosure. Usually the caveat is added that the disclosures should be made within a "safe" context of mutual promises that nothing said will be held against either person. Many counselors who speak on "communication skills" recommend that a couple engage in a *series* of dialogues, each slightly more revealing and intense than the last. When the partners come to their final exchange, and all emotions and thoughts are laid completely bare, these counselors promise that now nothing will stand between the two of them; they will know each other deeply and be joined (but not too joined, it's always added; certainly not codependent).

If it were possible to unite egos, this would be a logical solution. But it's not possible. Communication techniques that call for "intensely honest disclosure" may make the partners feel better temporarily but will also plant seeds of misunderstanding and suspicion that will surface later. Planned disclosure programs will tend to:

---

* See also "Is Miscommunication a Cause?" in Chapter Three, and "Is Confession Necessary Communication?" "Is Confession Honest Communication?" and "Is Confession Ever Appropriate?" in Chapter Nine.

- define each partner within the relationship
- spawn unconscious resentments
- solidify each partner's opinions as given within this dramatic context
- give birth to secret concerns about each other's normality, which will surface later during marital crises
- cause the couple to think their relationship has failed when the ideal degree of "openness" is never achieved

The couples we see, and whom many of the counselors we know personally are seeing, are harvesting the entangling off-shoots of this kind of honesty, which has been preached and practiced in various forms since the sixties. It didn't take the generation of the encounter group and T group long to realize that venting the ego does not work with one's parents, boss, or friends. But now it's somehow supposed to work with one's spouse.

During the last stage of "ever-increasing intimacy," the partners are advised to be "deeply honest" in this dialogue about such subjects as "the worst thing" in each other's sexual performance, what they "really feel" about one another's parents and family, what they find "most disgusting" in each other's personal habits, the weirdest thing they have ever fantasized doing sexually, the most "shameful and dishonest" thing they have ever done, the most violent thing they have ever done, the one secret they would "least want to reveal," and on and on, deeper and deeper into the sewers of hell. Unfortunately, hell (we've been told) has no end of sewers.

As a couple gets caught up in one of these disclosure programs (invariably it's recommended that they be ongoing), the initial boost of energy, the release of erotic feelings, and perhaps even the welcome numbness that comes from making forbidden revelations and extravagant attacks, gradually begin to lessen, and they must probe even deeper into their psyches for more and more outrageous statements to make about each other and themselves. This is not as difficult to do as might be imagined.

Even old reactions that have been seen through and let go of can always be recalled and felt again. As part of their methodology, many actors routinely recall and express the emotions of their past. Once strongly experienced, any feeling can be dredged up again if one so chooses, but the act of doing so does not prove that this is still the way one feels about one's partner or about anything else.

Once the darker thoughts and imaginings begin bubbling up, they can build upon each other very much like false memories and become increasingly bizarre the more they are indulged. Every day, the ego, which grows stronger the more it is exercised, can find new grounds for grievances in even the common friction of two people being thrown together in ordinary routine. But if the two are in a disclosure program, each of these minor clashes must be highlighted and disclosed. No scrap of negativity can be simply dismissed.

At some therapists' urging, children are also brought into these disclosure sessions. Although it's often advised that the sessions be specially designed and controlled for them, the rule is usually "no secrets allowed," and a surprising number of "mental health care professionals" recommend revealing to the children that one of the parents has had or is having an affair, if this is the case (which statistically it often is). In our opinion, this is an extremely violent form of communication between parent and child. It is certainly not "mental health care," and in a number of cases that we are familiar with, has been no more than an act of revenge of one parent against the other, insincerely carried out in the name of "respecting children's equality."*

---

* There is also a trend to present children, who of course are politically and economically powerless, with a frightening view of what is happening to their environment through books, movies, and songs directed specifically toward them, as if they could somehow act more responsibly than the grown-ups who create and sustain the problem. It is as if an

One of the assumptions made by advocates of so-called open communication is that the partners (or other family members) have reached a level of maturity where they can see the purpose of the disclosures and "negative feedback" so clearly that they will not take them personally and turn them into resentments and suspicions. Having received verbal or written promises from each other that they won't react in these ways is somehow supposed to assure that they won't, and also guarantees, presumably, that their unconscious minds won't load up.

Token warnings are often made that partners don't have to reveal information they think is "just too personal" to talk about with this person who is their life companion, their closest relative, their best friend, their lover, their confidant, and the one who so much wants to be close to them if only they would "open up." Just where to erect this wall of privacy within these sessions designed to "tear down all walls" is necessarily left to the "not-open" partner and his or her mood that evening. (Couples are often encouraged to have these guided conversations in the evening, or even after they have gone to bed, when most people tend to be slightly discouraged, physically tired, and not as mentally sharp as usual—in fact, the very hour that many of these same authorities have said is the worst time to make a decision.) Thus, what seemed like a good thing to say the night before may not seem so good the next morning—or the next, or the next, for the following fifty years.

It's interesting that many advocates of disclosure dialoguing report that these fears are the very resistances that their clients feel before starting one of these programs:

· My partner might think that I don't respect her or him as much as I did before.

entire generation of adults has abdicated maturity and accountability and has displaced their burden onto the backs of their children.

· My partner might think of me as weak, contemptible, mentally disturbed, or sexually perverted.
· My partner might use what I say against me later.
· My partner might withdraw and begin acting funny.
· My partner might get furious and leave me.

Could it be this is common sense rather than "resistance"?

Although the workshop leaders and other advocates go on to reassure their couples that all of these fears will be handled in the course of the communication program, our experience is that they rarely are. Not only do most of the fears later come true, we have also noticed that many of the couples develop a familiar hardness in their attitudes toward each other.

Naturally, in these communication exercises opportunities are also given for positive disclosure: "What are your three most important moral values?" "Tell me the last two times you did something nice for someone." "The thing I like best about our life together is . . ." "The nicest thing about your body is . . ." "Name four of your achievements in life." In most plans these are included in the earlier, "less intimate" dialogues that the couple is instructed to have, or they are scattered at random among the more numerous and darker communication cues.

The final dialogue, which the couple leads up to, requires "the greatest degree of sharing" and offers "the most satisfying closeness." In these, which are the "most rewarding of all forms of communication," the couple is instructed to make disclosures at "the deepest level." Specifically, they are to reveal their corruption, terror, deceit, sexual anxiety, betrayals, embarrassments, and acts of violence. They must do this so that they can "embrace each other's darkness" and nothing hidden will remain between them.

In most of the disclosure systems of which we are aware, it's assumed that a couple's most negative thoughts and feelings are located on the "deepest level," and that by sharing these they share their real selves. The terms *sharing, openness, revealing oneself, intimacy, honesty, truthfulness, tearing down walls, open-ing up, dialoging,* and *feedback* are used by disclosure advocates to refer mainly to the negative contents of the mind. When sugges-tions are made to couples on how to give each other "positives" or "affirming, supporting, empowering communication," it's clear that many of the writers or speakers think that sharing posi-tive reality means talking about career goals, mutual attraction, magic wishes, personal accomplishments, common interests, nice vacations, and the "three reasons I think we should end world hunger." In other words, they seem to believe that positive com-munication occurs on the level of agreeable concept and pleasant memories. Even the spiritual and sacred—if it's given a place in the dialogues—is put on the level of opinion: "It's really impor-tant to me that you believe in God," or "The three reasons I don't believe in God are . . ."

Clearly all that's really being shared here is positive ego rather than negative ego. We are still being made to slide in silly circles on the surface of our being. Only the shape of the spins change. But where is the Splendor for which there are no words? Isn't communication also sensing the warmth of our partner's heart? Isn't there closeness in feeling our partner's eyes bless the back of our head? Where in all of this wrenching disclosure is the oneness of God, which is our oneness? Why can't the soul, or whatever one wishes to call that deep place of stillness that joins every one of us, also be communicated?

Disclosure theory mistakenly assumes that our essence, the part of us that is capable of uniting, is corrupt, anxiety-ridden, and full of rage. Our essential nature, however, contains a reality that any-one who wishes to can experience. When we reveal the most de-structive urges of the ego to each other, we don't reveal anything that can be received by the heart. The words may be heard and understood, but no bridge can be built from person to person out of the past alone, no matter how damaging a past it was. A love-less reality simply cannot be extended from heart to heart.

Obviously it's essential that you be deeply aware of any darkness in your nature that could control you. It is also important that you feel comfortable enough with each other that anything that is important to either of you can be discussed, remembering always that the purpose of such discussions is the strengthening of the bond between you and that no topic, no matter how therapeutically correct, is ever worth risking your marriage over. To attempt to make the ego part of the mind your most profound store of topics and the foundation of your intimacy is to misunderstand what real communication is.

what is communication for?   Jordan has recently decided to learn to pitch, perhaps in part because his older brother is a pitcher. Hugh has been working with him for five days now, but he takes so much time with each pitch that to date he has thrown only eighteen to twenty pitches. Despite Hugh's advice that he must first learn how to be accurate, he continues to experiment with a different stance, grip, and delivery with every throw. Of the eighteen or so pitches, maybe three have been strikes—approximately half the number that have sailed over the wall into our neighbor's yard or onto the clumps of prickly pear, for which his throws have a strange and unnatural attraction.

Throughout these practice sessions there's a bubbling stream of happy questions. "That was really a good one, wasn't it?" "Dad, do you think I'm a good pitcher?" "You don't think that was a strike?" "Now *that* was a fast one; don't you think that was a fast one?" "Did that curve?"

If a team of relationship experts were observing and were actually to apply some of the same ideas that we have heard them give on TV talk shows, they might say, "He's not being completely open with his own son." "Yes, I think there's some hidden stuff there." "This secret of what he really thinks of his son's curve ball is polluting their relationship." "Right, and have you noticed the disturbing tendency toward escalating positives? You've got to be honest if you're going to access the relationship."

The ego part of our mind can tell us whether the words we are saying are *literally* honest. It doesn't matter if anyone else would agree with the assessment, it is still confident about when we are being accurate and when we aren't.

To our ego appearances are everything. It's interested in form, not content. **The ego concentrates on making each word literal yet ignores the actual conclusion the other person is coming to.** When we use it as our guide to communication, we think we are doing our best when we are verbally accurate. Yet something far deeper than superficial truthfulness is needed if we are to achieve real communication.

Many people already understand this fact, at least within certain areas of their lives. For example, in dealing with a young child, loving parents do not make verbal accuracy their priority. When their son or daughter shows them a first drawing, a poem, an "invention," or when they taste the child's first try at cooking, the comments they make come from their heart, not from their "honesty." If the parent were to be "honest" about the taste, texture, and presentation of the food and were to point out every stain and spill left behind in the kitchen, the child would surely never try cooking again.

Emphasizing verbal accuracy, full disclosure on all behaviors past and present, and complete venting of every emotion and idle thought also has very little to do with building ordinary friendships. In fact, it wouldn't even occur to most people to use this kind of "open" communication with a friend. They like the person too much.

When we moved to Patagonia, Arizona, there was an old friend living there whom Gayle hadn't seen for about ten years. She and Gayle began occasionally running errands in Nogales and having lunch together in Tubac. At first Gayle wasn't sure if her friend had changed over the years, and she asked Hugh if he had noticed anything. He said he certainly had. Her husband was the richest man in Patagonia, and as Hugh's grandmother would have said, she had "taken on airs." Even though Gayle's friend was more self-admiring than in the old days, she was still a dear friend, and Gayle continued their relationship.

Several months later, Gayle met another woman in town whom she realized she enjoyed being around more than her old friend. She could have gone back to the old friend and said, "I've met someone I like better than you. She's a person I can really *talk* to. Besides, she knows better places to eat than Tubac." And the friend might have said, "Why? What have I done wrong? Just tell me, and I'll change." And Gayle could have answered honestly: "You're not the person I used to know. You're sort of conceited and full of yourself. And no, there's nothing you can do. It's all over."

We all know that to "hold nothing back" doesn't work, isn't kind, certainly isn't necessary, and does not take into consideration the possibility, even the probability, of change. We know this is true for children, parents, other relatives, the boss, co-workers, and in this case, an old friend. But somehow it isn't true for our spouse—especially if we have something to say that is almost guaranteed to damage the relationship. **Don't underestimate your ability to make things worse.** It's an ability we all have in common.

Gayle actually never said a word to her friend about her perception of her, and they even continued to have lunch in Tubac.* In time, either the friend changed or Gayle became less sensitive to her "airs," because over the years she has grown to realize that her friend has a side that is remarkably generous and considerate.

No one can experience oneness and still believe that "sharing" the ego is the most important form of communication. Two people would make more progress toward a real relationship if they paused a minute a day to surround each other in light—and never

---

* Also, she so completely disguised this story that her friend couldn't possibly recognize herself.

did anything else but talk about the weather—than they would if they spent every waking hour trying to reveal all of their elusive "shadow side."

If disclosure theory were accurate, hearing-impaired adults who couldn't speak and couldn't sign—and there are many—would never "achieve true intimacy." Yet they do achieve it. Young children, who don't even know what a shadow side is, would never bond. Yet they do bond. In fact, none of the creatures of this earth would ever know love. Yet there is abundant love and intimacy in many earthly forms of life. To have true closeness, you and your partner do not have to torture each other with disclosures. But if you have been doing so, and your ears are burning with all you have heard, complete this exercise: Wink at each other and say, "Just kidding!"

CRISIS (ALSO CALLED THE ACUTE PHASE; PERIOD OF ERUPTION; IMPASSE; BEING TESTED; BETRAYAL; ABUSE; TRANSFORMATION)

This mindset is a state of deep confusion and pain. Usually something jolting and unforeseen has happened, such as an affair, a death in the family, one partner being struck by the other, an unexpected pregnancy, one partner causing financial disaster, parents getting a divorce, a spouse announcing that he or she is moving out, or even an argument in which particularly vicious and unexpected things are said. Both partners may be in shock, and soon the question of whether to get a divorce surfaces with surprising force. Very few relationships escape these periods, and although they occur infrequently, sometimes only once or twice in the course of a marriage, they are the times of greatest danger *and* the times of greatest potential transformation.

Liz and Maurice had no children of their own, but Liz had brought Rodell, an adopted boy—age six at the time—with her from her first marriage. Maurice had liked Rodell from the beginning and he and the boy quickly became pals. The relationship between the three of them was fairly stable until just after Maurice's fifty-first birthday. The textile manufacturer for which he was the head floor manager decided to go public. To improve their financial statement they laid off twenty percent of their senior employees as well as a token number of younger employees. Maurice's pension would have been financed in a year and a half and he felt deeply betrayed by the company where he had spent most of his working life.

At the same time that this was happening, Rodell was entering puberty and withdrawing from his family, as most teenagers do. Suddenly Maurice found himself without a job and without the companionship of Liz's son. He became deeply depressed, withdrew into his garage workshop—which had a La-Z-Boy and a TV —and began drinking beer early in the day.

At first Liz was very supportive. They had saved their money; their expenses were low; she was a part-time consultant for a local foundation; Maurice was now drawing unemployment, and so, despite some retirement plans that would have to be postponed, she knew that their income for the foreseeable future was adequate. Maurice had never had a drinking problem and even though he was now drinking throughout the day, one beer would sometimes last him several hours. She decided not to make an issue over this and even went out of her way to keep the garage refrigerator stocked with his favorite beer.

Maurice made some job inquiries, went out on a couple of interviews, but quickly realized that he would never be offered the salary he had spent years attaining at his old company. And so he stopped looking and went back to beer and TV. Liz's goodwill lasted about three more months, then she started losing her patience.

In most marriages, when one partner experiences a loss of confidence, the other partner begins attacking. This is the trap Liz fell into, all the while telling herself that she was trying to motivate Maurice. When it became obvious that he couldn't be motivated, she continued her attacks anyway because now he was "ruining" her life. She was on the brink of divorce when she called to have us confirm that she was making the right decision.

We told Liz that although divorce is sometimes a necessity, she would have to make that decision herself and we would be happy to show her how to gain clarity. When she first met with us, her list of grievances against Maurice was long indeed. Because of frequent bouts of impotence and a general lack of desire on Maurice's part, they had stopped having sex. Maurice no longer wanted to go out in the evenings or help drive Rodell to activities. He had stopped reading the classifieds and didn't even return the calls of the employment agency. In fact, he barely spoke to anyone. Despite all of this he refused to go to a doctor to get anything for his depression. "He just lies around like an old dog," Liz concluded.

"Do you like dogs?" Gayle asked out of curiosity.

"Yes, of course—we have one. Well, two that is, if you include Maurice."

"Is he any more trouble than your dog?" Hugh asked.

Liz laughed bitterly. "I suppose not. Maurice at least feeds himself and picks up his own messes."

This rather off-beat exchange eventually led to a serious discussion of what is commitment and who deserves it. Liz decided to postpone filing for divorce.

In the following days she was able to identify her prime thought, which was: *People don't love you; they just use you.* From all she told us we were also able to guess Maurice's: *I'm the only one I can count on to take care of my needs.* (Several months later Maurice confirmed this to be accurate.) These two prime thoughts had combined to form the couple's core dynamic: *One who has difficulty seeing commitment* (Liz)—*One who has difficulty showing commitment* (Maurice). In other words, they were perfectly matched! We knew from experience that if they could form a real relationship they would heal each other's primary source of unhappiness. Put in spiritual terms, they would dissolve each other's defense against the peace of God and experience lasting oneness.

We pointed out to Liz that in every marriage there are times when one partner must carry the candle of their love, because the other partner is momentarily too weak. Clearly, she was now the stronger of the two and if she wanted to save their marriage, she was the one who must shelter the light through the storm they were in. Her reluctance to do so stemmed from the difficulty she was having in seeing Maurice's devotion. She was convinced that his behavior for the last several months proved that he had never really loved her and now was taking full advantage of her. He was staying merely because it was convenient. If he really cared for her he would go to a doctor for his depression; he would answer the unemployment agency's calls; he would at least try something.

Liz's prime thought is not unusual. Many of us focus on how other people act and fail to discern how they truly feel. We think that a real friend is one who always takes our side. A loving parent is one who lends us money. A good teenager is one who takes out the trash. And so forth. But devotion is not always expressed outwardly in the ways our ego would prefer. Not all animals like to be petted; not all babies like to cuddle; not all children like to hug; not all elderly relatives like to discuss their feelings. We often accept this and other less than ideal behavior from the very young and the very old, but what we have come to expect from our spouse—the one toward whom we should be more lenient and understanding than anyone else—is a standard of attitudinal, sexual, and financial performance that is impossible to live up to. Thus, when our spouse falters in some severe or protracted way, we are poised to reject this one we have promised never to reject.

Maurice was not "ruining" Liz's life. Her judgments and expectations were afflicting her far more than he was. Certainly he was not "meeting her needs," but he wasn't abusing her or bankrupting her or plotting against her. He was profoundly shaken and depressed and was not snapping out of it.

The breakthrough for Liz came after about five weeks of watching her mind for all traces of her prime thought. One day she suddenly recalled that in her marriage vows she had promised to cherish Maurice in sickness, and that he was like someone who was very sick. Those who cherish the sick often do not get sick themselves, but Liz had been angrily fighting Maurice's mindset of withdrawal and in so doing had been infected by it. Now she had discovered a vital truth: Those who judge are controlled by their target; those who forgive are not. She decided that she would simply remain by Maurice's side, even if he *never* rose above his problems. "In my vows were the words 'whom God hath joined together,'" she later wrote to us. "Marriage is a promise we make to God, and so it was out of my love of God that I decided stay."

As so often happens when one truly lets go, little miracles of change began to occur. The first was that Maurice told her that he wanted to adopt Rodell "because he won't be a teenager forever, but this way he'll have a father for the rest of his life." Liz wept when she heard those words, because she realized that Maurice had always loved Rodell—not just liked him—but her prime thought had kept her from seeing this. Slowly she began to recognize that he loved her also.

Today (four years later) Maurice is the cost manager for a small chain of local restaurants. He is very good at it. But he is even better at being a husband and father.

We hope that this book, and the knowledge that there are many who have weathered the great storms of their marriage, will make a difference when you come to a crisis point yourself. We went through several such periods during the first half of our marriage and now have come to know a peace in each other's presence beyond anything we could have expected. We also have had the good fortune of knowing well several other couples who have been through a long and violent night and awakened to see a dawn they didn't even know existed, a sun shining on them so gentle and warming in its blessing that all they had gone through seemed an insufficient price for *this*.

We wish we could take the two of you by the hand and bring you before each of these couples, so that you could sit with them and *feel* what we have only been able to hint at with words. If we could do that, the separating and anxiety-producing effects of the world's bloody dissidence and of this current psychological movement would be gently washed from your hearts. You too can have such a relationship if you will only persist in looking in your own heart for the innocence that is in your partner's heart. You don't have to be on the same spiritual path or any path at all; you don't have to work alike or play alike; you don't have to eat the same diet or vote for the same candidate. All you need is to share a vision of gentle understanding when you look upon each other's face. If you have this, the day will come when you will love every line and wrinkle you see, every inch of stoop in each other's walk, every creak in each other's disposition—because they will all eloquently sing to you of the effort that this dear friend has made for *you*, of all that your beloved has gone through, yes, all that your beloved has gone through and did not leave.

what do you want this crisis to mean?   As the victim of this crisis (and *both* of you will feel a victim of it to some degree), aside from rushing into divorce, the primary trap that lies waiting for you is getting stuck in an angry, resentful frame of mind. Naturally, you can't help feeling a host of very strong emotions after this crisis, whatever it may be, engulfs you. Yet you must be on guard not to begin slowly forming the *habit* of blame and thereby deeply poisoning your mind and permanently altering the relative position between you and your spouse. Anger may be

unavoidable, perhaps in this case rage may also be, but after you have worked through it—which may take a long time—clean your mind thoroughly of any negative patterns of thought that were set up. Do not stop this work until it is completed.

Movies, books, paintings, plays, sculptures, speeches, TV programs—that are happy—are often dismissed by critics as "lightweight" or "unrealistic." Words such as "powerful," "profound," "piercing," "revealing" are usually reserved for the unhappy ones. The ego assumes that the more negative something is, the more truthful and real it is. Unless you are very alert, this will also be your attitude toward whatever has just happened. After the string of cruel remarks, for example, the other partner thinks, "The truth comes out at last!" After one partner has an affair, the other presumes, "He never loved me," or "I can never trust her again." After one partner announces that she's moving out, the other partner begins acting as if they were already divorced. Or after being struck, a spouse thinks, "I've married someone insane."

confiding in friends   None of these interpretations is correct, and yet many people would jump to the same conclusions— and they will do so on your behalf if you allow them to. As we mentioned earlier, your confusion will usually be increased when you discuss your problems with those outside the relationship. Even to hint at marital problems starts minds spinning and mouths flapping: "You don't need him." "You're wasting your life." "There's no point sticking with something this bad." "To ignore the pain is self-destructive." "Your body is telling you to leave." Soon a consensus forms, and you stand to make your friends think less of you if you don't take their advice.

Many who have been through a breakup will encourage you to do the same and will make "being self-reliant" seem more fulfilling and exciting than it is. As the news of your troubles spreads (the ego "lusts to know"), the feeling within you will grow that the problem has been taken from you and now you seem unable to decide anything. Your tendency will be to build an ever-stronger case against your marriage and finally to succumb to your friends' desire to see your partner get what he or she deserves. In highly charged circumstances like these, the advice that comes from friends often springs from anger or jealousy. Many people in the world want everyone who lives differently from themselves to be punished. Perhaps you have already noticed that there are those who are not entirely unhappy about all of this happening to you and even a few who think that you brought it on yourself.

fear, panic, and self-blame   Another reaction that is very common during a period of crisis—especially if you are the victim of an affair, a physical assault, an unusually cruel verbal assault, or some other form of direct betrayal—is the feeling that this is all your fault, that somehow you had this coming, and so you panic and try to make amends, try to apologize, ask how you can change, perhaps even plead to be given a second chance— although you are not quite sure what you did wrong—yet every gesture you make only seems to make things worse.

When we love someone, and that individual is having a problem, our ego will try to involve itself by taking on the same problem. So, for example, when a friend at our place of work becomes angry at another person, we also become angry; when one of our parents becomes depressed, we become depressed; when our child's feelings are hurt, our feelings are hurt. This, however, is quite different from sharing that individual's burden and in fact hinders us from sharing it.

Likewise, even though they may be very angry at them, those who have in some way been betrayed by their partners still love them and do not want to lose them. Becoming entangled in their emotions and assuming the role that those emotions dictate is understandable. Yet you must recognize the danger in this.

If you can at all help it, do not cast yourself in a weak, fearful, apologetic role. Of course you want to make any change that would help the relationship, but that doesn't mean you must endlessly analyze your contribution to what happened, wonder what you could have done differently, say you are sorry for things you are not even sure were mistakes, and hang on your partner's every word for a sign of whether he or she is going to leave.

Unless you and your partner are ready to sit down and talk honestly about how the two of you can work together to get past this crisis, the less you say, the better. Naturally there can be exceptions to this rule, and some couples' backgrounds call for more talk and emotion than others'. Even here, though, **if you have a question about whether to say it, don't say it.** Words at this stage tend to do more harm than good. However, from unfortunate personal experience, we also realize that the tongue is very difficult to control.

Please understand that we are not advocating that you slip into some morose silence or use silence as a weapon against your partner, but just that you be very conscious of the role your ego has chosen to play in all of this, whether that is the outraged victim or the simpering victim, the righteous victim or the stoic victim.

Your feelings of self-blame may also be coming from mistakes you think you made. Remember that the ego believes only in the past and future, and so to it, raking over your past behavior makes sense. Believing that what is over is still real, the ego operates as if it can be changed. But it can't be. Don't spend one instant trying to rewrite the past. You decided what you decided; you did what you did. You can't behave differently yesterday. If you want to act in the present, then do so. In fact, asking yourself, "Is there anything that I want to do about it now?" is an effective means of cutting short self-blame. You don't really know how another decision would have played out, but you do know that the desire to attack yourself does not come from your goodness and sanity, and certainly it doesn't come from God. You are not in a position to judge, even yourself.

is action called for?   If the answer to most problems were

"first sit quietly and do nothing," most self-help articles and books would never be written. And yet that is the answer, or very close to it. A little more accurate version might be: Stay with your stillness until you are clear. But would any expert be invited back on a national talk show if that were the answer they gave to every problem? Our entire media is now geared to "proactive" solutions, as if there actually were formulas to every perceived difficulty. Even in looking at our own nation's very unhappy history, which is a little less rocky than most, it's clear that there were many difficulties we would have been better off sitting with just a little longer. And we can all see this in many of our friends' lives if not our own—jobs left too quickly, surgery jumped at without a second opinion (not to mention one's own), expensive purchases impulsively made.

Obviously some emergencies require an unhesitating response, but today *everything* is an emergency. For example, regardless of what administration is in power, if there's the slightest pause from the Oval Office over any perceived problem, correspondents, commentators, and talk show hosts throughout the country begin asking why action hasn't been taken. Questions from reporters prod answers out of government officials before there are answers, political parties stake out their claims on solutions, experts who can be relied on to make instant pronouncements are invited on news programs, and soon the entire nation is locked into "doing something."

That is the atmosphere around you as an affair or other marital crisis falls in your lap. Your friends and advisers are probably not immune to the mania and will subtly and not so subtly milk you for a decision. Almost any magazine or book you pick up will give you fourteen things to do immediately. But where will they all be ten years from now—ten years after you have made your decision?

Even from the standpoint of not stirring up egos—yours or your partner's—it's usually best for the relationship if you don't take the role of initiator, at least not until your partner is ready to work with you. We understand that this is in contrast to the advice many books give. It's not that initiatives never work early in a crisis, but if you share our belief that the survival of the marriage is more important than the mistakes that occur within it, our experience is that rushing into action, especially action that comes from an outside source and not from your intuition, is likely to put additional strain on it. And yet this will be your tendency. Those who know that they love their partners naturally will want to reach out.

And so of course you will want them to remember the good times and the love you once had; you will want them to see the effect this will have on your children; you will want them to see the suffering all this is causing you; you will want them to know what getting past this could bring to both of your hearts. But first *wait* until you have gathered your peace around you. Once you know that you are connected to your self and that your intentions are gentle, you can do almost anything without damaging the marriage—but do wait until then.

separate therapists?   If you and your partner can find another couple, or a therapist who is in a permanent relationship, to talk to together, this can counter the insanity that swirls around you. Be certain that the counselor to whom you turn is showing you how to solve the problems of your relationship and not stirring up doubts and producing an overall separating effect. It's probably not good for you each to go to separate therapists. We have seen in our own practice—and have confirmed it through other family-oriented counselors—that very few relationships survive the separate therapist approach. Obviously there can be exceptions to any pattern, but it's a rare therapist who will help strengthen and heal a relationship, and the chance of finding two such therapists is improbable.

mental wounds   During the period of crisis, you will have many conflicting thoughts and emotions to deal with. One moment you will want to leave; the next moment you won't. You will get depressed; you will get sick; you will get angry. There will be times when you feel worthless and times when everything seems okay. You will have revenge fantasies, and you will make attempts to forgive. When your partner throws away his or her job, strikes you, has an affair, or in some other way displays extreme insensitivity, the episode can be like a death over which you soon begin grieving. These are the same feelings that partners experience in connection with divorce, and crises such as these can feel like a divorce, so deeply does your partner seem to have betrayed you. Your assumption that your relationship was special and above this kind of thing has just died. Now you know that you too face very difficult and ordinary problems. Both your personal illusions and your trust in your partner have been shattered. You have definitely been wounded, and now you must heal.

It's important that you be very patient with yourself if you don't immediately bounce back. Mental wounds take at least as long to heal as physical ones, and for a period, sometimes a long one, you may be out of control; you may do things that you know on one level are not helpful, but you can't keep from doing them. However, to the degree you are able, make as few demands on yourself as possible, do not allow yourself to become overly tired, and as much as is feasible, stay out of stressful situations. Eating a good diet and in other ways taking care of your health would be good, but many people are not able to deal with this or even to do the usual household chores during the period immediately following the crisis event. If you find this is true for you, don't condemn yourself for so normal a reaction. You can't expect to carry on your life as usual, and you don't want to. This is a time when you are trying to regain your balance and sanity, and that may be very difficult to do. But do *try* to make your life as simple as you can. Avoiding useless battles and arguments is definitely helpful, and therefore, if you have some degree of self-discipline, don't start discussions with your partner late in the evening when you are both tired. None of this is indulging yourself or turning to avoidance as an antidote. Rather, it is freeing yourself from distractions in order to rest, concentrate, and heal.

"cutting your losses"   There will be enormous pressure for you to leave precipitously. People tell with admiration how a friend of theirs discovered that her husband was having an affair and, when he lied about it, filed for divorce the next day. The stories you don't hear—because it would be considered an admission of weakness—are from the many clients who, in tears, say to their therapists that they left too soon, that it could have been worked out, and then go on to cite all the misery they have put themselves, their children, and countless other people through from this one so-called act of self-respect.

What will you have gained by precipitous action? You may end up getting divorced anyway, but if you do, you don't want to spend the rest of your life thinking about whether it was a mistake, as so many people do. You have all the time in the world. So take your time, and decide each day for that day alone. Do not be rushed by talk shows, books, or people who don't really know you —and who may have their own reasons for saying what they do that have no connection to your happiness.

Our relationship counseling, as well as the work we do as ministers, is separate from our livelihood. We personally don't charge individual couples and never have. When we give a workshop, we remain available, without charge, to any couple who attends. Relationship counseling holds the same place in our mind as our spiritual path because we now know that the partnership between two people can be a very direct and rapid road to the peace of God. It makes no difference whether the couple believes this or even believes in a self other than the ego. Time and again we have seen that if they will merely remain together and work as best they can at treating each other kindly, they will come to experience the reality that connects them.

discovering you are homosexual—discovering you are straight   Most heterosexuals will occasionally have homosexual dreams or fantasies and most homosexuals will occasionally have heterosexual ones, especially individuals in whom the sex drive is still strong. If you desire sexual gratification, as most adults do, you can expect your mind to imagine a wide range of scenarios in which you might receive it. The mind, especially in the case of fantasies, is merely exploring a variety of *mental* pleasures, just as one who likes to eat might explore the tastes of many unusual foods or one who likes movies might watch almost any subject matter. Of themselves, sexual dreams and fantasies, no matter how violent or ''perverted'' other people might consider them, do not have to be raked over for anxiety-provoking interpretations and are certainly not grounds for a major life change. Those married partners who truly discover they have a different sexual orientation may soon find themselves in a ''crisis of conscience.'' If you have realized that you are lesbian or gay, our work with opposite-sex couples who have this added factor to deal with has shown that for you to break up your marriage is rarely necessary. We know a number of very successful relationships in which either the husband or wife is bisexual or homosexual. **There is no moral imperative to act out homosexual feelings outside the marriage,** and there is no harm—physically or spiritually—in gently declining to do so.

In most heterosexual relationships, one or both of the partners occasionally feels sexually attracted to someone of the opposite sex. This is so common that it's depicted as normal in ads, fiction, movies, songs, and everyday expressions. ("You can look but don't touch." "When I stop looking, I'll be dead.") And yet it's also universally recognized that the happier course is to be sexually monogamous, despite the desire to be otherwise.

However, homosexual feelings are now being treated as somehow different, especially by many in the gay community. If one is gay, one is *"living a lie"* if the heterosexual partner is not informed of every dream, fantasy, or urge; a lie if the desires are not acted out with other bodies; or a lie if the individual *remains* in a heterosexual relationship. This line of reasoning is heartless, and on many occasions we have seen the miserable results it can cause.

Naturally, the same applies to long-term homosexual relationships. If you and your homosexual partner are deeply bonded, your sudden heterosexual urges are not "your opportunity to be normal." A sexual desire, no matter what sex it is directed toward, is never justification for betrayal or abandonment. The sex drive is not eternal, but love is. Your partner is your opportunity to see the face of God and nothing your ego can offer you can possibly compare to that potential.

In a real relationship, passion eventually evolves into love. Anyone can be loved, and "orientation" is not a factor. It is simply a mistake to abandon the one you are married to, whether that person is of the same or the opposite sex, or whether that person is oriented to your sex or not. We can tell you from our experience with numerous same-sex and opposite-sex couples that this problem can be worked out as easily as any other—as long as you don't try to conform to the loveless ideal that voices outside your own heart tell you is "honest" or "normal."

smart rock imagery   Whatever your crisis may be, within all of its emotional churning and confusion you want to try practicing stillness. This is certainly not easy, but nevertheless you want to make the effort. Picture yourself as a steady rock within a swollen and turbulent stream. Simply allow all of this swirl of thoughts, events, feelings, advice, and memories to wash over you and gently slip by. A smart rock does not attempt to move in the midst of a torrent. It would only smash against new and unknown objects. A smart rock feels its steady base and waits for the water around it to settle and clarify.

You are more than just a body. A part of you is grounded in the eternal, unmovable love of God. You have felt this before and can feel it again. This part of you is hidden away from the world and remains just the way it was created. It is exactly like its Source, as still and safe as eternal Truth. It cannot be betrayed, damaged, or abandoned. It cannot be touched by anything but Love. Its reality rests in the mind of God, not in the events of the world. This part of you is your core, your stillness, your peace, your essential self. That is why no matter how often you lose your footing, there is nowhere to fall except into the welcoming embrace of God. Let each mistake you make be a reminder of this kind of falling.

program of recovery   When you feel strong enough to do so, it will shorten and ease your recovery to put in place a step-by-step plan for how you are going to survive this crisis. Naturally, such a plan will be personal to you, because in times of stress what each of us needs—emotionally and physically—can vary greatly. However, there are certain spiritual needs that remain universal: the need for awareness; the need for honesty with yourself, with your own mind; the need for forgiveness and the mental stillness that forgiveness brings; the need for love, appreciation, and understanding of yourself; and the need for the peace of God, the gentle reality that the world has forgotten.

As a possible starting point for your recovery program, we will outline four steps that many people have incorporated into their own plan. Some individuals also include specific ways of protecting their health, simplifying their lives, and keeping their minds focused. For example, they may work out a daily schedule that includes regular meals, a period of rest, and exercise. In addition, a few spiritual practices can build up one's reserves of inner strength. Peaceful rituals such as a morning prayer, an afternoon meditation, and the evening routine of releasing the day can be highly beneficial.

Please remember, however, that far more important than the particulars of the plan itself will be your willingness to carry them through. Therefore, make your personal guidelines ones that are likely to be within your strength to fulfill. As you go along, if you find that you need to scale down what you are attempting, then do so rather than give up on having any plan at all. Without a plan you are likely to be borne along on the present current of emotion, and we can assure you that it will not carry you to a place you would have chosen for yourself. As the tide continues to go out on commitment and family, it is not washing those who are caught in it onto the promised shores of freedom and fulfillment.

The following are four steps that we recommend be a part of any plan:

1. LOOK DIRECTLY AT THE UPSET.

There may be many aspects of this crisis that you find deeply disturbing, and you may discover that often you are unable to make any effort on your behalf. Yet you will also have respites, moments of comparative strength, although at first these may be short and fleeting. Whenever you sense that you can do so, focus on the upset and not on the person or event that appears to be causing it. Simply look closely at all the thoughts and emotions that constitute your distress. Do not interpret them. Examine them the way you might look at some strange insect that is crossing the sidewalk in front of you. You don't know where it's going or where it's been, nor are you interested. You have never seen this particular insect before and you want to take in as much detail as you can while it is before you.

Each moment of upset is slightly different than any other. There is often a progression to our thoughts and feelings that indicates we are making more progress than we may suspect. The mistake we make is that we think we can know what we are feeling without looking closely. We tell ourselves and others how we are feeling, but we don't quite have it right. We look at our *word* for the emotion and not at the particular thoughts and sensations we are experiencing *this* time. We think: I'm depressed; I'm angry; I'm sad. We name it and immediately ask ourselves *why* we are feeling it. This question shifts our focus out of the present and blocks healing. The ego asks why in order to assign guilt, our own or another's. But blaming is not an efficient road to recovery.

Please trust us when we tell you that you will heal a little, you will strengthen a little, every time you are able to look at your upset—whatever form it's taking at the moment—without interpreting it. This may not be easy to do, but we assure you that it is worth the effort. When your mind is in the present, the door to God is open.

2. CONSULT DEEPLY WITH THE STILL PART OF YOUR MIND.

Because of the state you are in, this may be difficult to do. And in even making the attempt, you will be tempted to fight the agitated part of your mind.

Never fight the ego. The ego cannot be perfected; it can't even be improved. We make progress by adding God to the upsetting thought, not by changing it. In non-spiritual terms, we make progress by bringing into our awareness the deep, peaceful core of our mind.

Whenever you notice that you are once again caught up in some upsetting aspect of the crisis, this second guideline is gently to interrupt your line of thought and remember the reality of God. Don't fight the thought; simply fail to complete it. Pause for an instant and touch your peace. Only a few seconds is needed—

about as long as it would take you to lean over and pick up a thread. Don't be afraid to use any trick that allows you to do this, whether it is taking a deep breath, saying some words of truth, listening to the sounds around you, drinking a glass of pure cold water, offering a prayer, or sitting on the edge of a chair and leaning over to let all of this chaos flow out of you.

When you are able to do this much, then begin trying to stay with the peace a little longer. Listen to it like a long-trusted teacher, for in reality it has never let you down. Accept its assurance that you are not alone. Follow its gentle leanings, its quiet preferences. Gather in the peace of God and not the opinions of every willing listener.

3. GENTLY BEGIN TO FORGIVE WHATEVER YOU CAN FORGIVE.*

We will be discussing forgiveness in a separate section, but for now perhaps it is sufficient to recognize that these defensive conversations that we script in our minds, these paybacks and fantasies of revenge that we play over and over trying to get just right, these dark characterizations that we cherish and build upon, do not make us happy, do not bring us needed insight, do not increase our strength or our perspective. Throughout this book, much is written about how to handle these thoughts and why it is essential that we do so. While you are in the throes of a crisis, however, forgiveness may seem not only impossible but ridiculous. Yet forgiveness, as we will amplify later, is not an act of kindness toward another person. It is the process of gently transforming your mind from something that tortures you into something that comforts you.

The basic forgiveness process has three steps: Examine the thought. Interrupt the thought. Turn your mind to another line of thinking that has some chance of making you feel better, of add-

---

* See also "Forgiveness," page 181.

ing to your energy, of healing your soul. As difficult as it may seem, you wish to make this little effort on your behalf whenever you can. As with all spiritual efforts, there will be a cumulative effect. And also, as with all spiritual efforts, forgiveness implies no behavior—neither phoning nor not phoning, arguing or not arguing, saying no or saying yes. Forgiveness is a mind cleanser and a restorative. It is an entirely separate process from deciding what to do.

4. MAKE EACH DECISION FROM PEACE.*

Once again, we realize the urge you may feel to act quickly or the pressure you may be getting from others to come to a conclusion about this or that aspect of the crisis. Conclusions are basically an illusion. The ego tries to make sense of the future by telling itself little stories with beginnings and endings. But please note that life never comes to a stop and that the moments that follow any action are equally real as the moment that preceded it. If all you have done is finalized a divorce, or moved out, or given an ultimatum, or begun a trial separation, there is no more God in your mind than there was before. Decisions made without peace will have little effect on your basic experience of distress. Your afflictions may now appear to come from a different source, but they still come. Make just one decision in peace, however, and peace abides in you.

In terms of your journey to oneness, there are no big or little decisions, just decisions made in the spirit of oneness and decisions made in the spirit of separation. You walk away from your connection with Love or you walk toward it. The decision to divorce, for example, can be made in peace, but you will accomplish nothing if you decide out of conflict and anger.

Thus the fourth guideline is to consider each small choice in

---

* See also "Making Decisions," page 237.

terms of the state of mind you are in when you make it rather than in terms of what you hope or fear the ramifications will be. You don't know the ramifications, and please note that your mind can't come to rest while trying to guess them. The ego seeks to see its way through, whereas a more attainable goal is to make the small decisions that are before you today with as much serenity as you are capable of at the moment.

Still your mind as best you can, and once you are satisfied that you feel at least some connection with God, with Love, that you feel at least some connection with other living things, ask yourself what is your preference, in what direction do you lean—not what is the perfect answer, or the right answer, or the answer that will solve all your problems, because none of these exist. You seek merely the gentle feeling that perhaps this course is the one you feel the least conflicted about. So for now this will be your decision, and you will not reconsider; you will not discount the goodness of your attempt by questioning it. If later circumstances change, perhaps you will consider repeating the decision-making process at that time. Otherwise, you will honor the effort you made and trust that it is impossible to ask for inner help and not receive it.

EIGHT

Consolidation Stages

FORGIVENESS
(ALSO CALLED PERIOD OF
RENEWAL; PERIOD OF
RESTORATION; RECOMMITMENT;
HEALING; MENTAL DISCIPLINE)

forgiveness and judgment defined   Judgment is what
the ego adds to insight. Insight is merely seeing how things are
now; judgment is deciding that what is seen is a permanent condition. Judgment "decides" about someone, and you can often notice yourself making up your mind, building a case, about another
individual. One clue is that you will feel dislike.

This feeling tells you that your mind is no longer flexible and
that you aren't responding well to what is actually happening. A
good shopper can see the difference between two cars but does not
hate the one that is inferior. When judgment is added to this activity, people can lock themselves into certain choices that are limit-
ing. For example, if they have trouble with one or more General
Motors products, then angrily conclude that these should never be
bought, they can keep themselves from making a good decision in
the future, when, as always, the choice will be between the individual cars that are available at the time.

We once talked to a trainer at Marine World who could discuss
in amazing detail the personalities of each of the dolphins she

worked with, and she obviously loved them all. We asked if she had ever known trainers who started disliking some of them. "A few," she said. "And they don't last long, because they aren't good trainers."

Growing up playing baseball, our son John has had a number of Little League coaches. All but a few provided abundant material for this section on forgiveness. One in particular took perhaps the most experienced and talented team on which John ever played and by midseason had made every boy scared, depressed, and remarkably inept. This coach had played semipro ball, was an excellent strategist, and was tightly in control of his emotions, but could see only the imperfections in each team member's play. He gave lip service to their good play and to their having fun, but all of his energy was in his calm, manly, quietly delivered criticisms, which fell like the blades of a guillotine throughout the game.

On a well-coached team, players are not afraid to go all out, to extend themselves, to take risks. On this team, time and again two excellent players would stand back, hoping the other would go for the ball, because both were terrified of making a mistake. On a well-coached team, players remain positive and resilient when they are behind. When this team started losing, it would become depressed and lethargic. During the course of the season, it never once rallied.

Like John, many of us have had judgmental coaches, and we can remember how off the mark their comments were. People who can see only the decision they have reached about someone no longer react to what is unique about that person—because they no longer see it. Nor do they see the changes and developing potentialities that are right there before their eyes. Not to judge is simply to continue seeing.

Absence of judgment does not mean that you advocate that dangerous inmates be paroled from prison. It doesn't mean that you stand by and allow your child to be attacked by a bully day after day at school. It doesn't mean that you silently listen to

criticism of your spouse. It doesn't mean you must never physically step back from a relationship, never take legal action, or that
after a divorce you must now spend quality time with your ex-
spouse. **Forgiveness is not a kindness to someone else.** It isn't
even a way of determining what your behavior should be. Forgiveness is simply the most effective way of protecting your mind.

training the mind   And yet who can have total absence of
judgment? No one. Everyone has an ego, and the ego judges everything. This is where the very effective, very ancient, and very
misunderstood tool of forgiveness comes in. Forgiveness means
"to for-give," to give over or give back. In other words, you give
back to your ego your excessive, unnecessary thoughts. Remember that judgment is merely surplus baggage, an ugly embellishment, tacked onto vision. Forgiveness is also the lovely sense that,
within your own mind, you have given back this person's innocence, which you had mentally taken away.

Forgiveness is usually thought of as an unselfish act, and yet
it's highly selfish in the sense that it benefits you far more than the
person you forgive. In the stream of the mind, little electric eels
are always swimming by. Most of these we don't pick up. But
when one attracts our attention, and we grab it tightly, we immediately feel the discomfort. Censure does not feel good. It splits the
mind and destroys one's sense of the peace of God. All you need
do is put the eel back. In other words, don't complete the thought.

As we discussed in the section on prime thoughts in Chapter
Five, when your mind has latched onto an unhappy idea, you must
first look at it—unless it's immediately apparent to you that it
comes from your ego and that you don't believe it. This applies to
thoughts of self-reproach as well as decisions against others, but
very often you will think that you want and need—and are a good
person for cherishing—attacks against yourself. If to see through
this takes examining the thought carefully, or asking the thought,
"What are you telling me to do?" don't be afraid to focus your

full attention on this process. As we mentioned earlier, by doing so you are not making your mind more negative. The thought is already there, so look closely at it to see exactly what is troubling you about yourself. Do this every time it comes back. Where does the thought lead you? How does it make you feel? What does your ego's purpose seem to be in handing it to you? Once you have seen that feeling guilty does not lead to correction of the mistake, then cut these lines of thought short and return your mind to stillness, to light, or to some other form of constructive and practical thinking that you have already planned.

the danger inherent in a period of forgiveness   The willingness to forgive is a mindset that you will use throughout your years together—in fact, throughout most days—and so in its usual form it is a habit or safeguard that is the outcome of mental discipline. Yet in most marriages there will be one or more times when either a single event or an accumulation of grievances will call for an intense period of mind purification, a profound willingness to start over and thereby to continue the considerable progress toward a real relationship that has already been made.

The danger is that the couple won't see how far they have come —not necessarily in terms of time, but in terms of effort—and will discount their gains, end up throwing away all they have worked for, and even more tragically, set themselves individually a far more difficult task than they had before they began this relationship. Fear of forgiving is not a guide that leads to happiness. Ironically, couples often give up just on the brink of a breakthrough. There are many reasons for this, but certainly among the most powerful is the thought that they will sacrifice their identity and autonomy if they don't stop now. They *think* they are fighting for their soul. And the enemy they believe is threatening them is love, devotion, and forgiveness.

consequences of holding back The opportunity for a real relationship can come in the form of a child, a parent, a best friend, a first love, or our present highly flawed spouse of many years. But it does come. Again and again a door is opened. The opening of an imperfect door is an opening nonetheless, and if we don't give everything we can to the effort of passing through, we will suffer consequences.

Much has been said about the "risk" we take when we give our heart to another and make a relationship our priority. Much has been written about the damaging effects of devotion, endurance, and forgiveness. And there is always a song that strikes the same chord. One that was recently on the charts used all of the popular catchphrases. It spoke of the danger of "loving somebody too much," of how you "can't trust" your heart, and concluded with the bromide that "love ain't enough." Unquestionably, most of us have suffered enormously from rejection, breakups, or divorce. But what we don't look at carefully, especially during a crisis, are the consequences of *not* devoting ourselves, of keeping our distance when the possibility of love stands before us. What we don't weigh against the hurtful effects of abandonment and betrayal is the long-term damage that can result from holding back until we can see our way through, of dampening our efforts until we know for certain what the outcome of the relationship will be. Until we commit, there *is* no relationship.

Not only can a relationship not thrive without a permanent commitment from both partners, it can't even be experienced. A relationship is the spiritual entity to which a couple gives birth. It is a piece of heaven that two people call down upon themselves to surround and bless them. But today no one wants to be the first to begin. Both wait to "see if it's going to work out." This is no different from refusing to put a roof over their heads until they can prove it will keep the rain out. Someone has first got to build the roof.

It's true that kindness, generosity, openness, and even self-sacrifice can sometimes achieve no outward benefit, can even appear to be the reason we feel used and worthless. But what are the consequences of *not* being generous, of *not* giving someone a second chance—and a third and a fourth?

We first began to understand the answer to this question in the late seventies, when we were crisis intervention counselors working with alcoholics, adults and adolescents who were suicidal, battered women, rape victims, and batterers. One year, just days before Christmas, the little boy of a couple we knew suddenly died. Our friends were devastated, and so were we. Nothing is more shocking and confusing than the death of a child.

In those days we had limited experience with grief counseling, and so the four of us set out to find a support group they could attend. We quickly discovered that nothing was available and made the decision to start one of our own. What we experienced in that group over the next several years changed us profoundly and permanently. Many of the people who came were parents of children who had died as newborns or as infants. One of the fundamental lessons we learned is contrary to the advice that some (but certainly not all) doctors, nurses, and especially relatives subtly and not so subtly give.

If her baby is born prematurely and is likely to die, a mother may be advised to ''leave it in the hands of the hospital'' and try not to become too caught up with its progress. Multiple visits are sometimes discouraged, although in oblique ways, and the actual touching of the baby through the gloved access holes in the incubator is prohibited altogether in certain hospitals. Directly and indirectly she may be given the message that if she gets ''too close'' and the baby dies, her pain will be far greater than if she had detached herself emotionally from it. The striking evidence we saw over and over was that the opposite is true.

Although there are no behavioral rules for how parents should act toward a dying child, there *is* a mental one: No matter what he or she may be going through, love your child with all your heart.

Those parents who do everything they can to express love to their dying child, whether it is praying for it, visiting it, quietly surrounding it in light, or participating fully in its actual physical care, suffer less and heal more quickly than those who hold back their love. Action is not required, but love is.

Not only in that one group but in the years of grief work we have done since, we have seen that mothers and fathers who try to harden their hearts and feel nothing carry with them a much deeper, more inaccessible grief than those who give their hearts over completely. The question is, does this same principle apply to a love relationship between two adults?

does devotion have the potential to harm?   In those early years we also had to work with people whose partners had apparently made the mistake that had led to the death of their child: Permission was given to go hang gliding; something poisonous was left within reach; the gate to a swimming pool was not closed. One mother backed up out of her garage without looking and ran over her baby. If ever mistakes are unforgivable, it seems that ones such as these would be. But even here, the choice of how the spouse looks upon the one who made the mistake was clear. They had to forgive or else be forced by their own belief system to be the living proof of their partner's guilt.

From a spiritual standpoint, one of the more obdurate problems that divorce tends to create is that it locks a judgment in place and thereby undermines the practice of forgiveness in all other aspects of our lives. By seeing our divorce as justified and the case we have built against our old partner as permanent, we believe that we must hide away this one area from the logic and light of our mind, whereas all we need is to acknowledge that we made a mistake—then forgive both ourselves and our former spouse. This of course is done only in the present, and only when a grievance comes to mind. Forgiveness is never for the future, never for all time, because that merely sets us up for disappointment when the unforgiveness once again surfaces, as it may do for many years. What you seek through forgiveness is to make your mind a clean, still mirror on which God's peace can shine.

Not forgiving is choosing to stay damaged. And there were indeed a few who passed through our grief group who had made a life-decision to remain bitter and had taken down their surviving children, their marriages, and most of their friendships with them. Whereas even if divorce resulted, those who tried with all their hearts to relinquish guilt and come back together ended up being far less damaged than those who held back, and they were certainly more likely to have a successful relationship the next time.

Likewise, when we became ministers and founded The Dispensable Church, we saw that the same rule of the heart applied to the couples we married and counseled. Those who held back their love, waiting to see if their partner was going to work out, suffered more and longer if a breakup came than those who had committed themselves completely to the relationship.

Perhaps the most dramatic example of this involves a friend of ours whose wife died, leaving him with three young girls. Two years after her death, he met a woman with whom he fell deeply in love. They each sold their separate houses and bought a new one, and the five of them moved in together. Within a few months our friend discovered that his new partner was admittedly and demonstrably afraid to commit. Periodically she would get upset, say she was through, and leave. But after a day or two she would always return. By the time he realized that this was a pattern and learned that it had also been one in her life before they met, his three girls had already bonded with her, especially the youngest.

Then the time came when she left, and instead of returning she moved all her possessions into a new apartment that she had secretly leased. He and his girls were very upset, and the youngest took the blame on her own shoulders. She said, "It's my fault—I didn't keep my room clean."

When, a few weeks later, she asked if she could come back, our friend called us for help.

In talking to him we asked several questions, among which were: Would his or his children's lives be in danger if she came back? Was she insane? Had she pretended to love him merely to take his money or for some other sinister motive? Had there ever been a time when he had loved her and seen the goodness in her?

He said that she might be emotionally damaged but she was definitely sane; that he knew she would never hurt them physically —although she had hurt them emotionally; that she had more money than he did; and that there had been a time early in their relationship when he had seen her goodness very clearly. We told him if that were true, he had another option beside saying no to her, or saying yes and continuing where they had left off, this time with even more misgivings than before. He could say yes but commit to her far more deeply than he ever had.

If he chose this option, we suggested that first he sit down with her, ask her to tell him every way she wanted him to change, then make the decision to become the companion she sought and, as best he could, live up to *all* her expectations. Second, he should stop making any demands on her, direct or indirect. For example, he should not pressure her to tell him that she loved him, or to set a date to marry him, or to make love more often. And he should stop thwarting or criticizing her in any way—unless he thought his children's physical safety was threatened. Furthermore, he would have to do all of this out of love for her and his children and therefore without resentment. We said that to carry this out would be extraordinarily difficult, surely the hardest thing he had ever done in his life—but it would not be impossible. Humans have a remarkable capacity to change their likes and dislikes, as most recovering alcoholics, heart attack victims, and others who have been forced to change their behavior and have grown to like the changes know from experience. We also told him that having done all of this, the relationship still might end.

The woman was very athletic, and one of her complaints was that he didn't know how to play tennis or racquetball, didn't like to take long hikes with her, didn't like to camp out, didn't like to take cross-country bike rides, and so forth. In the past his solution had been to try to find a new sport they could both learn, but this had never worked. Another complaint was that she had had her children much earlier in life than he had; they were now grown, and although she loved his girls, she did not want to take on the duties of a mother all over again.

It took our friend several days to arrive at the conviction that he wanted to accommodate her in all these ways and that he wanted to do so "cheerfully"—not all the while chewing on the question of who was giving the most. We told him that for her, simply to make the effort to come back and stay would be very difficult and probably all she was capable of giving.

He began taking tennis and racquetball lessons. He bought a mountain bike and began riding with her. He rearranged his schedule and set up child care so they could hike and camp out. He took over all duties that related to the children. He told us that even more difficult than the changes themselves was dealing with his tendency to monitor his partner's actions to see if she, too, was making compromises for him. During the times when his ego was in revolt, he would try to stay in the present, "put one foot in front of the other," and remain focused on the truth that he wanted to try this "as a gift to my three girls."

All went comparatively well for about five months, when suddenly the woman began complaining that he didn't make enough money for them to travel, that he was losing too much hair, and that there was a hump in his nose that he should have fixed. At this point our friend saw clearly that the woman's inability to commit had nothing to do with him personally, and when she left this time, he felt at peace that he had done all he could. His girls, having seen the dramatic accommodations their father had made, were also more at ease about the relationship ending, although it was still hard on the youngest, who kept showing him pictures of different kinds of noses in magazines.

The change that struck us most forcefully was the increase in our friend's confidence and inner strength. He had always spoken very softly; now even his voice seemed louder. Another unexpected result was that he was finally able to forgive his wife for dying and leaving them all alone.

It so happened that he had met and happily married another woman by the time (almost a year and a half later) the first woman called again to ask if she could come back. But there is no magic, and his marriage cannot be attributed to the process he underwent. We do feel, though, that because of his extraordinary effort, he was able to enter this new relationship remarkably free of baggage from the past.

The extreme our friend went to in order to commit is rarely called for. One would have to be very clear as to the reasons one was undertaking these changes, and most people are not willing to be that honest with themselves and so would not make the changes without resentment. The example merely illustrates that real devotion can't hurt you. In this case it brought a good measure of strength and peace to a father and his daughters, but it can also heal a troubled relationship as well, even if the devotion is exercised for a time by only one partner. In our own marriage, Gayle had to commit and single-handedly carry the relationship for almost fifteen years before Hugh saw the value of what we had and was also able to commit. During this period she unquestionably grew stronger within herself, and although she never condoned his affairs, she also grew more understanding of Hugh—a change in attitude that many would say he didn't deserve, but one that allowed him to change more quickly.

possible spiritual consequences of leaving

It's more likely that a relationship will work if we devote ourselves to it. That much should be obvious. But it should also be clear that each

time we fail to extend our purity, we push it further from our
awareness. The danger inherent in following current values is that
by not choosing to be decent to our partner and by not understanding why we *want* to be decent, we can risk losing contact with our
core. And without this contact, there is no chance at all of simple
happiness.

What comes out of you informs your mind of what is in you.
Goodness is in all of our hearts and in the hearts of every living
being, but it must be expressed in some way before it can be seen.
Otherwise, it won't be believed. In today's cynical atmosphere,
when goodness is discounted as a factor, you can very quickly
lose sight of what you are, especially if the outward flow of the
gentler contents of your heart is blocked.

Perhaps you have known a truly good person who entered politics, joined the police force, became a litigator, a probation officer,
an investigative reporter, or entered a hundred other fine profes-
sions, but ones in which a deep belief in guilt sometimes prevails.
And perhaps you saw this individual slowly lose contact with his
or her innocence. It takes study, concentration, and vigilance to
keep from becoming part of the general picture. We *will* drift
along with whatever tide we find ourselves in unless we make the
decision not to.

A much broader example is found in how we relate to the
children of the world. No one could deny that it is every adult's
sacred trust to protect children, and yet there is widespread indif-
ference toward them. Today, children are starving in many parts of
a world that could feed them if it truly wanted to. Millions of
other children are living in crushing poverty. In the United States,
kids are being beaten and abused at home, shot and terrorized at
school, shuttled between broken families that don't wholly welcome them, recruited into crime, and kidnapped right off the
streets. It has been estimated that half a million children (11,000
in New York City alone) are homeless. And remarkably little is
done about this. It's simply not a high priority in most adults'

minds. But no one can escape the heart's quiet insistence that it should be, and every time we betray that basic knowing in some small personal way, we can feel our integrity slipping away from us.

This same disconnection from the spirit also occurs during most divorces, because of the sacred trust that is implied here. Whether it should have been or not, for thousands of years the marriage promise has been so important a commitment that it was believed to have been made in the sight of God and blessed by God. Tennyson wrote, "Marriages are made in Heaven." This sacred symbol is deeply rooted in our shared consciousness. By their very nature, all long-term relationships carry with them a similar aura, and the unhappy consequences of treating this lightly are easy to see all around us.

a generation of yuppies   For several years now we have been noticing a remarkably consistent pattern: Individuals who abandon their partners tend to become more ego-centered and superficial in their values almost immediately, unless they are those rare few who divorce out of genuine love for their children or themselves. What was once a generous father, a man who would do anything for his kids, now that he has left is penurious with his money and stingy with his time in his dealings with them. A mother who never lost sight of her children's innocence, now that she has a new family assumes their guilt when issues arise between them and her new children. People who had little interest in money, social position, or possessions now pursue these as primary goals.

We also have noticed another, more advanced stage of this deadening of the soul that sets in after people have abandoned a *series* of partners. As with the group of people we will discuss later whose pattern is to break up relationships, **no category fits any individual entirely,** for everyone has at least one area of sanity that operates outside his or her ego. In general, however, although they may still be capable of short-lived passions, these individuals gradually lose the ability to commit permanently to almost everything—a place, a plant, a pet, a job, a friendship, a child, a spiritual path—and they begin thinking of their desire to reject all things as a virtue and a strength, possibly even as an indication of enlightenment. Often they are genuinely surprised at other people's inability to "let go," especially of them. They are like children with bonding disorders, except they are the ones who always leave. These individuals are not necessarily preoccupied with money—because even this is a form of commitment; their only consistency is in thinking that whatever their whim, it indicates the superior course of action.

Many have wondered why such a large number of the flower children of the late sixties, a generation that was so idealistic and so concerned with issues of human welfare, could turn into yuppies a few years later. In 1968 we moved to the Bay Area to be in the heart of the counterculture movement, and we stayed there long enough to witness its turn from love and idealism to reverse prejudice and self-interest. There were many factors that caused these young people to change. One was having their expectation dashed that goodness is rewarded. Drugs was another. But certainly among the most powerful factors was the epidemic of divorce and separation. Theirs was the first generation to experiment with wholesale abandonment, and many were, at least temporarily, gutted of their integrity as a result. Most of the people we knew had not only left their husbands or wives—in order, ironically, to work for a better world—but many had also left their children and had turned against their parents, sometimes in very cruel ways.

What happened to an entire generation can happen to anyone. We have not yet faced how deep and devastating a mistake is abandonment. Certainly many individuals don't change in this way after a divorce, but the large number who do is indicative of how the soul begins to harden when one deeply betrays another person. It is done, of course, because people want to be happy, and they think that removing this highly objectionable person from their lives will help. But they overlook a happiness of another kind.

Whether our ego likes them or not, certain people are a part of our lives and our minds. There are those with whom we came into the world; there are those whom we have helped bring into the world; and there are those whom we have given reason to believe that we will never abandon. These primary relationships are like the parts of our body: We may not like the way a hand or a foot looks or performs, but it is nevertheless entrusted to our care. To neglect this trust does not make us happy, but in addition to this, a discernible pleasure comes from taking excellent care of our body and all its parts.

Many of the rooms of our mind are already occupied. There was at least one moment when we recognized each of these beings as part of our being. Now we may have forgotten, but nevertheless we feel the pain when we try to cut one of them from us. Certainly peace, if not fulfillment, can flow from our simply saying, yes, this person is my father; this person is my sister; this person is my child; and here is the one I chose to be my mate. I may not condone what they do, but I will insist on their innocence within my heart.

When much of the world is starving and at war; when people's houses collapse from earthquakes and their families die in floods; when accidents, diseases, and genetic anomalies affect almost everyone; we do not "deserve" ideal primary relationships and the fulfillment of all our dreams. What we deserve is love, and we have it only when we give it.

the line your partner can't cross   You can't hear your decency over your ego without a deliberate effort. Even though the purity of the heart calls out in every mind, one must choose to listen. Attack does not work, and it betrays the heart. Yet attack will be turned to as a solution unless a couple steps back from the general atmosphere that surrounds them and chooses to focus on something deeper.

It's an interesting phenomenon that people often see their ex's good qualities only after the breakup, when their anger has decreased and their vision has cleared—*then* it suddenly hits them what they have thrown away. It would seem reasonable that they would learn a valuable lesson from this. But such is not the pattern. As they begin a new relationship, they are even more likely to keep their distance. The lesson they *think* they have learned is to hold back even more.

This is indeed a curious aftermath of breakups that were caused by lack of forgiveness, as most breakups are. One would think that the person coming out of a failed relationship would be more accepting, more willing to try, the next time around. But they are actually more insistent that their new partner be everything they think they need, and they are quick to spot trouble. Once again, they are assuming that by keeping their distance, remaining highly critical, and being vigilant never to give more than they are receiving, they are protecting themselves from the pain of breakup, should it come. And to some extent they are. But they are also sowing the seeds for an even greater pain.

In their first serious relationship, especially if it's a marriage, most people consider deeply the question of whether to leave before they act on it. For most, it is a wrenching pain. Before they take this step, they must first draw a line that was not there when the relationship began. This is a line of behavior so unacceptable that if it's crossed, their leaving is justified. Of course, no such line really exists; it's merely an opinion, and so they must decide what behaviors the line is made of and where to place it. Should it go just in front of their partner, so that if he or she makes just one more mistake, the relationship is over? Or should it be placed just behind their partner, so that all the abuse they have already received can justify leaving now? Whatever the decision, those who leave take the line with them into their new relationship, and now their love is highly qualified. Those who leave their second partner add still more unacceptable behaviors to the line. And if this pattern continues, soon no individuals can be found who are so perfect that they won't sooner or later cross it.

making damage permanent If you believe that you were damaged by your childhood, leaving your partner will confirm this damage. Thus it makes healing more difficult. After you leave, you are more likely to believe that the damage is permanent, because you and everyone else now have dramatic evidence of its powerful effects. Any guilt you feel will simply deter you from examining whether you *are* damaged. The case you built against your partner can't stand if you are whole. You *have* to be damaged, or else you can't explain why you pledged your love and loyalty and then withdrew it. Now you take with you a larger measure of pain and guilt, even though the new circumstances may seem temporarily easier for you. Now you wear a permanent badge of failure, legal and written proof that you did not emerge whole from your childhood. Leaving has also added another problem—the belief that you will choose poorly again.

This unhappy picture is held in place by only one decision: that your leaving was justified. If it was simply a mistake, you are free to see it as such and not repeat it. But if it was "right," then perhaps you will be right many more times to come.

a mistake does not make future action mistaken It will make your task in life more difficult if you leave your spouse, but if you have already done this, you must now release your mind of all that happened to you, or else you will judge your new partner by the same standard you applied to the old, and far more quickly. Rather than forgive, most individuals continue to build a case against the one they left, and each new grievance they add is still one more patch of mud into which their new partner may step.

All of these intolerable faults, cited over and over to yourself and others as justifications for leaving, must now be weighed against your new partner—if you are to appear sincere. And any mistake that this person makes that is even slightly similar to what your old partner made will throw your mind into doubt and confusion. That is why it's far better to say, ''Yes, I made a mistake, but I will not compound it by poisoning my new relationship with denunciations of the old.''

Those individuals who don't admit this are saying to themselves that what they did was called for. This means of course that similar circumstances would call for a similar response. Admitting a mistake frees you from having to repeat it. Don't be afraid to look closely at what thoughts or people led you into choosing abandonment. Increased awareness is a protection.

Leaving was a mistake—unless of course it was done for reasons of safety—but this doesn't mean that your new relationship is in error. **Making a mistake does not cause everything you do thereafter to be mistaken. If an act of joining follows an act of leaving, clearly they are not the same.**

But don't underestimate the pressure around you to believe that they are. Most divorced couples fall into this trap of guilt and stay in it by continuing to cherish a long list of complaints against their ex-spouse. They try to justify the mistake and thereby prevent themselves from seeing it.

Honesty is especially needed if you are now married to the person with whom you had an affair. If there are children or an ex-spouse who think you are guilty of breaking up their home, it's extremely difficult for you not to agree on some level. But when you do, you are taking on two separate attitudes about yourself: that you broke up the home, *and* that you are guilty. We have seen so many couples with this cloud of guilt, this aura of defeat, around them, just marking time until they get what's coming to them—and very often they are not fully aware of it. They aren't really giving themselves a chance, as the greater incidence of divorce among second marriages shows. When they do discuss the past, they expend their energy not on seeing it more clearly, but on attack. This leaves them with only an alliance against mutual enemies and keeps the guilt alive.

Don't be fooled into thinking that what we are saying here is a fine point, a precious distinction that matters little. What the two of you are attempting now is to unite in oneness, and there is no holier work. However, you will secretly believe that you are "living in sin," unless you see your mistakes and thereby put them behind you. Once you know that you are no longer capable of acting that way again, you have started your life over.

Unquestionably, your old partner made many mistakes and had many unpleasant attributes. That's not the point. What is crucial to acknowledge is that your mind continues to grip whatever you condemn. **You are controlled by your grievances from the past, not by the past itself.** So acknowledge your old lover's basic innocence—without trying to understand *any* of his or her behavior—so that you may feel your own innocence and begin anew. You don't have to *see* this person's spirit or being, but you do have to begin asserting the truth within your own heart. You want your mind to be a friendly place where you can roam freely, not a minefield of resentments that hurl you into misery.

No one is in a position to judge; it simply can't be done. We can see a person's ego clearly—and respond appropriately—but we are never so wise and all-knowing that we can hate that person honestly.

"NORMING AND PERFORMING" (ALSO CALLED CONSOLIDATION; PERIOD OF RELINQUISHMENT; REINFORCEMENT STAGE; PERIOD OF COMMITMENT AND GROWTH)

Now the partners have accepted their relationship, are committed to it, and have learned the basic concepts that can carry them forward. The time has come to turn ideas into consistent execution. They have a sense of a real marriage and think of themselves as a permanent team, and in many ways they now work from affection and caring rather than from fear and manipulation. They have most of the basic tools they need, and during this stage they will refine and simplify their approach.

In a sense they already know enough and must now go through a period of reinforcement in which they make the same mistakes again and again until they have seen through each one. Even though they "know better," they err anyway because of their fear of sacrifice. They are not yet convinced that all they will ever relinquish is what hurts them. Even though they must do many things that they will initially think of as sacrifices, where they expected drudgery they will find accomplishment, where they expected tedium they will find peace, where they expected inequality they will find love.

Discouragement is the danger posed by this stage. If your basic mindset is one of commitment, performance, and growth, it is unlikely that you will separate, no matter how discouraged you become. But it's quite possible to be delayed, and the danger is that discouragement will do so. To counteract this within our own relationship and to move us quickly past plateaus, we developed a five-point plan that included working systematically to dissolve the defeating residue from the past; deciding on and following set guidelines for resolving issues; concentrating on one difficult area of activity at a time until we got a breakthrough; scheduling a regular friendship practice period; and creating a simple daily program for spiritual advancement.

1. RESCUING YOUR RELATIONSHIP FROM THE PAST

the power of selfishness does not heal Your fear of sacrifice comes from lessons your learned in childhood, and so becoming more aware of what each of you went through will speed your progress, provided that you don't become so preoccupied with the past that you forget who you are, that you don't harden your judgments of your parents and other key figures in your life, and that you don't use other people's mistakes as justification for remaining a victim.

Great emphasis is now being placed on the dysfunctional family patterns that left their mark on most of us. Much of the material contained in the popular books on this subject would be helpful, except for the all-pervasive advocacy of selfishness that runs through them. Selfishness is not the solution to childhood damage.

If you "nourish" the damaged part of yourself, the damaged part will grow. You may feel stronger as you become more ego-centered and act this out, but you will eventually discover that this is a bitter and lonely strength that leaves you with nothing you really want. It seems like power merely because you are now doing many things that you did not allow yourself to do before and you are getting reactions from others that were not common to your experience. But this alone is not progress, no matter how empowered you temporarily feel.

Three weeks before the school year ended, Jordan's third-grade teacher, a loving and wise woman who had helped him adjust to a radically different school environment, called us, obviously distressed. She said that Jordan had not been himself for the last couple of days, that he seemed to be angry at her for no apparent reason, and could we talk to him to find out what was going on.

She added that if this continued, she would have to send him to the principal.

When he came home, we told him that Ms. Jacobson had called and was upset. He immediately assured us that he had done nothing wrong and had gotten in no trouble—but it was clear that something was bothering him. We asked him if he was mad at Ms. Jacobson. He said that he wasn't. What then, we asked, was he doing that would make her think that? He told us that he had been staring at her and refusing to speak, that he had tried this with his drama teacher, and "it had worked." "But your drama teacher had treated one of your friends very unfairly and you were mad at her," we said. "Yes," he answered, "and when I wouldn't speak, she didn't know what to do."

As we dug deeper, it turned out that he had inadvertently discovered that he could have a strong effect on an adult. He became curious if he could do this again and had been trying it out on Ms. Jacobson. But it was clear that he was not entirely happy with this experiment, even though he said he could see nothing wrong with it.

We reminded him that he loved Ms. Jacobson, that she had been a real friend to him on many occasions, and that for him not to answer her in front of the entire class was embarrassing to her, and did he really want to make her unhappy? As we talked, he could see that this would embarrass her, and he said that he definitely didn't want to do that. We left the conversation there and didn't bring it up again.

Ms. Jacobson later reported that she didn't know what we had done, but for the last three weeks of school Jordan was one of the most helpful and cooperative students in class. We had actually done no more than help him become aware of the *full* effect of his actions and to sort out his priorities.

By behaving in a separating manner, Jordan had indeed become more powerful and had felt that power. But because he had taken only himself into consideration, it was a power that blocked love and that had an unhappy effect on everyone. Empowerment that is not love-based can make you feel different, but it cannot heal.

Healing comes from feeling and extending the wholeness and wellness you didn't receive as a child, not by trying to get it or by trying to get others to give it to you. Indeed, it is essential to your relationship that your damage be healed, but this is accomplished through releasing into consciousness the undamaged part of you.

No experience, no matter how destructive, can cut you off from all of your being, from all of your core. A part of you always remains untouched. This truth is sometimes acknowledged in theory within separation psychology but is assigned no practical importance in the *means* to healing. **What you didn't receive as a child is not absent from your being; it is within another part of you.** This fact is easy to experience, at least for moments. And yet considerable work may be needed to open a *permanent* flow from your wholeness.

correcting childhood programming   If one or both of your parents were alcoholics, you are more likely to be one. If you were spanked as a child, you are more likely to spank your children. If your father abused your mother, you are more likely to abuse your wife. Even if one of your parents had allergies, you are more likely to have them also. And so if your parents were unable to resolve issues in a way that strengthened their relationship, or if one of your parents left, you must not ignore this added push to do likewise that flows from your past.

Many childhood lessons can work against your present relationship, but unquestionably the most powerful is the example of parents who in one way or another turned their backs on each other. The lesson Hugh was repeatedly taught as a child was how to break up. He learned it in all of its detailed and unhappy facets. For example, he learned to argue that there isn't any real problem and make your spouse feel paranoid. The art of making one's wife think that she is emotionally unstable has been passed down from generation to generation on the male side of many families, and certainly the Prather family is among them. Hugh applied this lesson cruelly and effectively to a number of women in his life and almost succeeded with Gayle.

Hugh was also taught that there is no value in permanent relationships. Virtually all of his relatives and step-relatives had multiple marriages. His mother was married three times and his father, four. Hugh learned from his father, who raised him, how to drive one's partner to leave, which he accomplished with his first wife but, once again, did not succeed with Gayle.

Hugh had to unlearn each unhappy lesson, and that required, not several weeks or months, but many years of hard work. Fortunately, Gayle did not turn on him during this difficult transition, but instead became a full partner in his efforts to heal.

Unlike Hugh's parents, Gayle's did not break up, but when they fought, they yelled and occasionally threw things. Gayle learned how to fight to win by raising issues quickly and at the moment when the other person is most likely to be defensive. She also learned to bring up the past, to interrupt, to state her position in the most personal and inflammatory terms possible, never to listen but only to think of what she was going to say next, and to end all arguments by doing or saying something that would not soon be forgotten. She also learned to react to her partner's failings (in Hugh's case, absentmindedness, forgetfulness, and judgments against Gayle as a woman) with irritation and outbursts of anger, and she applied this lesson even though she knew anger was very upsetting to Hugh.

Just like Hugh, it was important for Gayle to unlearn her ways of participating in harmful dynamics. She also had to overcome a certain pride in her temper and in the history of her family's ''classic'' arguments. Without Hugh's gentle persistence and determination, although she would never have left, Gayle probably would have resigned herself and given up trying.

• • •

The past actually doesn't repeat itself. There are always important factors that are different. That is why the "lessons of history" are so confusing and agreement is never reached on how they should be applied. However, there are *similarities* between present circumstances and those of the past, and these can and do trigger our past programming. Something familiar happens, and we immediately fall back into an old way of dealing with it that, when we were younger, was logical but now is not. This happens in little ways throughout the day. Often we can recognize such patterns more clearly in others than in ourselves.

We can encounter a complete stranger and within seconds see that this person is feeling competitive and acting aggressively, or feeling insecure and talking compulsively, or feeling superior and not listening, or any number of other ego patterns. If we were to say to the person, "You feel superior to me and aren't listening," he or she would not only deny it but would probably think we were mistaken.

When we lived in Santa Cruz, we had a neighbor who would make a suggestion or deprecating joke about our house every time we saw him. He was a builder who had built his home himself as well as many of the surrounding homes, and unfortunately for us the house we had bought across from him was bigger, more expensively built, and generally thought to be more attractive than his houses. Once, when we very indirectly brought up his attitude, he said that he joked about all kinds of things and that we had no sense of humor.

His feeling of competitiveness, expressed on many occasions toward others as well, did not make him happy and like all ego patterns was not an appropriate response to the present situation. We were not builders; there was no contest under way between our houses; we didn't think less of him because his house was smaller; and in fact the very features that he found threatening in our house were the ones that had made us hesitate to buy it.

Just as we could see our neighbor's ego more easily than he could, there were several professional people who could see Hugh's ego more easily than he the first time he had to read one of his books in a sound studio. Yet they knew how to use what they saw to help him. As soon as Hugh started reading, his memory of the experience of his first-grade classmates laughing at him whenever he was made to read out loud filled him with anxiety and self-criticism—even though he was in a very supportive atmosphere and any mistake would be immediately edited out. The other people in the studio, having encountered similar problems with other authors, knew that criticism would only make the situation worse. They also understood that Hugh's problem was equally the problem of their joint relationship. They were risking their time and money, and it was in everyone's interests that Hugh get beyond his past. They were therefore very patient and made several suggestions that Hugh would never have thought of on his own. Their approach was unlike the attitude most couples adopt toward each other's patterns from childhood.

scheduling past-reduction   We distilled these and other experiences into four guidelines that we used when carrying out our past-reduction plan:

· Be aware of your partner's personal programming, and
  take it on faith that you yourself have programming of
  which you are equally unconscious.
· Acknowledge that since your partner does not have
  the same programming as you (all egos are different),
  this is a person who is in a position to see you more
  clearly than you can see yourself.
· Don't use your knowledge of your partner's ego to
  attack more effectively; this will only make the relationship that you are in unhappier for you.
· Try not to hear your mate's insights as criticisms. If

you will allow them to, these perceptions can help you get past what was a logical way of being during your childhood but no longer is.

To help our own relationship, we scheduled a one-hour work period twice a week to do nothing but talk about our past experiences, going as far back into our childhoods as we could. The purpose of these sessions was not to establish blame or to justify current mistakes but to get a clear, uncritical idea of the characteristics of our egos and of what forces had helped form them. This is a very different way of looking at and using insights from childhood, and it is essential to understand the difference. Within separation psychology, the experiences of childhood tend to be used to justify selfish behavior, lack of maturity, and an unwillingness to change.

A woman we know, a social worker, an insightful, good person, calls herself a "rageaholic." She particularly has difficulty around the time of her monthly period and tells her husband and two children that they had better watch what they say and do. She thinks nothing of screaming at them during those and other times and basically has told them that they must simply adjust to her rage. She can cite every instance of verbal and emotional abuse from her dysfunctional childhood that causes her to be this way. She is still angry toward her parents; in fact, she has almost no contact with them and will not allow them to see her children. But since she didn't cause this behavior herself, she doesn't see that she is responsible for it. She therefore cannot change. And even though she has not lived with her parents for twenty years, she continues to see herself as their victim. Obviously, insights into one's childhood that are used merely to justify separation and the continuation of a negative family dynamic are not helpful.

To combat this tendency within ourselves, we later added to our work sessions exercises on forgiveness and short meditations to increase awareness of our true feelings. In this way we were able to determine more quickly whether an emotion or thought was coming from the past or from the heart. Because after several years we had exhausted its benefits, we eventually dropped the co-analysis portion of these sessions, but we continued the meditations, expanding them to include all aspects of our life and incorporating them into our spiritual program, which we will discuss shortly.

2. HOW TO HAVE A REAL ARGUMENT

the ten guidelines   Unlike *A Book for Couples,* this is more a book of ideas than a methodology. However, there are a few procedures that have been so essential to our progress that we feel we must include them. We first worked out (over a period of several months) the following ten steps as rules to guide us through an argument in a way that would not harm our unity, but we later discovered that this procedure also began dissolving the *residue* of grievances that we were carrying. We also encourage the couples we see to use these steps as a way of having the simple experience of success. A surprising number of couples have never had even one completely happy resolution of an issue. That is why rule 5 is crucial. You must begin giving yourselves reason for hope, so begin with the lesser-charged issues, and even with those, break off a part that you are almost certain to resolve well.

1. **Do not call each other on these rules.**

2. **Wait until a conducive time to raise the issue.** Most of us make the mistake of bringing up something our partner just did. If an issue has come between you, even a small one, you don't want to ignore it or let it fester, but neither do you want to make the situation worse by forcing a discussion when one of you is still angry or in an unreceptive mood. Whenever you feel a sense of

urgency to make your point and your mind quickly grasps a reason why this would be best, you can be fairly certain that your ego is speaking. ("This can't wait; it's happened too often." "If I let her get away with this, I'll become a doormat." "I need to show him what he does while it's still fresh in his mind.") Wait until you are clear that the reason you want to sit down together is to strengthen your relationship and not just to be right.

3. **Never dismiss your partner's unhappiness.** The *relationship* has a problem that needs to be dealt with, even if only one partner thinks it does. If you are not willing to address your partner's concerns at this moment, suggest a specific time in the very near future when you would be.

4. **Sit down.** What your body does symbolizes to your mind what you think is important. Don't raise questions or have little discussions while doing something else (while getting ready for bed, cleaning, driving, eating). Since your relationship is at risk when you argue, demonstrate that you value it enough to stop whatever else you are doing.

5. **Break the larger issue into several parts and take up only one small part at this sitting.** All of the big problems between couples are made up of many small provocations that have accumulated. If for example the issue is jealousy, take up only "provocative clothing" and only one item of such clothing; or only "how you joke about sex when we're over at the Smiths;" or only "you're never home when you say you'll be." If the issue is finances, take up only separate versus joint checking accounts, or checks received on birthdays, or "who pays when we have *your* friends over?" **Your goal is merely one small success;** you will try again on another aspect of the problem at another time.

6. **In turn, state your ego positions with as little attack as possible and without hinting at any other issue or bringing up the past.** Although this can be included if you wish, it's not essential that you "echo" or "reflect back" (say in your own words what you believe your partner just said). Nor is it necessary to

"state your demands" for clarification purposes. But certainly you can try these and see if you find one or both of them helpful. However, the most important guideline in rule 6 is to give your side without negative embellishment.

7. **The one who is listening should not interrupt and should silently repeat the words "(Name of partner) really means this."** When people disagree with us, the tendency is not to believe they mean what they say. They must have some other motive. ("No one could be that wrong and mean it.") If you will watch your mind carefully while your partner is disagreeing with you or criticizing you, you will notice a tendency to dismiss what he or she just said as not heartfelt. Even if it's an exaggeration, your partner means it. Even if it's a *lie,* your partner means it. Listen deeply, and you will be able to sense not only what is meant but even perhaps what is so important that he or she might lie or exaggerate. **Communication is not undermined by the differences between sexes, cultures, races, or past experiences.** Remember that during the honeymoon period these differences almost never cause deep rifts and misunderstandings. Communication is undermined by the desire to be right. Once you become defensive (withdraw into your ego), you can, and will, use anything to misunderstand your partner. If genuine concern motivates, you don't focus so much on the exact wording of your partner's side of things, but on what you can feel is meant. This is not a difficult or mysterious process. All that is required is your desire to *hear.*

8. **Restate your ego position, but this time strictly in terms of your fears.** It's easier to let go of what you fear than what you want. And it's easier to understand your partner's position when you understand his or her fear. You are never arguing about what you are arguing about, and this step is crucial to discovering what is really going on between you. Behind every demand is the fear of what the demand symbolizes. However, root fears are not easy to bring to consciousness—they may seem embarrassing or off the

point—so give whatever time is necessary to this step. You will often have to close your eyes and look very honestly at your thoughts to see what you are really feeling. Be careful not to subvert this step by simply rewording your criticisms or demands to *sound* like a fear. ("I'm afraid I've married a conceited, insensitive liar," or "My fear is that you won't ask me before you buy something that's not on the list.") Whereas the actual fears might be "I'm afraid you don't really love me and that you'll eventually leave," and "I'm afraid you'll see me more clearly and discover you can't accept me as I am."

9. **Close your eyes and remember what you love about each other. Use any trick necessary to accomplish this.** The first few months that we argued in this new way, we were often so angry that only by listing ten things that we liked about the other (or things that were thoughtful, funny, forbearing, and the like, that we remembered the other doing for us or someone else—saying these out loud, taking turns one by one) could we get past the anger. On several occasions Hugh had to set his watch to go off every twenty minutes, at which times he would think of ten new positive things about Gayle. He would continue this until once again he felt his love for her. Only then could he sit down to have a structured argument.

10. **With your eyes still closed, think of three gifts you wish to give to the relationship.** If you have truly completed rule 9, you should have little difficulty in thinking of "gifts" you want to give. These should not be vague or grand gestures or mere sentiments but should **relate very specifically to the issue you have been discussing.** Before completing rule 9 you would have thought of these as compromises or concessions, but now you realize that each one improves the quality of the relationship you are both in. After you have each thought of your three gifts, open your eyes and share them.

We worked out these guidelines through trial and error. You can do likewise, or you can use ours. However, we urge you to have no more unstructured arguments. Otherwise you will continue to accumulate defeats, inequities, and resentments. This is the ever-darkening cloud of memory that most couples add to each time they have even a small discussion. It eventually causes them to overreact to almost anything their partner says or does. Any strategy that allows you to have a satisfying argument, one that adds to your feeling of closeness, is sufficient. But reaching a state of numbness by yelling at each other is not the same.

3. ONE AREA OF ACTIVITY AT A TIME

are you many couples in one?   Our progress was greatly accelerated when we stopped trying to get an overall transformation of our relationship and began working on only one recurring circumstance at a time. We set aside an hour each day to do this.

"Everything's going along fine." "We've been doing just great recently." These are comments we hear often from some of the couples we know, and they usually indicate that either the couple has not recently engaged in the particular activities that give them the most trouble, or it can indicate that they are in a heightened state of love and acceptance and have indeed "risen above" their usual petty reactions. Perhaps every couple has had moments of "being above it all"—in a peaceful rather than an arrogant sense—and if not, the honeymoon state probably gave them a sense of what this could be like. Therefore it's natural for them to wonder why it can't be like that all the time and even to conclude that there must be something wrong with their relationship that it isn't.

A state of consistent well-being must be learned and practiced, just as we learn to perform consistently in any other field, through study and application. Learning is not a curse, especially learning how to be at peace, but you will progress more rapidly if you will make your goal a small gain each day and not look for one all-inclusive transformation.

We found that a simple way to practice this was to divide our "relationship" into all the little ways we related. After we had done just that much, we discovered something very interesting: Our marriage was a series of separate marriages. In many ways we were a different couple in each activity, with different attitudes and personalities. Just describing those various "couples" was helpful in itself, because we became more aware of the parts of our personalities that we drew on that set up patterns of conflict in each circumstance.

For example, when a diaper had to be changed, Gayle was assertive, arrogant, and efficient, whereas Hugh was tentative and defensive. On the tennis court Hugh was the all-enduring guru, and Gayle was the giggling adolescent. We found that we were a different couple when we fixed a meal together, shopped together, made love, went out with friends, trained the dog, did housework, or balanced the checkbook.

We dealt only with those areas in which there was an unhappy pattern operating—but in our case that covered almost all activities. We would take up one area and decide together how to try to make it more pleasant. If our plan didn't work, we would try something else, and we would continue this until we got a small breakthrough. Making love is an area where we had great difficulty bringing about change and actually had to start over in order to do so.

resurrecting our dead sex life   We hope no one will interpret what we say here to mean that we believe it's helpful, happy, or even possible to restore a couple's sexual communication to the newness and titillation of the honeymoon period. That kind of sex is a stage, not a goal. Here we will describe our having *no* sex life, but also wanting one. If partners are not relating sexually—and they are both comfortable with this—there is no reason they should change. Many happy couples have infrequent or no intercourse. These "passionless relationships" do not break up or deteriorate into cold, businesslike alliances more than other relationships, as is frequently claimed. This idea comes mainly from anecdotal reports of therapists who advocate breaking up a marriage because the sex is less than they believe it should be. Many divorced individuals who thought that sex was very important and yet did not receive the kind or amount of it from their partner that they wanted, do blame their sex life for the breakup. In cases like these, our experience has been that the issue of sex, not sex itself, comes between the partners and is more a factor in one partner's mind than the other's. (Both partners seldom agree on the cause of a divorce.) Certainly, many couples who had great sex have still gotten divorced.

The day we finally got down to concentrating on it, making love had already become such a conflicted and unhappy time that we had virtually stopped. There were many reasons for this, but unhappy childhood lessons were a major part of the problem. Unlike Hugh's father, Gayle's parents appeared to have had no real interest in sex. Gayle's mother, however, was fascinated with reports of violent crimes, and almost the only times Gayle heard sex mentioned were in the context of newspaper stories about rape and murder.

In contrast to Gayle's parents, Hugh's dad believed that sex with new partners was a means of renewing his youth and energy, and so sex to him was like lifeblood. He thought that a woman's primary function was to be attractive and to bring pleasure to men. Hugh's mother, on the other hand, thought bodies and bodily functions were somewhat disgusting and she appeared to have an aversion to sex.

An example of how these attitudes played themselves out was that Hugh had an aversion to performing oral sex for Gayle and yet believed it was his due from her. Gayle's underlying feeling was that Hugh's pressure on her was tantamount to rape. This is just one of several patterns that would kick in whenever we would try to make love.

To restore sex as a pleasant and satisfying way of relating, we worked out a detailed plan for starting our sex life over. We realized very early on that the most important factor for us was to be mentally free of grievances while we made love, and so we first spent several weeks helping each other understand the attitudes we had each picked up as children. Your partner can almost always see your family more clearly than you can, and if you will receive this information without becoming defensive, it can be enormously helpful in getting over past programming and sensing your true feelings. If it causes too much conflict between you to attempt this analysis, a loving, nonjudgmental sex therapist—one who supports your relationship and, preferably, works with both of you together—can be equally helpful.

After we felt that we had a fairly good grasp of what was going on emotionally, we scheduled a "date" once a week. This was a time alone in the evenings in which we brought each other some form of physical pleasure. For the first month we had a strict rule that there could be no erotic pleasure of any kind. We played music. We ate foods we did not ordinarily allow ourselves. And after the first week we began scheduling nonerotic massage—first with clothes and then gradually less clothing. Finally, we began including, in a very mild way, the erotic zones; but no lovemaking as yet.

During this period we slipped once and tried to make love but realized quickly that it was too soon because of the old patterns that it instantly triggered. We went back to being very patient and included a new rule that there would be no analysis or discussion of our past problems during the period of the "date." If either of us found *anything* that was happening unpleasant or fearful, that person had the right of veto, which the other person agreed never to question. We tried to plan these dates carefully, however, so that objections would not arise. We discovered that the key to success was going slowly and never pressuring each other.

When we first began to include lovemaking, we always decided beforehand what we would do, making sure that neither of us found the plan threatening. If ever we discovered that we had tried too much, as did happen once or twice, we would return to less threatening forms of sexual activity and gradually work our way back. We discovered that it was beneficial to be creative and to try things we hadn't tried before, which, because they were new, didn't have the old negative charge.

openness to options invites healing   With sex, as with other issues, we kept working until we got a breakthrough or series of breakthroughs. Sometimes a problem area would be particularly resistant—how firm to be with our children was one such area—and other times a problem of many years would melt away almost instantly. The key factor was isolating the activity and being receptive to any idea or plan that might make us feel more compatible during that time. Only couples who dismiss options before they are tried, or who tell themselves that there is nothing else to try, are doomed to live out their days with the same unhappy pattern always in place. A mind that is flexible and willing to start over remains open to healing.

One game we used to play to loosen our minds was to make a list of options that might help in the area of activity we were working on and to begin the list with wild or even insane ideas. For example, we used this when we were working on the issue of hair. The pattern we were in was that when we would come back from having a haircut, we would try to find out what the other one thought, and invariably we did not like what we heard. We had once solved a similar problem with the dinners we would each fix by making the rule: Unless you can't keep it down, you must say that whatever was cooked is just wonderful, and no matter how closely questioned, you can't back down. Since cooking has never been a passion of either of ours, this rule worked beautifully, turning a running unhappiness into a running joke. Haircuts, however, involved the question of whether the particular hair stylist should be used again.

The mind-opening portion of our list included such crazy things as murdering all the hair stylists in town so that new ones would move in; each of us wearing a turban; becoming hair stylists ourselves; shaving our heads; and so on. The more serious possibilities were ideas such as accompanying each other to make sure that the person who cut our partner's hair followed the instructions given, and increasing our budget for haircuts so that we could try the more expensive shops. These last two we did try, with mixed results, but the one that ended up working came from the crazy list. Hugh ("Mr. Hugh") began cutting his own hair, then Gayle's, and now, after experiencing a few bad haircuts themselves, both our boys occasionally ask him to trim theirs.

Having to iron out a multitude of difficulties is not an indictment against a relationship. Even the loveliest garden needs extensive weeding occasionally and will always need maintenance. If you will approach them in the one-at-a-time way we are suggesting, the number of problems between you will begin to decrease. And yet your egos will still clash, and unless you are ready to ascend, you will repeat some of your old mistakes from time to time. In a sense, almost everything in the world needs repair and maintenance, and relationships are no exception.

Don't underestimate your or your partner's resistance to working on your marriage. We have been conditioned to believe that true love requires very little effort. And even though it's often quite difficult to begin a healing program, the rewards arc far greater than can be imagined. When you find that your ego is fretting about the amount of time your new program takes, don't underestimate the time you spend fighting in the old way, worrying about whether you should break up, feeling depressed and lonely because you aren't close, talking to friends and relatives about your lousy relationship, and so forth. A sick relationship wastes more time than one that is in the process of healing.

4. SCHEDULING FRIENDSHIP

The fourth step in our plan was, once a week, to block out an hour
or two, sometimes more, to practice friendship. This grew out of
our lovemaking "dates," which had as their purpose bringing
pleasure to each other. We realized that very seldom in our marriage had we experienced times that were truly carefree, but our
"dates" had shown us that we could give this to each other—
provided it was our single goal. These new dates were times when
we did something we both enjoyed, like taking a walk, a hike, a
drive, or going to a special restaurant. Our rule of thumb was not
to bring up any "unhappy subjects" such as how our relationship
compared to others, mistakes we had made in the past, or any
other area of conversation that contained an issue that would divide us. This is also the unspoken rule between most friends.

We have always loved to talk about our children, politics, our
neighbors, our spiritual path, and a few other subjects, and so we
stuck to those. We practiced making each other feel good, practiced having fun, practiced being comfortable together. In other
words, we practiced being married, and we still have these dates
today, even more frequently.

5. A DAILY SPIRITUAL PROGRAM

The last part of our plan has had the most far-reaching results. We
worked out a daily spiritual program that included setting our
purpose for the day just after rising in the morning, a period of
meditation in the afternoon, and letting go of the day just before
going to sleep. Our children join us for this evening meditation on
the bed, and before we release the day together, we surround anyone in light who we think could use the help.

To this basic program we have also added brief meditations (a
few seconds each) at the little beginnings and endings of daily
events. For example, we pause just before we turn the car ignition

on and just after we turn it off. This allows us to see what we want our focus to be when we go into a store, a school, our home, one of our parents' homes, or whatever other new situation we are about to enter. And, once we get back in the car, it allows us to let go of whatever we have picked up that we don't want to continue carrying.

If everything else fails, we have always been able to restore peace to our relationship by increasing our spiritual efforts. It's not only our belief but our consistent experience that no one is alone, and that those who turn their thoughts to Love, to God, to the stillness of their being, or to whatever one wishes to call that which cannot be named, and do this every time it occurs to them, peace will begin to blanket the harsh events of their lives. This is especially helpful during times of crisis, because the mind tends to get on an unhappy merry-go-round of miserable thinking that amplifies sorrow and anger. Because these thoughts usually involve another person, one way to stop them is to interrupt each thought as soon as you become conscious of it, then surround that person in light. If you will consistently do this, your mind can become a friend and a place of peace. It's important to remember that there is often no obvious reward for your spiritual efforts within the circumstances of the world, but there is a change in atmosphere and outlook that is profoundly happy.

ATTAINMENT (ALSO CALLED UNCONDITIONAL LOVE; TRUE LOVE; SECOND HONEYMOON; FRIENDSHIP; A REAL RELATIONSHIP)

Most of this book is about reaching this stage, and we have already described it in many ways. We would like to add here a few personal experiences of what our own process has and continues to be. The conflict that a couple experiences during their journey, however extreme, exists on the surface only. At their core level, they have always shared unlimited similarities. As they were learning that their happiness is in each other's safekeeping, their interests were gradually shifting to a common ground, and they were growing increasingly compatible, even on an ego level.

Hugh's family's core dynamic was their unshakable belief in their superiority (coupled with the ideal of behaving humbly) and their conviction that whatever they felt, whatever they wanted, was always right. A belief in one's superiority is very separating and, because it is closed to help, is particularly resistant. To break up this mindset, for years Hugh said this little chant: "Today I need no opinions. Gayle's opinions are sufficient. Today I need no ego. One ego is enough." (A man who had been married for fifty-three years stood up in a workshop we were giving in Boston and revealed a shorter version. He said that he had finally learned the key to a happy marriage; it was always to answer "Yes, dear.")

Hugh was able to say his chant sincerely because he had seen that Gayle was intelligent and that she had no malice. Although he would have chosen to do many things differently than she, he knew that no real harm would come to anyone by letting her approach be the approach of the relationship. Naturally, if she wanted Hugh to make the decision with her, or if she just *wanted* Hugh's opinion, he would give it.

Hugh now knows from long experience that one does not become less a person by relinquishing defensiveness. The opposite is true. As he gradually dropped the need to be right, he became more complete, more whole, in fact, more interesting. For example, a sense of humor that he didn't know he had began to surface; he became more intuitive and a better listener. He also became more willing to let Jordan and John learn from their mistakes, less afraid of their anger, and much more deeply bonded to them.

We don't recommend this approach to any who believe that their partners would take advantage of them or would become more ego driven as a result. We include it in this book because of the tremendous fear so many now have of being swallowed up by love. Many people, especially women, find themselves pushed into the role of family drudge, and this is not good for them or for anyone else. While they are in this role their creativity may seem to dissipate; their humor and happiness may all but vanish; and they may indeed appear to have been swallowed up by love. And yet there are others who thrive on the same set of duties, so obviously it is not being married or having domestic duties that causes the fire within people to dim. The problem, and it is a universal one, is that a real friendship has not evolved that embraces both partners fully.

Eventually, the relationship itself, the shared consciousness, must become aware of all the needs of each family member. This state is difficult to describe to any who have not experienced it, because what in fact happens is that an overlapping of thinking, a shared mind, begins to develop, and *it* watches over the family. You come to have an intimate awareness of your partner, and the two of you develop a joint conscience that causes you to feel extreme distress if circumstances have become unfair to either of you. You will actually feel this more strongly over your partner's deprivations than your own.

In the early stages of a marriage, the needs you each have or that your children have can seem so numerous and at variance that the task of accommodating everyone appears impossible. Most attempts to do so result in a kind of chaotic battle scene. And yet all you need do is begin, and to start over wherever you are able to start over. As this new form of thinking begins to develop—thinking from the *standpoint* of your friendship—all your needs will very gradually come into mutual awareness. Then still another remarkable and unexpected process will start: the needs themselves will begin to "marry."

A couple in love for many years will often like the same entertainment, pastimes, and friends. They will tend to agree on what type neighborhood to live in and if and when to move. They will develop similar tastes in furnishings and decoration and will usually embrace the same political and religious philosophies—often making changes in these at the same time. As their sense of inner oneness grows, they may even begin to have the same illnesses and injuries, possibly even dying at or near the same time or at times that are connected in some obvious way.

We don't really know why this external harmony develops, but in our case at least, it has been a source of amusement and pleasure. Now, for example, when one of us strains a muscle or bruises a limb, we laugh that it won't be long before the other does the same. Last week in a restaurant we discovered that, without consciously deciding to do so, all of our family had switched to having our sodas the same way. A waiter who had served us before said, "Oh, I know you, you're the no-ice family." In southern Arizona this is not a logical preference.

We realize that this description of a permanent relationship will be frightening to some students of separation psychology, because they will see it as still another indication that devotion leads to loss of identity. But in many ways a real relationship merely enters into a second honeymoon, and very few couples experience the honeymoon mindset as a threat to who they are. It is true that in the light of love, the *ego* self begins to lose its grip on the mind, and this is what allows the second honeymoon to be permanent. The partners become less defensive of what they truly don't want and choose what they do want.

PART III

Protecting and Perfecting a Real Relationship

MANY PEOPLE GIVE LIP SERVICE TO SOCIETY'S NEED FOR SOUND, LOVING families, but as yet there has been no widespread effort to protect them against what is perhaps their primary form of destruction. In the first two chapters of Part III we will give you ways to think about and react to affairs, ways that can save your marriage.

Some researchers now estimate that at least one partner will have an affair in over 70 percent of all marriages, and that infidelity or the threat of it is a factor in almost every divorce. Whether one accepts these high-end figures or the only slightly more conservative low-end ones, the numbers are overwhelming. It would seem that adultery can now strike almost any marriage at almost any time. And this is the behavioral footing on which we begin the twenty-first century.

NINE
Affairs

THE SILENT PLAGUE

In a sense, the problems that couples have are always the same:
Something has been made more important than the relationship.
In the case of an affair, the "something" would appear to be a
competing love. It is not real love, but one partner, at least,
doesn't know this. The approach that the couple would ordinarily
use with any other problem—working to restore their relationship
to its priority position—is undercut by one partner's having sym-
bolically thrown the relationship away. This leaves only the other
partner to carry the candle of their love, and suffering the betrayal
that he or she feels, this is extraordinarily difficult. Still it is not
impossible, and we will devote a large part of this chapter to
helping the one in this position. Naturally, most of what we have
already said about this in the "Crisis" section on page 159 applies here also.

The type of affair we will discuss is always a breach of trust.
We will not take up the more unusual forms of extramarital sex—
swinging, swapping, mutual consent, sex with a prostitute, sex
when one's spouse is permanently disabled, and so forth—except

to say that in our experience "mutual consent" is seldom truly mutual (one of the partners is often being pressured) and that sex outside of marriage is not only life-threatening from a health standpoint but is also likely to obscure the spiritual bond between you. We personally know of only one marriage besides our own that survived an open marriage period—an ideal that many of our friends shared in the sixties and seventies.

how it starts   All problems are problems of the relation-ship, and as such both partners are responsible for solving them. It's also true, and very helpful to see, that both partners partici-pate in the upset, the arguments, the attacks and counterattacks. If your participation in the distance that you now feel is not apparent to you, then you must simply take it on faith that you are contrib-uting and proceed as if the problem were equally yours.

However, it does not follow that the actual event—in this case, an affair or series of affairs—was caused by both partners.

Because of the emphasis on codependence and co-blame within separation psychology, there is now much confusion over how guilt should be distributed. In our marriage Hugh was the one who had the affairs. Gayle didn't somehow "manifest" or "draw" those experiences into her life. Nor should she have known that Hugh was someone who would have affairs. Hugh didn't even know that about himself. He had been married briefly once before and had not had an affair, and he didn't start having them until six years into our own marriage, when *Notes to Myself* became a best-seller and suddenly there were many opportunities before him.

The concept that it was Gayle's faith in Hugh and her trustful-ness that "enabled" Hugh to have the affairs is not only cruel, it is insane. Enabling does of course take place, but loving another person and seeing his or her goodness is simply not what allows that individual to be destructive. The alternative to love is always some form of judgment, and who has ever been helped by being judged?

Although her perception of his basic goodness went unjustified for many years, just at the time all of her friends agreed that Hugh was hopeless, he began to justify it. Today Hugh knows absolutely that he couldn't have turned his life around if it hadn't been for Gayle's faith in him, because only one other member of his family has ever broken out of their pattern of disloyalty. Not only didn't Gayle leave, she wouldn't leave, and as Hugh's appreciation of her intuition and intelligence grew, it began to dawn on him that maybe what she saw in him was actually there.

Perhaps more believable to those who want to think that their spouse always shares responsibility for the mistakes they themselves make is the explanation that Gayle somehow encouraged the affairs or drove Hugh to them. In counseling sessions we have heard these arguments many times. Most people try to justify extramarital sex by revealing that their sex life at home was inadequate or nonexistent. ("I had to make an appointment with her." "My husband had a little problem that no one knew about." "She put on a lot of weight and wouldn't do anything about it.") Or they simply cite unhappiness at home, as if everyone has the *right* to be happy at home and the only remedy is adultery. ("I have a right to a life." "I have needs too.") In Hugh's case, he could make no such claims—he was comfortable with our home life, and most of the time our sex was fine.

Even though there are numerous ways to satisfy one's sexual needs beside infidelity, our culture tends to quietly condone it if it's practiced under these circumstances, and there are a surprising number of therapists who suggest that an affair can "stabilize" a marriage and even improve the *quality* of the couple's sex life. This general pretense of being "understanding" of the problem of an inadequate sex life does not make affairs any less destructive to children, families, and older adults, and it does not lessen their brutalizing effect on society.

can affairs be motivated by love?   Loving concentration and increased devotion to the relationship would be your response if your spouse had been in a serious accident or developed a catastrophic illness. What prevents you from this now may be your belief that by having an affair, your partner has stopped loving you and is no longer your partner. However, an affair isn't motivated by love; it is motivated by any number of complex ego patterns. **An act of love doesn't cause lives to be torn apart, people to be thrown into pain, and children to be emotionally burdened for life.**

Perhaps you think that your wife has taken her love for you and given it to another, but this could not be what has actually occurred. It may be of little consolation to know that even though she chose another man's body over yours, she did not do that out of love for him; nor could he have participated out of love for her. In the vast majority of relationships that lead up to an affair, the two participants do not even share a real friendship. This is not to say they don't *think* they love each other, but what passes for love in most "illicit" relationships is primarily a combination of hormones and self-suggestion.

Although your husband has had an affair, there is still love between you, and you don't want to obstruct it by trying to force him to do things that merely give the appearance that he loves you (spend more time at home, call more often from work, be on time, have more sex, move back into the bedroom, go out more with the usual friends, talk about the future). The ego values the appearance of love more than the fact, and it will sacrifice the fact to get the appearance. So don't allow the fearful part of you to lead you into this very common mistake. Your partner will devalue what you thrust at him, even when it's the appearance of a loving relationship.

There are of course friendships that can form outside of marriage, and occasionally these individuals choose to betray their mates. It is very interesting, though, that when real friendship comes first, even if the two people later discover that they are in love, they usually choose not to act this out, and in fact they will step back from the friendship as a protection to each other's family. If the friendship does lead to betrayal, the act of the affair itself is a loveless act and throws the relationship back to the level of all affairs. This is why it is essential to the protection of your marriage that you stay focused on the most important thing that you and your spouse still share, which is the bond you have already formed. Staying focused, though, does not imply a particular course of action. It is an act of the heart, a permanent decision to love.

"you deal with it."   Although the affair was not caused by both partners, as with all other difficulties, both partners now have the problem that has resulted from it. The aftermath of an affair differs widely within each relationship, and the two partners participate in determining the nature and duration of the upset. They must work together to move their marriage past this rupture. The attitude, "It's your problem—deal with it," accomplishes nothing except further distance and resentment. Those whose partner had the affair adopt this stance because they feel that since they didn't make the mistake, they don't need to change. Their partner, however, must completely transform. Those who had the affair, on the other hand, may think that the problem is not the affair but their spouse's overreaction.

The attitude that will take you furthest is, "This happened to *us,* to *our* relationship, and we will work it out together." You can begin with this approach yourself, even though your spouse may not be ready to. Instead of focusing on Hugh's behavior, Gayle found a therapist who supported her marriage, and for eight years she worked on her problems from childhood and her insecurities. If at any time the therapist had suggested that she think about getting a divorce, she would have stopped seeing him, because that is not what she was there to decide.

Once Hugh was ready to work, we set aside an hour each day in which, one by one, we took up each unhappy aspect of our relationship. We continued this for several years. We are not suggesting that every couple has to devote this much time daily, but your relationship does have to be placed above everything else, and some symbol of this commitment is vital.

Remember that you will *both* make mistakes—many more, in fact, after this one. Granted that in the eyes of most people this is a very large mistake, still you need each other more than you need the illusion that life can be made to seem always fair. We are a society inundated by sexual images, and it's simply not reasonable to expect that our relationships won't be affected. We are certainly not condoning affairs, but to expect your partner to be completely immune to that which is all-pervasive is unrealistic.

When you stumble, a good friend does not walk on, but stops and tries to help you. Likewise in this crisis, eventually you will need to decline the temptation to turn your back on your partner. This doesn't mean that you must make unasked-for suggestions or go through the motions of being "helpful." But when you are emotionally able to do so, you wish silently to bless and hold in light this person to whom you once pledged your friendship and understanding.

THE ONE WHO DID NOT HAVE THE AFFAIR

We understand very well that if your partner has betrayed you and if you are not going to leave, you will be very confused and not know how to react. There may be a period when the affair is not over and your spouse appears to be deciding between you and this other person. Or there may be a string of affairs, as there was in our marriage. You are probably very conflicted. You want to hang on—*and* you want to punish. You are willing to change—but you are not willing to change. You want to withdraw and heal—*and* you want to move forward and get this over with.

Nothing you alone do will guarantee that this marriage will last. Your partner may leave you. Perhaps you and everyone else can see that he or she would be walking straight into misery to leave you for this other person, and yet that may be exactly what happens. All you can do is the best you can.

rage and the ego emotions   It's unrealistic to think that you can get through this without anger or possibly even considerable rage. It is possible, but very few people are that centered in their cores. We assure you that *we* are not. However, there is one mistake that you can probably avoid making. Do not ignore your ego emotions, especially until you have had ample time to examine them closely. In a sense, anger can be your friend if you will expose it fully in a safe situation, because it can point you down a stairway that leads first to fear, then to understanding, and finally to empathy or love. It can't take you there, because anger is too superficial an emotion to know the place of love, but it can provide an opening that your awareness can pass through.

Many years ago there was an elderly woman in New Mexico whom we both thought of as a close friend. She was much too judgmental to be a good candidate for a mother figure, but in his own mind Hugh managed to turn her into one. She had some health problems, and so we ran errands for her and helped her in many other everyday ways, at one point even bringing her into our home to live. The three of us used to spend a lot of time together, but one day, without any warning or apparent provocation, she told Hugh that she liked Gayle better than him and preferred that only Gayle visit her from now on. She did not say any of this in a gentle way.

When Hugh heard her words, he felt the deepest sense of betrayal that he could remember feeling since his mother left him at age six. Although Gayle, on her own, decided to cut off her relationship with the woman, in the days that followed Hugh began having murderous fantasies. One day he caught himself planning in detail how he could actually kill her. He was in his car at the time, and he was so shocked at how far his anger had gone that he drove home and went out to the woodpile. He began throwing logs on the ground one at a time. He would picture the woman's face at the center of the log, chop until he split it, then throw down another one.

He thought this would get his anger out where he could see it more clearly and thereby dissipate it—and this did in fact occur—but something else happened that he was not expecting. Suddenly Hugh could feel what the woman was feeling. It was as if he temporarily became her and realized that she didn't hate him; she simply liked being with Gayle and found him overanxious and burdensome to be around.

Looked at from his standpoint, "overanxious and burdensome" would seem like criticisms, but since Hugh was seeing this from *her* eyes, it didn't feel like a personal attack; it was just a fact.

Although that relationship never resumed for either Gayle or Hugh, neither did Hugh's rage. He learned from the experience something of what it feels like to be betrayed as an adult—and this was by a woman he had known less than a year, to whom he was in no way related, who certainly had never pledged her devotion, and who simply preferred to be around his wife and was blunt in saying so. The early loss of his mother had obviously entered into his emotions, but everyone has had *something* traumatic happen in childhood. For us, to see how one can work up a murderous rage over a minor betrayal of friendship has made it more understandable how a wife or a husband might do almost anything under circumstances in which a far more substantial betrayal occurs. Hugh also learned from this experience how important it is not to let anger, jealousy, fear, sadness, and the other ego emotions fester and get out of hand. It isn't necessary to "vent" them on others—this merely adds complications—but it is essen-

tial to our mental stability that we bring them fully into consciousness and dissipate them.

guilt   Attack, either outwardly or inwardly directed, is the
most common mistake that people make in response to an affair.
Books and articles are still being written advocating the use of
revenge in relationships, as if ten thousand years of it were not
enough and if we just tried a little longer, maybe it would turn out
to be the key to healing our wounds and correcting each other's
shortcomings. Also a part of the self-help literature, as well as
conventional books and entertainment, is the notion that to be
critical of oneself is an expression of humility, a first step to
reform, and a constraint on future destructive behavior. In other
words, by valuing some forms of attack we will stop valuing other
forms.

   You can't prevent thoughts of guilt from coming into your mind
(the ego is always seeing enemies), but you can decline to get
caught up in any one of them, and this is to your advantage. What
you do with blame or self-censure *once you notice it* will determine the effectiveness of all your decisions throughout the day.
Guilt can't be contained; it spreads like barking. No dog in the
neighborhood can resist, even though the original cause has long
since been forgotten. If you think attack thoughts about yourself,
soon you will be thinking them about your spouse. If you think
them about your spouse, soon you will be thinking them about
your children, and so forth. Just as no one can silence all the
neighborhood dogs, you must simply allow your ego to bark—but
make sure that you have better things to think about with the rest
of your mind.

the two- and three-chair approach   There are many
possible ways of bringing your anger and guilt more fully into
your awareness: hitting a mattress with a bat, punching a cushion,
writing hate letters (that you do not send!), screaming into a pil-

low, painting or drawing exactly what you feel, tearing up photographs, stomping something to pieces, exercising to exhaustion. If you decide to destroy something, choose objects that you won't want later, and of course don't take out your rage on your spouse's treasured possessions. However, it's obviously better to attack these than to attack your spouse.

One very effective procedure is to set up two chairs about three feet apart, sit in one, and picture your spouse, the third person, in-laws, disloyal friends, or your own "guilty" self sitting in the other. Take time to imagine this individual in detail; include, for example, typical gestures and clothing. Then bluntly say to this person whatever is on your mind. Be as emotional as you wish. When you feel yourself pausing or coming to a stopping point, get out of your chair and sit in the other one. Now take a moment to become this other person. Assume the attitude, the posture, and so forth that this individual would have. Staring at yourself in the opposite chair, answer back what was just said and add anything else that comes to mind. Be honest and very direct. When you feel finished, return to your old chair, once again become yourself, and answer back.

Continue switching chairs in this manner until you feel finished, then go about your day as usual. Don't read great meaning into anything that happened—simply allow the procedure to have a settling effect on your mind. Repeat this as often as you need to in the days to come, remembering always to include switching chairs and becoming the other person. We stress the switching because this is the point when you will feel the greatest resistance to the procedure. Your ego doesn't *want* to know what the other individual feels and thinks (or more accurately, what you believe that person feels and thinks).

If your spouse or someone with whom you have a long relationship is the one you picture in the opposite chair, you can use a version of the "How to Have a Real Argument" process we detailed on page 208. After you have finished exploring the ego positions from both chairs, return to your original seat and again express to your imagined partner your position, but this time solely in terms of your fears. Then switch chairs as before, and as your partner, answer back with his or her fears.

When you feel that you have vented as fully as possible the fear level in "both of you," set up a third chair facing the other two. As you sit here, you wish to represent the *relationship*. So take time to sink gently into your stillness, and from your quiet wisdom and your peace, say to both partners what comes from your heart.

While in this third chair, some find it helpful to imagine that Jesus, Moses, a being of light, the Buddha, their Higher Power, their Higher Self, or some other figure of wisdom is sitting there. And perhaps they are.

When this stage is complete, return to your original seat, and, with your eyes closed, think of three gifts you wish to give the relationship. Open your eyes, and state these to your imagined partner as promises.

"it wasn't the affair so much as the lying." By far the most common explanation we have heard as to why people divorce a spouse who has had an affair (and also the bottom line that many relationship books give) runs like this: "I could have taken the affair. I wouldn't have liked it, but I think I could have forgiven that. It was all the lies. Even after it all came out and was obvious to everyone, the lies and the cover-up continued."

Almost all people who have affairs lie. We have yet to meet anyone who was covering up an ongoing affair who was not also using lies as part of the cover-up. Unquestionably, it would be best if once the affair became known or strongly suspected, and the involved partner was directly confronted, that he or she would make a clean break and become completely honest. But that simply is not what happens in most cases. The affair is deceitful and the lying is deceitful, and the distinction between the two is lost on most people who are still in the grip of a betrayal. **If you are going to forgive an affair, you will have to forgive all of it.** Any therapist, friend, or adviser who leads you to center on the lying simply does not understand the mindset of an adulterer. People who are addicted to an infatuation are not morally superior to people who are addicted to drugs, power, fame, or anything else. Who, for example, would expect an alcoholic to be honest while still drinking?

Most people who are having affairs are in an intensely selfish period and are simply not going to listen to reason or to calls to their better nature. They think they have found something that is making them happy. They don't really see anything wrong with it. They probably think that their life up to now justifies all that they are doing. They very well may have friends who support what is happening, and certainly their lover does. And in most cases they are not going to let anyone or anything stop them. Of course, there are those who feel guilty and *want* to be stopped, but those individuals, especially in this era, are a minority.

Once, when Gayle requested that she and Hugh have a session with a couple who were marriage and family therapists, he reluctantly agreed. The couple asked Hugh if he had ever had an affair, and since Gayle knew that he had, Hugh said yes. The therapists began strongly lecturing Hugh (in a therapeutic way) on the inadvisability of this, and Hugh argued back that he thought it was an essentially harmless practice. After a while he got bored with the exchange—it was obvious to him that he was not going to change their minds—and began acting as if they were convincing him. Finally they asked Hugh to swear never to be unfaithful again. He thought about this for a moment, smiled, and solemnly pledged to be monogamous.

After the session Hugh went around to some of his male friends and told them what he had done, and they all doubled over laughing. "I've found the key to being left alone!" Hugh declared. They all agreed that he had, and some of them said they were going to get their wives and try it too.

We tell this simply to show how selfish and insensitive a person who is pursuing other bodies can become. Hugh now knows from years of helping other men with this problem that what he did is not an extreme example.

Some form of selfishness is probably what you are up against. Your wife (or husband) may be fed up with running short on money every month, fed up with emptying the cat box, fed up with your never wanting to go to the movie she wants to go to, fed up with the endless fights and mess and chaos, fed up with you. If there are children and a career involved, she may be fed up with those too. To her, the affair seems like a godsend, a sudden release from jail. When she is with her lover, all her worries are swept away. He understands her. He is always there for her. He makes no demands. And the sex is new and great.

making decisions   If you are determined to weather these storms, you can often do so. But it will not be easy. And you may not get a lot of support from anyone. Now more than ever, you need to turn within, to your own sense of another reality, and begin trusting in what you already know. Above all, don't make things worse by taking action you are conflicted about taking.

In the section "Core Dynamics" on pages 88–90, we briefly described the pattern in which one partner chases and the other runs away. This is also a frequent pattern between the betrayer and the betrayed. It's not necessarily the central dynamic of the relationship. (If over 70 percent of all marriages experience an affair, that would leave very few relationships to have another dynamic.) But it usually surfaces and can be plainly seen when the relationship is in a crisis triggered by infidelity. It means that your tendency will probably be to act, to initiate, to encounter, to reach out, to solve, and it will be your partner's tendency to want to withdraw, to run away, to be left alone, to escape from all emotional and physical contact. Neither position is higher or better, but as we said before, the betraying partner is almost always in a selfish state, and any approach you use—simply because it's an *approach*—will probably be misinterpreted and used against the relationship. Under these circumstances, waiting for clarity can be extremely difficult.

We wish we could tell you to seek professional help, or help from your friends and family, but in most cases their desire will be to get you to leave. Many therapists focus on the autonomy and strength of the ego, and thus the effect of the therapeutic process is usually to strengthen every tendency you have to be separate. It's important to remember that the divorce rate for therapists is just as high as it is for the general public.

Fortunately, there are some professionals who understand what one must go through to build a real relationship. Sometimes you can identify these people from their ads, sometimes from word of mouth. But you want to guard against continuing to see anyone who raises questions about your relationship rather than shows you how to solve them. The Jungian psychiatrist Gayle went to for the eight years she was working on herself knew that Hugh was having affairs and yet, when the subject arose, encouraged Gayle not to leave.

As with all questions, the safest answer to what you should do comes from your peaceful mind. Your *un*peaceful mind tries to decide by weighing alternatives and foreseeing outcomes. It gets on a mental merry-go-round, and each new factor you think of starts it spinning faster. Since there is no end to the considerations, no end to guessing how to weigh each one, no end to the consequences that could flow from any choice you make, the merry-go-round never stops. This is always the cue that you are using your unpeaceful mind to decide: you will keep going over and over the same considerations and never reach certainty about the future. Obviously, there *is* no certainty about the future, no perfect answer to be found. You can come to know what you *believe* is best, but not what *is* best. Taking the time to discover your deepest belief of what will be best for you and those your life touches places your decision on a firm basis of awareness and compassion. In the course of your life, the quiet answers of your heart will gradually lead you toward peace—but they will not magically solve anything.

Life-changing questions usually cannot, and should not, be answered all at once and in their entirety. Break the larger question into the one or two steps you could take today. Then wait for tomorrow for tomorrow's options. Don't be concerned if you can't see where these little decisions are leading. Simply make each choice in peace. For example, if you are torturing yourself by trying to decide whether you should get a divorce, become as peaceful as you can and then ask yourself if you want to call a lawyer now. If the answer is no, commit radically to your relationship for the day, and do not allow your mind to resume its unhappy focus. If it does, interrupt the thought and remind yourself that you have made the decision to commit for this one day.

Instead of focusing on the question, focus instead on your state of mind. Once you have made your mind as quiet and relaxed as you can, you will feel a leaning, a peaceful preference. This is a possibility, an option, that comes from your heart. Don't analyze it; simply give that answer a try. This is a perfectly adequate way of getting through a crisis, and whatever conclusion you eventually reach about your relationship, you will know that you reached it from the center of your being rather than from the passion of the moment.

detaching from the problem, not the person

Just as the wife of an alcoholic learns not to count beer cans to check up on how much her husband drank the night before, or the husband of an alcoholic learns not to ferret out where his wife hides vodka, so the spouse of an adulterer does not want to get caught up in the little games the partner may be playing or be swept up in the partner's emotional turmoil. You can't help someone out of quicksand if you jump in too. Nor do you wish needlessly to increase your pain and fear by doing so.

Therefore, if confessions are a part of your spouse's affair pattern, as best you can, try not to be taken down by them. For example, try to keep from asking for details of the kind of sex the two of them had or are still having; try not to become obsessed with the other person; don't attempt to get assurances of what your partner is going to do now; don't ask your partner to measure his or her feelings for the other person against his or her feelings for you; don't try to find out who knows about the affair; and so forth. Each time you play into another aspect of this soap opera, you will want to know still one more miserable detail, and you will be less able to help either yourself or your partner. Making threats also sets you up for the same kind of involvement, because now you must wait to see what your spouse will do, and having your actions dependent on your spouse's illness is exactly what you do not want.

threats and pronouncements   If you can help it, you wish not to stir up even more pain and chaos than you are already in. Nor do you want forever to remain walking evidence of your partner's guilt. And certainly you don't want to get divorced just to make a point. Staying damaged will punish you more than it will your partner. Making threats or pronouncements about the future will not heal either of you. Verbal attack does not correct, and no matter how reasonable they may sound, ultimatums are almost always issued in anger.

It should be remembered that affairs, abuse, drug relapses, and many other crisis-precipitating behaviors are very hard to control. And of course the tongue is even harder to control. You may not be able to keep yourself from saying things that aren't helpful. But since threats merely drive your partner further from you and put still another cloud over your relationship, make as few as you possibly can. Naturally there will be the thought that your partner shouldn't be allowed to get away with treating you like this, but vengeance is not your province. You will have to work hard to keep in mind that this relationship, even under these disturbing circumstances, contains far more potential to benefit you than does your pride.

The central misguidance that most books and articles that address adultery are giving is that they emphasize stopping the affair more than saving the relationship. The relationship is more important than the affair, because the *relationship,* if it takes its natural course, will heal all dynamics, not just this one. Once again, this unfortunate emphasis is coming from the belief that everyone has a right to a life free of suffering: Adultery causes hassle, mess, and pain—no one should have to put up with that—therefore either your spouse stops imposing this on you, or you call the lawyer.

Many writers will openly say that the marriage "must be risked" if you are going to end the affair. The effect on *you* for having risked and lost your marriage is not fully described. The effect on your *children* is certainly not fully described. And the effect on the *adulterer,* who is now left without a best friend, the one person who could have eventually helped her or him get past this, is never described. All that is *fully* described is how you are now being afflicted. But affairs are not always easy to end, no matter how many lives you are willing to risk hurting.

In the twenty-four years that we have been counseling people in various forms of crisis, it has been our consistent observation that all marriages, like all individuals, have their measure of grief. As Paul Tsongas said when asked by a reporter how he felt about his cancer having returned, "We all have something, cancer is just mine." Naturally, one doesn't sit back and forever do nothing. But neither does one act from the complicating belief that problems, even severe problems, are an aberration.

the planned ultimatum   Some therapists advise presenting the betraying partner with a carefully thought-out ultimatum ("setting limits," "drawing lines") as a way of helping that individual control his or her behavior. In some cases this might work, but you should turn deeply to your own intuition before you use such an approach. Clearly an ultimatum does not work with many addicts and alcoholics, and in our experience it usually doesn't work with repeat adulterers. The problem with trying it in the latter case is that if it isn't successful, not only is the behavior not stopped but the marriage is broken up when the threat is carried out. And if the threat isn't carried out, the partner who is not having the affair feels weaker and more vulnerable.

Anything you do in order to manipulate your partner's behavior (since you can't know for sure that you *will* leave, this is what you are doing) is risky because it depends on the reaction of other egos. There are plenty of tapes, books, and magazines that tell their readers how to get their partners to change (how to make them love you more, how to turn up their sex drive, how to keep them from taking you for granted, even how to make them go to the doctor, and so on). Many also suggest strategies to use when adultery is suspected or discovered—forced contracts, confronting the third person, withdrawing love as a technique, trial separations, hiring a detective, laying traps, calling in others to confront one's partner. No one can devise a perfect rule on how to respond to an affair, and all we can do in this book is give you our experience. Ultimately you must take these very difficult and complex questions into the stillness of your heart and wait for your answer.

In all of the examples we have just cited, our experience has been that they often—but not always—misfire, and sometimes they are disastrous. The planned ultimatum, for example, will not work if your wife is having an affair *because* she is already leaning toward divorcing you. It will not work if your husband has affairs because of his unconscious hatred of women. It will not work if your partner is in a self-destructive state of caring about no one. And certainly it won't work if your spouse is a martyr. Possibly it will work if your partner can't say no without the aid of your absolute firmness. And it might work if your partner needs shocking and being brought to his senses.

In Hugh's case, his mother left him, his first wife left him, and Gayle was supposed to leave him. If she had, Hugh's view of women would have been confirmed once again. If she had even declared an ultimatum, it would have been confirmed. But after Hugh had done everything that he had been taught, and still Gayle didn't leave, he was very confused. Eventually this confusion prompted him to question his view of women.

When the planned ultimatum *does* **work, both partners may suspect that the involved spouse is staying because of the threat that hangs over his or her head.** This alters the basic balance of the relationship. The prospect of divorce can carry with it the prospect of damage to one's career, loss of property and income, separation from one's children, and so forth. Clearly there can be many reasons for not wanting a divorce besides loving one's spouse too much to leave, and since these other reasons are known by everyone, cynical suspicion may undercut the rebuilding of trust.

A man who came to us for help with his marriage told us that when he was a child, his home life changed from a consistently happy atmosphere to a consistently unhappy one after his mother laid conditions on the marriage. She had caught his father in an affair and threatened to leave him if he ever had another one and if they didn't move out of the small town where the woman lived. A divorce could easily have ruined him professionally, and so, although these seemingly reasonable requirements stopped the affairs, they also increased the destructive effects of the father's original mistake, and four children were damaged in the loveless aftermath.

When love is conditional, the partners are no longer equal. A mistake committed by only one of them has been singled out and given a special category and ranking. Affairs are a tremendous mistake, but there are worse mistakes. We have known a woman who forgave her husband for leaving a ditch uncovered that their one-year-old crawled into and drowned in—after she had warned him to cover it. We know a man who forgave his wife for falling asleep at the wheel and killing their three-year-old daughter. We have met many inmates whose spouses have remained married to them and visited them religiously for years, even though they had committed armed robbery, arson, murder, and the rape of children. And as deep a betrayal as affairs are, is divorce any less a betrayal?

We have been strongly questioning the often rigidly stated advice of making planned ultimatums, but we want to stress again that we are not saying they can never work. One woman who had an affair and deeply regretted it gave her husband not only written assurance that she wouldn't do it again, but also stated that along with her accepting a divorce if he should want it, she would take no share of their community property. She saw that this would give him the reassurance he needed to heal more quickly, and she said, it was "the least I could do after how I had behaved."

punishing   Closely linked to threats and ultimatums is punishment. It can come in many forms: verbal lashings, endless nagging, withholding sex, refusing to take care of the things you once took care of, withholding money, saying things to others that embarrass your spouse. **In marriage, punishment does not work.**

Many parents recognize when their children have reached an age when they can no longer act punitively toward them without driving them further into the mistake, and yet they forget this lesson when relating to their spouse. If parents do punish a child past this point, in the child's mind the unfairness of the parents' behavior is so much greater than the mistake itself that it pales (becomes unimportant) in comparison. The bond between parent and child starts out as a very deep one, yet perhaps you have seen fathers or mothers who have made this mistake one too many times and ended real communication. Naturally, your attempts to punish your spouse can have the same effect. And even if they don't, they will make *you* unhappy.

forcing a choice   To force your spouse to choose between you and the other person once again makes appearances more important than content. To the ego, a divorce *looks* like an end to uncertainty, to hard feelings, to recriminations, to revenge, and many people who run out of patience opt for this seemingly quick way out. But it's quick in name only. You may believe that if all this chaos doesn't end soon, you will go crazy—and perhaps for your own emotional health, you do need to break from the situation or in some other way distance yourself from what your spouse is doing—but what most people don't see is that to force a divorce (because that is what a forced choice often brings) will end very little of the chaos and may actually increase it. There will be the property and financial divisions, the encounter with lawyers and the legal system, the reactions of your children, relatives, in-laws, and mutual friends—all of which tends to bring out the worst in people and to create grievances that last for a lifetime.

Even more apparent will be the fact that your partner is now a permanent part of your mind—and not a very happy one. During each new day of "freedom," familiar names and places will come to remind you of this. If there are children involved, you have embarked on a lifelong series of encounters with your ex-spouse over them (their crises, financial support, discipline, school problems, and family occasions like Thanksgiving, birthdays, graduations). None of this means that a divorce is never the wiser choice, but divorce won't stop all difficulties between you. It ends one set of problems but creates another.

One reason that people force a choice is that they panic about their state of mind. Either they feel as if they are going to explode, or they become stupefied with the endless series of burdens and issues and march, zombie like, ahead. Eventually this scares them. If you sense that you are no longer making good decisions, do something emphatic to restore your mental balance. For example, if there is a place you can go to be quiet and renew your soul, then go—and do so as often as you need to. If you must ask a friend or relative to take over your duties while you take this break, don't let pride keep you from protecting your sanity and health.

which partner has to change most?   One obvious way that what we have been saying could be misunderstood is that the reader might think that because we repeatedly point out that the victim of the affair did not have the affair, that person has not made an equal number of mistakes—some perhaps just as destructive to the relationship. In our experience an affair often indicates that the relationship was having some serious problems before the affair and that both partners were contributing to them. We state this carefully. *Often* does not mean "usually," and again, it never means that the cheating partner was driven to cheat.

We used to get the same argument from batterers—that they were so provoked by their wives that they attacked. Instead, why didn't they run out of the house and have an affair? Why didn't they shoot up or go on a binge? But again, none of this means that both partners may not have a substantial amount of changing to do.

Yet the ego asks "What mistakes did *she* make?" or "How does *he* have to change?" and of course this approach to healing is ineffective. The problem you *both* have is the division and conflict between you *today*.

Walk to your TV right now and turn on any program of any kind, and you will probably hear someone blaming someone else for something. It may be sung, reported, acted, laughed about, or animated, but it's the favorite pastime of the ego, and in practical terms, it's a waste of energy. In practical terms, when a problem arises on a baseball, football, or soccer field, the officials huddle together to move the game along. You don't see them shouting and pointing the finger at each other. Thousands of fans are watching and they *must* be efficient. Blame is not efficient. And it's a luxury you can't afford to have in your marriage. Blame is also an illusion.

There can be no fire without fuel, oxygen, and an ignitor. If one of you stacks the wood and supplies the match, and the other one strikes it, who is most to blame for the fire? And who should work hardest to put it out? An atmosphere of extreme alienation can't exist in a relationship if one partner is wholly at peace, regardless of what the other partner did to start it. So despite the preoccupation you see all around you to assess blame for every team loss, every new disease, every rise in unemployment, every natural disaster, every lost election—in fact, every social, economic, and political problem there is—your marriage does not have to fall in this trap. Once blame starts, the only way a relationship can be saved is for the blaming to stop. Shouting won't stop it, or threats, or hitting, or trial separations; not even divorce will stop it. It comes to an end only within your own mind.

what children shouldn't see   Your mind can also protect your children against your making a decision that is too narrowly focused on blame. In most of the written advice for those who are victims of affairs, an alarming lack of attention is given to the *effects* of the advice on the children involved. Advice that appears to help one person "fulfill himself" or "declare her independence" but that throws kids' lives into chaos and trauma will not deliver what it promises. If the sentiment "It's a shame but it can't be helped" is guiding you, you're heading down the wrong road.

"It isn't good for the kids to be around all this fighting" is only partially true. It will not harm children to see their parents fight— if they also see them eventually work it out. Obviously, this doesn't mean parents should flaunt their arguments in front of them, but what a gift it would be—because they have seen it so many times—to know that there is nothing that can't be worked out between two people if they really try. And isn't that the very thing we have been telling our children all their lives—that "you should never give up," that "nothing is impossible"?

But most adults don't think they're obliged to stay with an "impossible situation" when it comes to marriage. "If it doesn't flow, let it go," they say (and sing) to each other. And yet when their child brings home bad grades, they say, "You aren't really trying. I don't care what grades you make, I just want you to do your best." When they discover a chore that their child hasn't completed, they say, "Always finish what you start. Always see it through." How many times have we all heard parents yell from the bleachers or sidelines, "Get in there! Keep your head in the game!"? Even at amusement parks and the play areas at McDonald's, you can hear parents urging their kids on: "Don't be a quitter, son."

Out of all the fights Roberto Duran had, the principal event he is remembered for in this country is the one in which he said *"No más"* and refused to finish fighting Sugar Ray Leonard. Adults choose to remember the past in this way, not children. Yet children everywhere are now seeing their parents fight and throw in the towel. What if they saw them fight and fight and fight and finally break through to real friendship? and the next time, when things *really* got bad, the same thing happened? What would be the effect on *that* generation of children? Is it impossible for adults to stay committed to an uncommitted spouse? Is keeping a family together such a heinous burden that no one should be asked to make such a sacrifice?

When a friend of ours explained to her little boy that his daddy was leaving, he said, "But he can't—he's part of our family." She told us that was the first time it really struck her that "you are not the only one who gets the divorce." Bluntly stated, when you divorce your spouse, you take your child's home away and, very often, your child's mother or father as well. Yet when you struggle until you finally work it out, it is worked out for your child also.

What greater gift could you give your kids than a family to grow up in and an example of how to succeed at something that really matters? And what greater gift could you give the world than children who come from a place where love triumphed?

THE ONE WHO HAD THE AFFAIR

is confession necessary communication?* If you have recently had an affair or are currently having one, your tendency may be to make decisions quickly and out of guilt. Although it's true that you made a mistake, you certainly don't want to compound it. The place of quiet knowing within you has not left, but it may take you longer to reach than before. Please don't begrudge yourself this time. Make your decisions about what to do with as much stillness as you can. A mistake doesn't require endless bouts of anxiety and guilt; a mistake only requires correction.

If your spouse doesn't know that you once had an affair, nothing in your relationship *has* to change. You may choose to change it, but you don't have to. Hugh's aunt didn't even tell his uncle that she was dying. She not only didn't reveal this to him in the final months of her life, but as the family found out later, it was likely she knew the morning she saw him off to work that she would pass on before he returned. When he came home that evening and heard the news, he looked back on the last few months they had had together and saw that she had made them the happiest time of their lives.

---

* In these first four sections on the question of whether to confess, we have expanded this subject into a general example of how the current stream of relationship philosophy has impacted one simple, practical question. Within the same context, we have also described what we believe real communication is, and what it is not. Also see "Is Miscommunication a Cause?" in Chapter Three, and "Are Disclosures Communication?" and "What Is Communication For?" in Chapter Seven.

Most experts now appearing on talk shows would probably argue against this woman's form of idealism, but she gave her silence on this subject as a gift to her husband, and he received it as a gift. And in the Prather family, it is a story that still evokes a gentle memory of this woman who was remarkable in so many other ways as well.

Death has a way of becoming known, and so the decision to keep a terminal condition quiet would not be happily received in many families, and most people choose not to take Hugh's aunt's approach. However, several studies estimate that 45 to 70 percent of wives and 65 to 70 percent of husbands have one or more affairs—and that the majority of these go unconfessed. So of course it's possible not to tell.

Hugh's aunt and her sister were related to the Prather family through marriage, and neither of them had the patterns of selfishness, disloyalty, and infidelity that plagued many other members of the Prather family. Hugh's aunt was loud, dramatic, and very funny. There was nothing closed or secretive about her, yet she was also the one who quietly went about helping the black sheep and rejected members of her extended family.

She and her husband were very close, and she loved to kid him and play tricks on him. At Sunday dinner, for several weeks in a row, she dramatically asked him in front of all the family why he wouldn't eat margarine. "Because I hate the damn stuff!" he would roar. "But you haven't tried it!" she would yell back, and he of course would insist that he had.

One Sunday everyone watched as he dipped his knife into his separate dish of whipped butter as usual, but this time they knew that his wife had filled it with margarine that she had whipped and colored to look like butter (in those days margarine was lighter in color). After he had eaten his buttered biscuit, she dramatically asked, "Why won't you eat margarine like the rest of us?" And when he roared out his usual answer, everyone screamed with laughter.

Why would a woman such as this suffer for months in silence

and not ask her best friend in life to share her burden? Those who knew her could answer this question easily because they had seen many of the things she did for people and after her death learned of many more. She had developed her capacity for quiet, selfless, anonymous giving. Anyone is capable of developing that capacity, but as a generation we have lost the habit.

If you have had an affair, naturally this knowledge may in many ways be a burden to you. You may feel guilty, and you may not like the fact that here is an important event of your life, possibly the only event of your life, that you and your partner have not shared ideas about. It's one place you can't go in your conversations, and you may chafe under this self-imposed restraint. For you to make the decision that, as a gift to your partner's trust and peace, you will work this mistake out yourself, that you will not burden him or her with this information, that you will not risk your marriage and family by telling, is of course anonymous giving. But no one will congratulate you. No one but you will even know the "sacrifice" you make by not "unloading." So putting aside for a moment the question of whether you should tell, here are a few love-based reasons why you might choose not to.

is confession honest communication?   Husbands and wives who have been unfaithful say, "I just can't keep this a secret any longer."

"Why?" we asked one woman. "You've stopped the affair. You have a good marriage. Your baby has a mother and father. Why do you want to change that situation?"

"It's not honest."

"Why isn't it honest?"

"Well, because he doesn't know. I'm living a lie by not telling him."

"Of all the things you have done this last year that you haven't told your husband, why is this one 'living a lie'? Have you told him every time you picked your nose or scratched yourself?"

"Of course not."

"Do you tell him everything you have done at the dermatologist's or hairdresser's to make yourself look better?"

"No."

"Many people think masturbation is a form of infidelity; have you told him every time you've masturbated?"

"No."

"Have you told him every one of your sexual fantasies that don't involve him?"

"No."

"Do you tell him each time you forget to buckle in the baby, go over the speed limit, run a yellow light, turn your back on the baby when he's in the high chair, or in any other way take a risk with him?"

"I never forget to buckle in the baby, it's automatic."

"You get our point."

"Yes, but an affair is different."

Here are some of the other arguments we have heard people use who want to confess an affair. The sentences in parentheses are paraphrased from comments we have read or heard from advocates of separation psychology:

"My partner will find out sooner or later." ("The news will have less impact coming from you than from someone else.") Actually, surveys indicate that of those partners who don't divorce (many things come out during and after divorce), surprisingly few find out. This is not to say that undetected affairs don't have harmful effects on marriages, because they clearly do.

As to whether it's better to tell rather than to let your partner hear it from somewhere else, it is probably best that it come from you—that is, if the subject is going to be brought up between you at all. Some husbands or wives, on receiving this kind of evidence, prefer not to confront their spouse, and this decision is *not* always based on denial. However, many partners do confront, and if yours is a relationship in which this is likely to happen, you are definitely taking a risk by not bringing it up first. But do you really know yours is such a relationship? Consider too that telling is also a risk, and against the chaos that your confession will unleash, it may or may not be a reasonable risk.

You can see here, just in one paragraph's worth of consideration of a tiny aspect of only one question raised by an affair, the degree of confusion and anguish that an affair generates. The far better question is, why have one at all?

"We agreed to tell each other everything." ("You have always been honest with each other; don't start lying now.")

Clearly there was greater trust between the two of you before you had the affair—whether your partner now knows about your infidelity or not. You simply can't engage in an act with this kind of ancient and violent symbolism without it creating distrust. But to argue that you can't break the faith between you now, by withholding a confession of your faithlessness, is insincere. You have already thrown it away.

"My partner doesn't know where this feeling between us is coming from; I owe it to him/her to tell." ("When there is a contaminating secret between two people, they can't achieve true intimacy.")

This is the same logic that compels newlyweds to name everyone they've slept with in order to "get off on the right foot." If you are having an affair, you are deceiving yourself if you think you are being motivated in life by what you "owe" your partner. That is not the reason you want to confess.

As to whether telling your partner that you have been having sex with someone else is the path to "achieving true intimacy," only a theorist could come up with such an unrealistic idea. So many couples we see today are afraid to use their own common sense. Simply ask yourself, "Am I more likely to hurt my partner and my children—in fact, am I more likely to damage them permanently—if I confess the affair or if I don't confess it?" *Stop-*

ping the affair—and all other forms of betrayal—is what will build intimacy.

"The affair will continue unless I confess it." ("The adulterer must confess to his spouse in order to be forgiven and start over.")

The affair will stop when you choose between kindness and selfishness. Only you can forgive your own self-blame, and there is little possibility of accomplishing this as long as the affair continues even emotionally. What you need is to purify your mind, not darken your partner's.

Naturally, if you are confronted and you see that your partner believes that you are having an affair, you admit the truth. But here the affair is already known, and you are merely not adding deceit on top of betrayal.

"I have developed a heavy heart. To lighten it I must be able to share with my best friend." ("Complete disclosure dissipates sadness and guilt.")

The person confessing feels better; the person hearing it feels worse. Unquestionably you can get temporary relief by shifting a burden. Then what happens? Is your partner really more forgiving of you because of this "act of courage"?

No, what actually happens is that before, you had feelings of guilt, fear, and estrangement, and this discomfort was about the size of a horseshoe that you carried around your heart. That was the situation you were in. After you confess, the discomfort grows to the size of a horse that flattens you. You have solved one problem and created another, or as one woman said, "I put out a grass fire around my feet and started a forest fire around everyone."

Sometimes we hear a wife whose husband has had an affair say, "I just can't go on like this. Keeping this secret is driving me crazy. He and I are just going to have to sit down and work this through."

And sometimes statements like this come well after his having had an affair that has so shocked the husband that it has brought him to his senses and as a result he has become a much more alert and attentive partner. Then suddenly he feels an urge to change all of that by confessing. And make no mistake, he will probably change *all* of it, including the progress he has personally made and the improvement he has facilitated in the relationship.

We have made the point before that we have become a generation of people who have lost the knowledge of how to suffer. We don't even *want* the knowledge, and our philosophies and therapies and even our songs encourage us to believe that "if it's not easy, it's not right." We think that we should not have to struggle to build and protect a friendship. So we run from all the guilt and inconvenience into a burden-lifting confession, just as we ran into a comfortable and undemanding affair. And when this too turns out not to be so comfortable and undemanding, we conclude that "nothing feels as good as letting go."

"Unless I confess, I will never take responsibility for what I have done." ("Confession is the first step to acting responsibly.")
Today even the concept of taking responsibility has been made dependent on other people. Not only did our partner drive us, or "enable" us, into having the affair, but unless our partner will hear our confession, we can't even take responsibility for our part in it.

Surely it's clear what this concept sets up: Our partner will *not* hear our confession—she or he will get very upset and interrupt after we have barely started! And this will deprive us of our right to take responsibility. But now we can walk away from the marriage free of blame for both how the affair started and how the marriage ended.

Let's think straight here: You had the affair. You can take responsibility for it. You are not dependent on your spouse, who didn't have the affair, in order to do that.

•   •   •

"Honesty is a virtue."

Indeed it is, especially if what we are trying to accurately reflect within us is worth reflecting. As well as thoughts of betrayal, there are many other cruel and petty thoughts floating around in our minds. Would any of us want a loudspeaker on top of our heads broadcasting our thoughts to everyone wherever we went? This, of course, would be complete honesty.

What if instead of that kind of honesty, we could have a transmitter placed over our heart and connected to the deepest reaches of our spirit, so that the love we felt for our children, our friends, our partner, and all those unknown millions who have to walk the same path we do, could somehow be received and felt by them?

In our relationships we try for this kind of honesty, we long for it, but none of us has attained it, and there is no rule of behavior that will give it to us. Yet the ideal today is that unless our relationship is 100 percent pure, it's not worth having. Unless our spouse can stand up to "the complete truth" and, no matter what we have puked forth, still be there for us afterward, she or he was never someone we should have been with in the first place.

One couple who had been married twelve years, had three children, and obviously loved each other immensely, became interested in honest communication. In the course of their first "heart-to-heart" conversation, the husband told his wife that years ago he had had a brief affair with another doctor in the same hospital and had immediately felt very badly about it. In his words, he had felt "dirty." Never had he been tempted to do something like this again, and over time he had been able to forgive himself. Until the night of their conversation, he had not thought about it in years.

His wife didn't seem to react much at the time; in fact, she said that she was "much happier" that he had told her rather than continue to keep it a secret. But a few months later she began therapy because, as she described it, her feeling of how "perfect" their marriage was had been shattered. Eventually she asked for a divorce, and to this day (ten years later) she has not gotten over this one little confession.

Perhaps her reaction was extreme, or perhaps it was more normal than many think; nevertheless, the confession was absurdly unnecessary, but even as you read this, someone somewhere has just opened a book that says, "Love is nourished by the truth," and within a few hours that person will also shatter his or her marriage and wonder what went wrong.

hidden forms of burden-shifting   We write our books as a team, although only in recent years has Gayle agreed to have her name on the cover. We work out the ideas together; one of us writes the rough draft; then the other edits and adds to it. On two of the occasions when our family had to move, it so happened that Hugh was the one writing the rough draft, and each time for a book with a tight deadline. This meant that all the packing and unpacking fell to Gayle. We both love writing and hate packing and halfway through the second move Hugh began to feel guilty. He would go into a room where Gayle was working and say things like, "I'm sure sorry about this. I can't believe this is happening again. Maybe I should stop and help you a little." Gayle would snap, "You know that's impossible. We're probably not going to get this book in on time as it is. Just get out and leave me alone."

Still feeling guilty, and now with his feelings hurt, Hugh would dutifully go back to work.

A few minutes later he would return and say, "I just can't write when there's something between us. Can we sit down and work this out?"

This time Gayle would yell, "The movers are coming tomorrow! Why are you doing this to me?"

So carrying guilt, hurt feelings, and now rejection, Hugh would go back to writing.

But soon he would come back and stick (only) his head in the door. "I'm sorry. You're right. I don't know why I was doing that. Do you still love me, ha, ha?'' And Gayle would very quietly and evenly say things that our editor won't let us put in a book that contains a section on how to argue in peace.

Confessing an affair is an example of burden-shifting on a very large and obvious scale, but all relating will contain lesser forms of the same pattern until they are weeded out. Here Hugh had an uncomfortable feeling and naturally wanted it removed. But instead of working this out himself, he turned to Gayle, who was in no position to help, to do it for him. If he hadn't been so self-preoccupied he could have seen this quite easily, let go of his guilt, and extended silent help to her.

Naturally, partners in a real relationship help each other and rush to share each other's burdens, but in the ordinary flow of daily routine, there are *frequently* times when this is not feasible in an overt way. To hold your partner in light and, speaking directly to his or her heart, to give your silent blessing is always a powerful means available to you of extending your strength and support.

In a popular book on relationships, the author argues that an adulterer must confess to his spouse in order to be forgiven and start over. If we scale down this line of reasoning, we can see a similar thought pattern in the mistake Hugh made. He was doing something that seemed pleasurable to him but unfair to Gayle. He wanted to confess this in order to get rid of the guilt. So he told himself that the reason he was going into where she was packing was that he felt bad for *her,* just as adulterers tell themselves that confessing is "the fair and decent way" to treat their partners.

Even knowing on some level that our partner is going to react badly to our request for help, going ahead and asking for it anyway has another ego advantage. Notice that when Hugh kept going back to Gayle, merely "trying to work things out," only "following the rules" of "never letting stuff build up and go unhandled," just seeing if he could "make things right," each time Gayle would do something that he could say was unfair to him. In other words, **he provoked her into slowly creating a cumulative sin greater than his original sin.** We have often seen this same pattern in working with couples trying to heal the effects of an affair.

is confession ever appropriate?   As we have said, if your partner asks you to confirm what he or she knows or suspects, the damage is already done and you wish merely not to increase it by lying. So of course you confirm it. As to confessing what is not known, obviously there could be circumstances under which almost anything might be appropriate. Relationships are extremely complex, and there are no flawless guidelines. If your partner is aware of most of your affairs, has forgiven you, and wants to work with you to get you and the relationship past this addiction, then this would be an appropriate time to discuss anything that's related. Your purpose would not be to "confess" but to fill in the blanks so that your partner could help you see how destructive your pattern was, how it worked, and perhaps even where it came from.

We had this type of discussion many times, and by his laying out all the affairs, Hugh could see what type of women were his victims and the extent of the damage he had caused. He probably could not have grasped the whole picture without Gayle's help— but you must remember that Hugh was now beyond the behavior, and furthermore, Gayle had reached the point where she was no longer interested in attacking him. A good therapist also could perform this function—laying out the past so it can be seen and forgiven. But as we have said throughout this book, when it comes to permanent relationships, therapists must be chosen with extreme care.

Thinking over all the marriages that we are intimately familiar with, we know several partners who are very deeply bonded, believe in forgiveness, and have a long history of practicing it who could definitely survive a confession. In each of these marriages there is almost no chance that an affair would occur, but if it did, the marriage would not break up. However, these couples have also learned how not to burden each other unnecessarily—even in small ways—and so in the highly unlikely event that one of them had an affair, that person would probably work through this mistake quietly.

being ''fair'' to the third person   If you know that you want to try to save this marriage, you first must stop the affair in all ways. Until you have done that much, very little we or anyone else can say will improve the atmosphere between you and your partner.

The one who willingly entered into the affair with you did not do so as an act of love, but you have a chance to build real love within your marriage. Your first duty is to your partner. It is not, as your ego will argue, to ''treat fairly'' the person who joined you in the betrayal. And your ego *will* argue this in many ways for as long as you listen. Certainly you don't want to be intentionally cruel, but you are going to have to break off all contact with this person—letters, phone calls, chance meetings—if you are to give your marriage an opportunity to heal.

You may be aware that you have hurt this other person, but you deceive yourself when you think that you are presently in a position to help or comfort your old lover. You were not a friend to that person before and cannot suddenly become one now. You simply can't maintain a ''little relationship'' without the risk of giving false hope, setting yourself up for a resumption of the affair, and keeping the destructive symbolism of that relationship alive within your marriage. Again, you must arrange your life so that this person is completely out of it, and you must arrange your attitudes so that your sole focus is on the one who truly needs you.

Therefore, when your husband or wife criticizes this person, you are not more honorable if you "set the record straight" or in any other way defend that individual's character, behavior, or participation. Your interest is in your spouse and no one else. You have a long road to travel in order to regain your partner's trust, but it's by no means interminable. At first, you may have to begin the healing work alone and continue it unassisted for many weeks or months. Hopefully, your partner will soon join you, for now it is truly the relationship's problem, and you are both responsible for what happens from this point on.

what to expect from your partner

Assuming that you have taken this first step, you now must make the decision not to be defensive. Your partner may be extremely angry for a very long time, and you may be able to do little more than listen and be mentally supportive. Over and over you will feel the urge to explain why you did this or said that during the affair, but you must understand that no matter what you say, it probably will not make things better. Therefore, as best you can, try not to make things worse. For example, it's best not to go into more detail than you need to about what you did with this other person, especially sexually. However, if you are asked, answer honestly and directly. Your time for hiding is over.

Remember also that there is no "reason" for what you did. It was not reasonable and can't be justified, even though it can be understood. If it could be justified once, it can be justified again. So don't try to rationalize what was an irrational act. Instead, commit deeply to a healing program, and be very specific as to what you intend to start doing immediately to see to it that this will never happen again. (We will have some suggestions about this in the next chapter.)

As we discussed earlier in this chapter under "How It Starts," there is a great deal of nonsense within current therapeutic philosophy about an affair being "caused" by both partners. Once it has occurred and is known, it is definitely both partners' problem.

And it will be healed by both partners. But both partners did not have the affair. And unless the circumstances were utterly bizarre, your partner didn't force you into it. For your healing and the healing of your relationship, it's essential that you not tell yourself that there are probably little reasons that make what you did okay. These little reasons (how you have been unfairly treated in this marriage, how you have been unappreciated sexually, how your spouse should have seen this coming) will keep your mind essentially closed to change and will greatly protract the healing process. You are not forever to be condemned, but you did make a mistake in having the affair, no matter in what ways your partner needs to change. To see that a mistake is a mistake can be very freeing, and you want to be free.

affairs are a package deal   When you chose the affair, you chose more than just the act of intercourse. As obvious as that may sound, a majority of unfaithful wives and husbands act as if all the confusion and pain that surround an affair were not their doing. They make excuses for themselves such as: The in-laws have no business sticking their noses into it. The other person's spouse is obviously insane. The children wouldn't get hurt if adults wouldn't bring them into it. And above all, the marriage wouldn't be damaged if their partner wasn't overreacting (''It's over between me and her—you're the one who's making this a problem.'' ''He pressured me into it.'' ''It was just a physical thing.'' ''I never loved him—why are you destroying our marriage over this?'' ''I felt sorry for her.'' ''It was purely business.'' ''It was the alcohol.'').

Once you see clearly everything you are choosing when you choose to be unfaithful, you will never be unfaithful again.

A powerful example of this is from the life of a friend of ours who, when he was a young father, carried on an affair with his housekeeper within his own home. His son Jason, almost three when this happened, was not only in the house asleep at these times but was sometimes in a bed at one end of the room where they had sex. "I can remember thinking at the time," our friend once told us, "that even though it seemed odd having Jason in the room, he was in no danger."

For many years thereafter, even though his wife had forgiven him and he had never had another affair, Jason had a peculiar lack of trust in his father. "I did all the things a good dad does with his son," he said. "I played catch, attended his games, took him fishing, and so forth, but time and again he showed me in his attitude and in the little things he did that he deeply believed that I couldn't be relied on."

One day, when Jason was nine, our friend was so distressed about this that he asked his wife Ann to join him, and together they prayed for an answer. Suddenly he saw an image of his son at about age three asleep in his little bed, and our friend was standing above him holding a knife over his heart. At once he realized what he had done by having the affair. In a letter he wrote us he said, "I had totally disregarded his future, which was to grow up in a happy, secure home, loved deeply by his mother and father. This had been the promise implicit in Ann's and my decision to have a child. My affair could quite easily have wiped out all of that, but he meant so little to me at the time that the risk I was taking with his future hadn't even occurred to me. In fact, as I believe I once mentioned, I had actually told myself he was in no danger."

After this insight, it took our friend several years to gain Jason's complete trust. To do this he had to carry out meticulously any promise he made to him, even when a change in circumstances made that difficult. Today there is a deep bond between them, but this decade-long effect on their family was just one of numerous other effects our friend had chosen along with the affair.

TEN

How Not to Fall in Love

JUST HORMONES AND SELF-SUGGESTION?*

getting hooked   In a drug-induced high there is no thought of tomorrow. The euphoria you feel today is all you need. Having the drug is sufficient reason to be alive. Infatuation, with its half-dozen hormones flooding the system with rapture, excitement, serenity, invulnerability, and just plain lust, is also a high, a fix, but because of the magical presence of this other person, it seems that you have been catapulted into a wonderland of love where, with just a little scheming, you can remain forever.

The reasons for why we each behave differently when infatuated are complex and individual, but the euphoric state of infatuation itself is essentially self-hypnosis with a little body-chemistry backup, and it definitely can be understood and controlled. Many of the expressions used to describe falling in love hint at the mental state behind it: "mad for," "have a thing for," "crazy about," "dote on," "love to distraction," "moonstruck," "delir-

---

* Also see "Falling in Love Outside the Relationship," "What Does the Honeymoon Stage Look Like?" "Body Love," and "Infatuation," all in Chapter Six.

ious about," "stuck on," and so forth. The old blues song just endlessly repeats: "Got you on my mind. Got you on my mind," and finally concludes: "Can't get you off my mind." That is both the pleasure and the problem.

Mentally, infatuation is a form of sustained self-suggestion. We build, polish, and perfect our picture of this person, all the while becoming more and more enamored with the fantasy. And like the fantasy, we ourselves seem to transcend the mundane and become larger than life. We are more attractive, funnier, stronger, happier, and more flexible. Suddenly anything seems possible. And it should. We have been chosen by a god!

Unfortunately, the god is of our own making.

Preteens, adolescents, and very young adults are usually not aware of how they infatuate their minds; in fact, they unknowingly conspire together to induce it in each other. The marketplace where we occasionally have lunch is near a university, and we frequently hear two or three girls at a nearby table talking about a boy who just walked in or about someone the others think one of the girls should consider. Boys will also have these conversations, but they tend to be much shorter, consisting mainly of a few sexual comments. The conversations between girls seem either to take the form of a hard sell—if the girl doesn't know the boy—or of unqualified praise for the girl's choice, plus lots of thrown-in food for fantasy ("what it would be like" to go out with him, sleep with him, marry him, and so on).

The expression on one girl's face who was listening to her friends reminded us of the way a child might look on hearing the description of a newly opened video arcade—the child can imagine it clearly, is motivated to go, and can think of no reason why the experience won't be as wonderful as described. Commenting on the boy, one of her friends said, "He's dreamy"—an old expression but one that exactly fits what is taking place mentally. A dream is being constructed strong enough to dominate the waking mind. The cure, if one is already married, is either not to get caught up in the dream in the first place or, if one notices the beginning symptoms, to question the dream systematically and thoroughly.

the one who helps you abandon your mate   It's difficult to fall in love if there is no one to fall in love with. So if you are married, whom do you choose? We will shortly be exploring some of the people and places that are statistically most likely to figure in an affair, but cutting across these categories is a group of individuals that we will refer to as "spoilers."

Spoilers do not exist in any absolute sense. As with the roles played in the dynamic "Feminine Female—Macho Male" (discussed in Chapter Five) or the personality type that develops after a series of abandonments ("A Generation of Yuppies," in Chapter Eight), no *individual* will fit into a category exactly, and *all* will have some spiritual strengths outside of it. Spoilers are not evil, irredeemable monsters, and as we will point out, most of them are not even aware of their pattern of behavior. Varying degrees of this kind of behavior exist, and we have known and worked with a number of individuals who have acted out this role in its most destructive forms, who eventually turned their lives around and now help many more relationships than they once hurt.

Many who advise their friends or clients that they "deserve better"—a better city to live in, a better company to work for, a better partner to walk through life with—are looking only at one or two factors and overlooking the greater truth that they do not have the wisdom to see all the people the decision will affect or how it will affect them. We don't even know what is in our own best interests; how can we know what is in someone else's? And yet we give advice as if we do.

The ego loves excitement, and to this part of our mind, disaster is exciting. People will pull off the road and make themselves late for an appointment just to look more closely at an accident. A crowd will always gather to watch someone's suicidal jump from a bridge or building, some even yelling for the person to jump. Almost no one will walk past two men having a fight. And the news segments about crime, misfortune, violence, and disaster usually garner the biggest audience share. Although often unconscious, it is human nature to give people who are having trouble in their marriage advice that will lead to a more exciting outcome. Clearly, many people resist the temptation to answer quickly and superficially, but it is simply a fact that it's easier to tear down than to find approaches that might truly help a marriage.

Most of us know someone who is always coming between people, between friends, between boss and employee, between relatives, and will not hesitate to come between us and our spouse. Do not fail to protect your relationship against this kind of divisive influence. In our own marriage, these are people we will not allow ourselves to be around unless we are together or unless the contact is unavoidable. We know from experience that they can have a disrupting effect on our sense of oneness, and this is a loss we are no longer willing to suffer.

As unhelpful as these "minor spoilers" are, they often do not provide the final push that leads to the breakup. For this, a force must come into play that seems greater than the individual who is trying to decide whether to leave. Advice given in a therapeutic setting, advice from a spiritual teacher, advice from a very trusted relative or friend can provide such a force, but the most common source is a new relationship that seems unusually special, or one that offers the hidden prospect of sex. A relationship of this kind is often enough to overwhelm the remaining resistance to divorce.

Derek and Julie had been having minor trouble in their marriage for almost a year when Julie decided to attend a group devoted to helping its members become more self reliant. The group convinced her that the problems in her relationship were actually much worse than she had thought. In fact, she was told that her marriage "positively reeked" of codependence and Derek, whom none of the group had met, was diagnosed as a "woman-hating control freak." Julie was encouraged to leave him and find her own "power." Foremost among those moving her in this direction was Paul, a twice divorced man who had been coming to the group for several years. When Julie weakened in her resolve against Derek, Paul reminded her of what she had put up with in the past. When Julie voiced the fear that a divorce might hurt their children, he reminded her that it would be worse for them to continue living in a codependent environment. He insisted that she call him any time, day or night, if she needed to talk. He seemed to value everything about her—her cooking, her sense of style, her views on motherhood, her wit. He listened to her and made her feel special and appreciated.

Like Julie, Paul was right-brained. He was interested in plays and art and was charmingly spontaneous and disorganized. She could talk to him about anything and everything. Furthermore, he didn't seem to want anything from her—not sex, not housecleaning, not ego enhancement. In fact, it was Paul who offered to take her sick dog to the vet when she was frazzled and running late because of her daughter's softball game. He told her later when she was profusely thanking him that he was "just being what a friend should be": one who knew what she was going through and wanted to be there for her. He was so different from Derek.

Still, Julie was reluctant to leave. Derek insisted that he wanted to try to work things out. When she talked about this with Paul, he was skeptical of Derek's motives but claimed he would support her in whatever direction she wanted to go. After each discussion with Derek, she would call Paul and although he would sympathize with her in wanting to save her family, he would also point out Derek's lack of vision and creativity and above all his lack of appreciation of her.

The group had also convinced Julie that she was an abused wife even though Derek had never hit or threatened her physically. In fact, Julie's main complaint against him before attending the group was that he lacked passion, while she was a very passionate person. The group diagnosed Derek as a "passive-aggressive abuser—one of the worst kinds because they make you think everything is your own fault."

One weekend Julie called Paul and tearfully told him that Derek had yelled at her and told her he was sick of the whole mess and why didn't she just get out if she was so miserable. Paul said he would be right over. And indeed he was, along with several other members of the group. When he saw them, Derek stormed out of the house and drove away. One of the women from the group claimed he had looked like a madman or a psychotic killer and expressed her fear for the safety of Julie and the children. They convinced her that she had to get out before he came back with a gun. While two women packed her belongings and those of the children, Paul got on the phone and found her a safe place to stay.

Julie didn't leave a note. She filed for divorce the following week.

Because we heard this story from Julie's sister, Mary, four years after the divorce was final, we also learned what happened to the people involved. Julie was still a part of the group, as was Paul, but they were no longer close. Mary was convinced that Julie had believed that she and Paul would get together as a couple, but Paul had made it clear that this had never been his intention and further suggested that since Julie had so badly misread him, she obviously needed a lot more work on codependence. Julie's children had not coped well with the divorce and for a time were fearful of their dad, whom they had repeatedly heard described as angry, controlling, and potentially violent. At first they didn't want to see him and were reluctant to keep the court-ordered visitations. Mary felt that later they became merely confused about their father's true nature and emotionally torn between their love for him and for their mother, as if they had to take sides.

We asked Mary what her perception of the marriage and divorce had been. She said that Derek wasn't perfect; he was "a little bit of a cold fish," but basically "a nice guy, a decent guy who sort of balanced my whacky sister." Their problems just hadn't been that serious. Julie was just bored and dissatisfied and Derek hadn't taken her unhappiness seriously soon enough to do something about it. Mary thought the divorce was "unnecessary, stupid, and nobody came out ahead" except maybe Derek who had met a nice woman and was living with her. Julie was just as miserable, probably more so; the kids were wounded, and a basically good family had been added to the list of tragic statistics. Paul, she claimed, was still out there like "a little breath of ill wind coming between people."

Unquestionably there are many people like Paul who try to make themselves appealing to those who are in a vulnerable period of their lives. Winning over another person's spouse seems more interesting and challenging to them than confining their advances to people who are unattached. **Taking someone away from someone else is an ancient human practice, probably far outdating marriage.**

Greater awareness of those who play the role of spoiler and how they go about it can help protect your marriage. They come in many forms: an old acquaintance, a co-worker, a stranger in a bar, and especially a platonic friend or a potential lover. In our experience these individuals are almost never aware of the role they have chosen, even when they have a history of this behavior —as they very often do—nor are they deeply conscious of the suffering they help launch or the number of lives it affects. In other words, they are usually convinced that their motives are good. This lack of awareness, however, does not excuse their behavior.

Although a spoiler may have given the final push to a spouse leaning toward divorce, the one who was left may also have participated in many unloving ways. In addition, that partner probably did not actively pursue every avenue to save the relationship. There also could have been influences from relatives, friends, or lawyers that contributed enormously to the breakup. Blame, as always, is impossible to assess, and in this section we describe the usual patterns of the spoiler as an aid to protecting your relationship and not as a way of classifying and condemning still another group of people.

The *force* with which you will feel yourself drawn into a relationship with a spoiler is a form of falling in love, but because it may not include sexual attraction, it can seem like merely a deeper and purer form of friendship than you have ever experienced before. Of course, it is not.

From the standpoint of the ego, to enter a victim's life at a critical moment and push that individual toward a decision that will leave a permanent mark on the lives of many is interesting and empowering and often has the added spice of danger, intrigue, and illicit sex. If in addition the spoiler is motivated by jealousy or by hatred of the opposite sex, it can also feel fulfilling.

Since you wish to protect your marriage, you should understand the usual patterns of approach that people who are caught up in this form of attack use. There are of course those who will "come on" to you strongly and persistently, and you will have little difficulty spotting their intentions. The greater danger is from those whose motivation is largely unconscious. They often have a keen sense about, even a sophisticated understanding of, individuals who are feeling doubts about their relationships. It may be difficult for you to imagine, but your vulnerability alone makes you very attractive to them. It is the scent of blood—but they will never appear bloodthirsty in response. They will appear to be decent people, and most will seem like a good catch or a "good lay."

If at the very time you are having trouble at home, or are deep into a "something's missing" period, someone begins giving you more attention or merely begins showing up more often in your life, it can do you no harm to stay alert. Obviously, this first little sign may mean nothing. But individuals stuck in this pattern will not stop there. They will continue to do what is necessary to gain your trust and, above all, to show you that they want nothing more than to offer you friendship.

As you get to know them better, at some point it should become clear to you that they are now aware of the difficulties you are having. How you feel about your relationship *after* being around them will provide you with the first real evidence of what is really going on. If you feel closer to your mate, more willing and inspired to make things better, *and* if you do *not* find yourself thinking how much better it would be to be married to someone more like this new person, then you may be safe in continuing this relationship—although it's always risky to draw closer to someone of the opposite sex at the very time your commitment to your mate is shaky. **If you feel a little urgency or excitement about the small decisions you make to talk to or be around this person, your ego is more involved than you may believe.** Yet you still have available within you a far friendlier guide than urgency or excitement.

If the relationship continues—and if the individual is in fact a spoiler—there are other patterns that are common to people within this group. They will appear to understand you, to know you, and to accept you as you are. They will seem reliable and accessible. They always have time to talk, always are willing to meet with you. The impression therefore begins to form that this person will be there for you forever, that you have indeed found a friend, someone deeply like you.

But once you have left your partner, these individuals usually fade away. Often they withdraw in such a way that no blame falls on them and their pattern remains hidden. You will blame yourself or circumstances for things not working out, but the fact will remain that someone you had relied on being there is not there.

As you look back, you will see that this person was never a true friend. Many people who play the role of spoiler are in the grip of a destructive focus that contains no love, and this can be seen. In all the support they give you, they may give lip service to but never emphasize and clarify the effect on *you* if you were to leave your partner. Nor are they really concerned about how a divorce will affect your children, and yet they may seem to be "better with the kids" than is your partner.

All of this is disguised by the fact that these individuals seem solicitous of your happiness. Often they will not openly encourage you to leave; they imply that all they want is "whatever is best for you." And unstated is the obvious fact that they themselves will be one of the rewards when you are single. However, you can see their true motivation if you care to look, and much depends on your looking.

Ask yourself if this person befriending you is in a happy relationship or, if not, is deeply happy. How can someone who doesn't know happiness lead you to it? The relationship you are being offered is actually based on excitement, on a break with the status quo, on shared misery, and on common enemies.

Many of these alternative relationships are platonic in the beginning and remain that way throughout. This type of spoiler seems to offer you no more than a sincere friendship with no hidden agenda, or even when they are clearly in love with you, they are not physically appealing. Although sex is not a factor ("nothing has ever happened between us"), these relationships can be equally as dangerous as those that are sexually interesting, and sometimes even more so, because they may not be as obvious to you—and also do not attract other people's attention. ("They're just friends." "After all, he's gay." "She's too old—not his type." "Are you kidding? He's too short for her.")

There can be fascination and compulsion without infatuation. These "safe" relationships are far more commonly a factor in breakups than is generally recognized. Affairs get all the attention, because sex is involved, but having someone in love with you, or someone very attentive and solicitous of your feelings, can be equally intoxicating.

However, sex often is involved, or at least the potential for sex. Many spoilers have getting you in bed a few times the finale they seek. Once you are used up, their interest begins to fade. Again, this pattern applies equally to male and female spoilers. In these people's minds, sex gets them almost everything they seek. It is a widely accepted symbol of victory and therefore proof of their accomplishment. It hurts a member of the opposite sex, against whom they frequently have anger. It quenches their jealousy of what couples have that they do not. It is an act so powerful that many lives may be left in ruin. It defeats the other man or woman. And it's exciting, forbidden, and physically pleasurable. Even though the spoiler may never meet your partner, the sense of competition can still be very great and the victory of getting you to be unfaithful very satisfying.

It's true that your having sex does not necessarily spell the end of your marriage—hopefully it will not. But in today's atmosphere it is often the fatal sting. Through sex the poison has been injected and the spoiler can now leave you, confident that your marriage is crippled and will probably die. Often these individuals will try to come back into your life if things begin to improve between you and your mate, or if you do break up and now have formed another relationship that needs crippling.

If you sense that your relationship is becoming vulnerable, immediately take steps to protect it. If you and your partner are having trouble, either turn deeply to the counsel of your own stillness or seek out someone you are certain is a friend to your marriage. But don't start talking to several different people. When you make this mistake, you not only open yourself to confusion, you also disconnect from your own quiet wisdom.

AT THE FIRST SIGN OF SYMPTOMS

what do you want to happen?   You are no longer seeing this individual as just another person. Something has happened within your mind, and you have started looking at him or her differently. That "something" was a little thought, a little fantasy about the future. Your ego has been adding to it ever since it began. So first you must determine what fantasies you have stored away.

Whenever this person is in your thoughts or in your presence, study your mind for any sense of excitement, happiness, anticipation, sexual stimulation, or anxiety. Once you notice it, freeze it in place and address it directly:

"What do you (speaking directly to the excitement) think *could* happen?"
"What do you (the anticipation) think *will* happen?"
"What do you (the anxiety) *fear* will happen?"

In other words, with your eyes closed, gently demand that this part of your mind "tell" you what is the promise, the potential, in this situation that is causing you to see this individual as different. If you can put words to the answer, that is helpful; if only a general impression of an answer comes, that is sufficient.

Next, project into the future what you personally would like to come of this relationship. Fantasize about this until you have thought of a number of possible outcomes. With your eyes closed, say to yourself,

"In my relationship with_____, I want_____to happen, and _____to happen, and_____to happen. . . ."

When you have thought of as many outcomes as you can honestly, notice where there were conflicts between them. Also notice if there was a progression toward your deeper, kinder feelings the more outcomes you thought of, or at least that some of your wishes felt as if they were coming from a deeper part of you than others.

If you did these exercises thoroughly, you should now be aware that you are (a) conflicted about what you want; (b) expecting outcomes from this relationship that are not connected to the relationship; and (c) making demands that it would be impossible for this person to meet.

what do you want to do?   From the first set of exercises, you should have some idea of the fantasies you have been having that made this person seem different. Now it's important that you determine where they end, that is, at what point in the future they dare not pass.

In the world, life proceeds uninterrupted to death. For most people that is not a happy thought. In order to derive pleasure or even meaning from thinking about the future, the mind must tell stories with beginnings and endings, and these must be severely edited. If they were not, and if they were totally accurate, they would take as long to complete as life itself. Therefore fantasies must be very unlike life to achieve their purpose. What then is the purpose of your fantasies? That is the point on which your ego is being silent.

With closed eyes, briefly review each fantasy that you suspect is a factor in your feelings about this person, and note carefully at what point in the future it ends or tapers off. Now turn back to whatever emotions (happiness, excitement, sexual titillation) that you originally had in connection with this person, or are still having. Take a moment to distinguish between them, if there is more than one, and then describe each one, as specifically as you can:

What does it feel like?
From where in your body does it appear to radiate?

What is the shape or outline of the area where it is located?
How would you rate its size or intensity? For example, what size
container would it take to hold it?

Now say directly to this feeling, "What exactly are you suggesting that I do about this relationship? Do you want me
to_____? Do you want me to_____?"

(For example, "Do you want me to rip this person's clothes
off?" "Do you want me to lie down on the floor and say, 'I'm
helpless; do with me as you will'?" "Do you want me to let it be
known in little ways that I'm still available, and if so what little
ways?" "Do you want me to plan out a long-term seduction and
carry it through?" "Do you want me to file for divorce on the
way home?")

After each question, pause long enough to compare the answer
you sense with what *you* want. (If, say, the feeling seems to be
urging you to be sexually aggressive, picture yourself acting that
way, and try to sense if that is something you would truly want to
do.)

As you answer each question, you will now sense some hesitancy about what you want to come of this relationship. When you
feel uncertain about any answer, ask it again, then project your
fantasy further into the future. For example, don't stop just at
letting the person know that you are available, but continue the
fantasy to the next day, and the next, and one year from now, ten
years, and on to the people that you can see it still affecting after
your death.

This exercise—directly asking your ego what it wants and pro-
jecting its answers into the indefinite future—is a powerful tool
for you to carry with you from now on. It can be used in any
situation in which you find yourself slipping into an unwanted
emotion about another person.

DISSECTING THE OBJECT OF YOUR FANTASY

defusing the body image   By now, it should be clear what your ego is up to. When you have questioned it, you have noticed that its answers are often indistinct and conflicted, but when you have carried any of its vague plans well past the point to which the excitement or anticipation reaches, you have seen what is really in store for you—the destruction of the bond between you and your partner.

There is unquestionably a part of ourselves that works against our happiness. As we have said, the ego, being a pretend identity set up in the mind to function autonomously, will always defend itself, just as an imaginary playmate will. The playmate knows that a real friend would be the death of it, and our ego knows that our bond with our partner poses its greatest threat. Having someone who truly loves us gaze on who we are enables us to look at our true self also. In the light of this relationship, our ego can do no harm—if we are alert to it. But if it's allowed to operate in the shadow of denial, it can easily destroy everything that is truly dear to us. So let's examine the one who is being offered as the driving wedge between you and your partner; let's strip the dream from the person.

With your eyes closed, mentally bring this person before you, standing straight and still as one might stand in a police lineup. On the screen of your mind, your ego has already flashed the physical image of this person countless times. But what is left out of the picture? Ordinariness. The ordinariness of this person's body, which you would see very clearly after ten years of marriage, or ten months. It's possible to see that now, and it certainly can't harm you to do so. So look at this person's hair and say:

"That is just hair. I don't need that hair to be happy. Nothing I see can control me. Nothing I see will last."

"That is just a forehead. I don't need that forehead to be happy. Nothing I see can control me. Nothing I see will last."

"Those are just eyebrows. I don't need those eyebrows to be happy. Nothing I see can control me. Nothing I see will last."

Continue this straight down the person's body, being certain to include the parts that you think are of most value to you. As you proceed, watch your mind closely for criticisms of certain bodily features. Until now, you may have overlooked or minimized these shortcomings because they would interfere with the fantasy. Don't be afraid to recall the weak chin, the short torso, the dyed hair, the questionable taste in shoes, the excessive makeup, the dandruff, the nose that's not quite right, or whatever other of your negative judgments you sense.

In the days to come, when you catch yourself dwelling on the thoughts of specialness that your ego presents you, insist also on the thoughts of ordinariness, and dwell on those for as long as you did on specialness. If it would help to carry a list of the ordinary features with you and review it whenever you notice that you are thinking about this person, then of course do that or anything else that occurs to you that will speed your awakening from this little dream.

defusing the personality image   Next you want to do a personality and personal-habit inventory.

Once again, with eyes closed, bring this person before you. This time, however, see her or him going about all the usual kinds of activities that this individual would ordinarily be involved in.

Each time you notice some posture, mannerism, attitude, habit, or way of speaking that is peculiar to this person, say:

> "When (name of person) does (mannerism or trait), what meaning does this have for me?"

(For example, if you think of the habit this person has of cocking his or her head when listening to you, you might say, "When _____ cocks her/his head, what meaning does this have for me?" Be as precise as possible. Instead of asking yourself what meaning "being nervous" has, specify the form of nervousness (rubbing the hands together, blinking, coughing, fiddling with the wedding ring).

Before, you were trying to sense what promise or potential you have read into this person's body. Now you wish to do the same with behavior. So pause after each question, and see if you can detect what is in your mind about the personal trait you have just focused on, and when you have finished with that trait, say:

> "That is just the way (person's name) is. (Mannerism or trait) has only the meaning I give to it. Nothing I see can control me. Nothing I see can last."

A magazine article might say, "If he fiddles with his wedding ring, he's ambivalent about being married." Whether that is an absurd assertion or not isn't the point of the exercise, which is designed to question the meaning *you* are assigning to the fiddling. If this person often looks up and smiles, what does this mean for you? That you have a bright future in store for you? That this person is kindly and good? That this person loves and understands you? That this person wants sex?

As you went through this exercise, you undoubtedly focused on behaviors that you did not feel entirely positive about. Like the

negative aspects of this person's body, these judgments are of use
to you in reaching a more balanced view of this individual's personality. If in a marriage, dwelling on a single fault can lead to
divorce, certainly your repeated acknowledgment of several faults
can awaken you from infatuation. If this person smokes and smoking would ordinarily turn you off, then dwell on that. If you can
add to your grievances eating with the mouth open, bragging,
chewing the nails, slips in grammar, scratching, or any other traits
you find objectionable, then add these without hesitation. If it
helps, write it all out and review it often.

This part of the exercise is not teaching you to judge. It's purpose is to make you fully aware of the judgments you already
have, which you are overlooking in order to maintain an emotion.
We generate dislike the same way we generate infatuation—by
what we dwell on. Naturally you are not trying to hate "your
type," but merely to have these people take their place in the
ranks of ordinary mortals, where in reality they already are and
where you or anyone else would soon consign them after a few
years of marriage. **No one is your type once you look closely.**

WHY YOU NEED TO PROTECT YOUR RELATIONSHIP

infatuation as guide   Perhaps you already know where
the peace of your heart leads you. Maybe you have walked that
gentle path many times before. But now a guide of a different sort
is calling to you, and many voices in the world are assuring you
there is nothing to fear. In fact, the sensation of falling in love is
itself so powerful that it will drive away all the gnawing rats of
fear. Perhaps you have been overwhelmed by this sensation before
and know well how it can make you feel. But where will it lead
you? For when its force is spent, you will not be where you are
now.

And perhaps that is another great appeal this guide has for you, that everything in your life might be torn apart. Wouldn't it be good to start over, burn all of it to the ground, and erect a new edifice? But to *what* will you erect it?

Perhaps, though, this guide's promise is far more humble than that—just a little parting of the drab clouds, just "a sex thing," while you remain "emotionally monogamous." Don't hundreds of people claim that they have pulled this off, and that affairs actually "stabilize" marriages, give the involved partner "new sexual insights" that can be used at home, and actually improve the overall quality of the primary relationship? Look across our country and around the world, and ask yourself if *you* see the millions of stabilized marriages brought about by the millions of affairs. The peace of your heart offers you far more than a stabilized marriage—but so does the guide of infatuation! So let's look closely at what affairs actually offer.

Some think that although having extramarital sex may threaten other people's marriages, their own marriage is safe. Perhaps they have put this belief to the test several times, and sure enough, nothing happened. If you had gone through the waist-high stack of relationship books* that we have recently finished, you would not deceive yourself about the atmosphere of opinions and influences that your spouse breathes daily. In all but a few, the authors proudly cite cases in which they brought clients to their senses who were too unaware or too negatively programmed to know that they were being "emotionally abused."

Many talk with astonishment about the endurance of some cli-

---

* In the research we have done, we have been disappointed in the superficiality of many of the relationship books we have come across. Some, however, were deeply thoughtful and quite practical. Of those, we especially liked *The Shared Heart* by Joyce and Barry Vissell (Ramira Publishing, P.O. Box 1707, Aptos, CA, 95001), *Love Is the Answer* by Gerald Jampolsky, M.D., and Diane Cirincione (Bantam) and *The Way of Marriage* by Henry James Borys (Harper San Francisco). You may have to ask your bookstore to order them. Naturally, we are also fond of *A Book for Couples* (Doubleday) and *Notes to Each Other* (Bantam).

ents who have forgiven their partners for not just one affair but a second or even a third—before they came for help. The authors describe how they finally got their client to see how abusive the situation was, and how, after the client's partner refused to get help, how hopeless it was also. Now their client is happily divorced, has lost twenty pounds, is earning more money, and all the kids are on the honor roll.

And these are just the writers of *relationship* books, people who presumably have an interest in helping couples get past their problems. If your spouse does not know what you are continuing to do, please understand that people report an affair more quickly than they report a mugging. And if your spouse does know and is continuing to remain married to you, please understand that virtually the entire adult population is out to "raise" his or her consciousness, even if they too are having affairs. None of this means that it's inevitable that your partner will either find out or be talked into leaving you, but we are speaking here of risks, and any needless risk you continue to take will weigh on your mind, your marriage, and your spirit.

Here are threats to you on other levels. We have written these in a form that can be said out loud.

your position in the world

a) Affairs demean my role in the world.

b) Through them, I teach that commitment is a worthless value.

c) I teach that risking another's happiness can increase one's own.

d) I teach that we are not connected and that we can think and act without affecting each other.

e) If my affairs end in divorce, I will complicate my own life and diminish the lives of (name of your partner), (names of your children), (name of the other person involved).

f) This waste may be the only real inheritance I leave behind, if I continue making infatuation my guide.

your children

g) Affairs risk the happiness and security of (names of your children), with which they trust me.

h) Through nothing (names of your children) have done, affairs risk scrambling and entangling their lives at a time when their lives should be simple.

i) Whether discovered or not, affairs remove me spiritually from (names of your children) and diminish, if not destroy, my position as their example and teacher.

j) Affairs implant a pattern of betrayal, noncommitment, and lovelessness that would have its effect on (names of your children)'s future relationships, including those with their children.

your partner

k) Affairs remove me from the path that (name of your partner) and I had meant to walk.

l) They risk abruptly throwing (name of your partner) into humiliating and chaotic circumstances, a blow from which she or he may never fully recover.

m) They threaten to throw (name of your partner) into pain, confusion, anger, cynicism, and protracted suffering.

n) They threaten (name of your partner)'s mental and physical health.

o) They risk the loss of our mutual friends.

p) They risk changing forever the relationship that (name of your partner) and I have with our in-laws and family members.

q)   They risk changes to our shared income, standard of living, occupations, and future prospects.

r)   I am the one person in the world with whom (name of your partner) has chosen to remain. This trust would be betrayed.

s)   If I now fail to attend to my own healing, I risk the possibility that (name of your partner)'s life, my life, and the lives of (names of your children) will be rewritten as tragedies.

your core

t)   Affairs are acts of extreme insensitivity that diminish me spiritually.

u)   They split my mind between the single purpose of oneness and the scattered goals of indulgence.

v)   They make smallness the defining characteristic of my self-image.

w)   They raise the physical body to a position of control it is incapable of assuming, thus leaving me without control.

x)   They delay, and can even end, the possibility of my experiencing enduring love within this lifetime.

y)   Until I question the value of betrayal, I will not feel a guiding presence in my life.

z)   In the world's balance between awakening and sleeping, affairs add my life to the dream of loveless isolation.

The following exercise requires a greater commitment of time than the previous exercises, but is also more flexible in its format: Schedule into your day two fifteen-to-twenty-minute practice periods. Make these times a sacred commitment for one week.

Use the preceding list as starting points for your own deliberate and detailed fantasies about these risks coming true. If you are already in an affair, some of the statements will obviously apply already. Here, your attempt will be to imagine and feel more fully all that you choose when you choose to continue this affair.

For example, if you were to begin with (e), perhaps you would start by imagining telling your partner, and later your children, that you want a divorce. You might see your partner crying; you might see the bewilderment and fear on your children's faces. Maybe you would move on to the effects on the person you are involved with and his or her family. Your story might then go to a legal proceeding, where you would encounter your in-laws. There you would see the toll this has taken on your partner. Maybe you would end your fantasy by imagining your children arriving at your new home for a visitation period.

what rides in your wake?   You may be headed for a life quite like this, so what you are attempting here is to see what it would be like to go through a divorce, abandon your children, then find yourself married to this other person after all of that. Of the women we know of that Hugh's father betrayed and left (four wives and one long-term lover), two of them developed severe mental disorders, one of whom required repeated hospitalizations, including years of shock treatments; another went through a bankruptcy and developed several life-threatening pathologies; one became an addict, committed murder, and went to prison, leaving behind their child; and one (Hugh's mother) became a severe alcoholic for most of her remaining years. With the exception of his mother, Hugh knew all of these women before his father married them, and they all were happy, successful, fully functioning human beings. All of them have put their lives back together, but not without scars.

As he looks back on his own life, Hugh can see a similar trail of devastation left by his affairs, including two women who developed mental disorders needing hospitalization, and four marriages that ended in divorce after he broke off relations with the wives, whom he had led to believe meant more to him than they did.

We tell these things not for shock value, for we suspect that a similar trail of pain can be found behind many of the other 30 to 70 percent of adults who have had affairs. Hugh loves his father and knows him to be a kind, thoughtful, and generous person. It was certainly not his intention to destroy lives. Nor was it Hugh's. Neither of them was devoted to evil. In fact, in the years following the breakup of his last marriage, Hugh's father worked very hard to become a real friend to his former wives, and he succeeded in forming good friendships with all of them. It should also be remembered that Hugh and his father were not alone in causing the pain they did. For example, the married women Hugh slept with also knew that he was married, and most of them were friends of Gayle.

Much of what occurred in the early years of our marriage was part of the culture we lived in, but fifteen years after we have put all of that behind us, the culture is still here and appears to be growing even sicker.

This has not been an easy book for us to write. Our feeling all along has been that unless we told how we personally participated in many of the common problems of marriage, we could not be as effective in helping others get past their mistakes. We want you to realize that the paths that Hugh and his father traveled for many years are only a few of the possible ones that infatuation may be leading you down also. Yet see just one of those possibilities clearly, and you will take the steps necessary to protect yourself. Here are some of those steps.

PROTECTING AGAINST INFATUATION

how infatuation enters the mind   First you must see clearly in what ways infatuation does and does not operate:

- **INFATUATION COMES IN ALL SIZES.**

It can range from a momentary "What the hell, why not?" sexual impulse with a stranger, to an all-consuming "this is my soul mate" intoxication that lasts for months or, if the circumstances are depriving enough, years.

- **INFATUATION CATCHES MOST PEOPLE OFF GUARD.**

The large majority of those surveyed who have had an affair say that they had not planned to, and of those, most report that it was an "accident."

- **INFATUATION DOESN'T BEGIN WITH A SINGLE, RECOGNIZABLE WARNING SIGNAL.**

Infatuation means merely that you begin looking at a person differently, and this may give you a sense of excitement that you will notice, or it may not. The process can seem instantaneous—the thunderbolt of love that the French speak of—but more often it is gradual, developing over a period of time. A condensed version can be seen nightly at any bar. Hours before, you dismissed the person sitting down from you as unworthy, but now after you've had a few drinks, he or she suddenly starts looking interesting. You think that you just overlooked this person's good points earlier, but you have actually added the good points.

· BEING MARRIED WON'T PROTECT YOUR MIND.

At the time they get married, most people assume that this is "the love of their lives." But real love has not yet been built, and theirs is a false sense of invulnerability. At the first signs that the marriage is not what they had hoped, a part of their mind begins looking for a way out.

· INFATUATION CAN'T BE PARTIALLY INDULGED.

It's impossible to do just a little of what your infatuation is urging you to do without eventually being swept up in the entire emotion. And it's the emotion that you want to avoid. "Affairs of the heart" are equally as destructive to your marriage as sexual affairs, because they block your experience of oneness with your partner. You can't have an occasional lunch with this person or an innocent hello hug from time to time, any more than an alcoholic can indulge in "just" an occasional beer without losing a little more control with each indulgence. Soon your purpose will be split and your life will be on hold.

two essentials of protection   Next you must devise an intelligent approach to protecting your marriage. Whatever you include in this plan, it must begin with an acknowledgment of the problem.

1. **Admit to yourself that you have this tendency.** People will brush their teeth after every meal, but they won't protect their marriage. They'll wear gloves and masks around AIDS patients, yet think it strange to protect themselves from falling in love, which can lead to AIDS. Several years ago, when Hugh took over kitchen duties in our family, it took him several months before he would admit that his hands crack from dishwater. That admission had to come *before* he would start wearing Gayle's rubber gloves. Affairs are not caused by the other person; they are caused by infatuation, and as long as you have this weakness, you must protect yourself, just as you would wrap a weak ankle before going hiking, or protect yourself from falling down stairs if you were a sleepwalker, or avoid bars if you get in fights.

2. **Avoid places and situations that call to this tendency.** In the West we have this ideal of the real man who never avoids a fight, of the supermom who does everything herself, of toughening up children, of going to war rather than ever negotiating with the enemy. If a stranger pulls out in front of us, we'll follow him for miles just to give him the finger. We don't like things that are simple, and we sneer when we say "the easy way." But are we consistent about this?

In fact, the areas where this ideal are actually practiced are quite arbitrary and are maintained through tradition rather than common sense. We certainly don't apply this philosophy to medicine. We are unquestionably afraid to fight off an illness. Hospitals are said to oversterilize, doctors to overprescribe, and our surgeons to be quick with the knife. We certainly don't apply it to our children. We are always getting out of little promises we made them. We are a nation that has long avoided tackling personal and national debt. Our politicians avoid difficult, unpopular fights.

And we ourselves avoid climbing stairs, making unpleasant phone calls, our relatives, and housework. For a people who have the ideal of never avoiding, we do an awful lot of avoiding—except when it comes to avoiding temptation for the sake of protecting our spouse and children.

Again, let us remind you that some researchers estimate that over 70 percent of *all* marriages will be affected by an affair. Whatever the chances are that it will happen to you, they are greater than your being hit crossing the street, your back getting skin cancer from the sun, your car being stolen, your home being burglarized or burning to the ground, or your mouth getting gum disease—all of which you protect yourself against, and in some cases, perhaps at considerable cost in time and money. Here are a few simple things you can do to avoid falling in love and risking everything.

co-workers   It has been estimated that over half of all affairs are with work-related acquaintances. Being required to relate every day with the same people, whom you probably did not choose in the first place, may be harder on you than you realize. Because of the discontent, disorientation, and conflict that can come from these forced relationships, the workplace is often a sexual minefield.

- If you must attend, **take your spouse along on company picnics, office parties, overnight conventions, and the like.** And unless there is no possibility that either of you could find the other of interest, **don't lunch alone with someone attractive of the opposite sex.**
- Frequently there is a strong sexual undercurrent in the workplace. Most people are not particularly happy in their jobs, and they think that to mix in a little sexual titilation will give them some harmless relief. So nat-

urally, **avoid going into isolated work areas where
you know someone who is attracted to you may be**
(stock rooms, vending rooms, deserted exercise rooms,
and so forth).

· **Before you leave for work, sit quietly for a moment
and imagine yourself going through your work day.**
Start at the point when you arrive, and systematically
fantasize the kinds of events that could occur, paying
special attention to anything that might be threatening
to your marriage. With each thing that you see happening, picture yourself responding from your peace
and your commitment.

casual encounters   Whereas two to three decades ago
there were only five major venereal diseases, today over twenty
different organisms cause more than fifty different sexually transmitted syndromes. In the United States, that is 12 million cases a
year. Most of those people thought they were having "safe sex."

· **Don't go into a bar or other night spot by yourself,**
because that is where affairs often begin, especially
ones with strangers. Either don't go—which would be
best—or take your partner, or go with a party of several other people.
· Of course, **don't bar hop or pub crawl with the
boys.** Be intelligent about a night out with the girls.
· **Don't go to sexually oriented events unless you take
your spouse** (dancing clubs and classes, topless restaurants, strip shows, adult movies, and so on).

friends   Some sex researchers think that about 40 percent
of all affairs are with friends or friends of the spouse. A relationship between couples may hide an attraction between two of the
partners that can seem under control for many months or years

before something happens. There can also be the same secret feelings for a friend of one's spouse. These are difficult circumstances because contact usually can't be avoided without awkwardly breaking up the friendships or informing one's partner of what is happening—which is seldom advisable. If you can't find some way to ease away from the relationship entirely, then try to be imaginative in reducing the number of contacts.

Don't allow yourself to be maneuvered into riding back alone from some event with this person, put in the back seat with her or him, or in other ways asking of yourself more control than is reasonable. Be prepared for these eventualities and have a prepared response ready. ("No, I have to sit up here, I have something about you I have to whisper in Pat's ear," or "I've been getting carsick recently, and my doctor said for me to try riding in the front seat.").

Each of these little efforts is a powerful symbol to your mind that you are serious about ending these feelings, and they will also have an effect on the other person's feelings about you. You may be able to enlist your spouse's aid—not by saying you're attracted to his best friend, or other such nonsense—but by saying perhaps that this person is boring to try to talk to by yourself, has bad breath, or has some other annoying trait that makes you prefer not to sit next to or be alone with him or her.

Naturally, your ego will say, "But those are lies!" In other words, far better to risk the happiness of your marriage and family than say that someone has bad breath.

Be inventive and persistent about what you can do, and you will receive a flow of power and peace that you did not expect, simply by having been willing to act quietly on behalf of your partner and family.

hugh's rules   My last affair was fifteen years ago. I consider it an affair even though it was an emotional involvement that not only didn't include sex but didn't include physical attraction.

It taught me that eliminating extramarital sex was not enough, because this relationship was almost as painful to Gayle as the sexual affairs. When I saw this, I immediately withdrew from the woman in every way. By that time in my life I had realized that above all I didn't want to hurt Gayle. I had become fascinated with this person's unusual psychic abilities, and the more I talked to her, the more I withdrew emotionally from Gayle. Which brings me to the first rule I made for myself during the approximately three years it took me to weed out the remaining fears I had that I might slip back into the old patterns.

• AVOID THE STIMULI.

As we have said, if you have been having an affair, you must stop all contact with that individual. If you haven't been having an affair, but feel vulnerable to one, still break off all contact with the person. One of several reasons that Gayle and I moved from where we had lived for fifteen years was to get away from the town where I had made so many mistakes. Avoiding stimuli also meant not putting myself in situations where I might receive the wrong kind of pressure from strangers —for example, not going alone to a woman's home to counsel her, not traveling out of town alone to give a talk or workshop. Now that I know that I could not have another affair, I don't have some of these rules, but that took several *years* of very hard work.

• ACT MARRIED.

I began wearing a wedding ring. I started saying "we" instead of "me" in describing anything that related to both of us. I stopped correcting Gayle when she told a story or exaggerated. *I never criticize her to anyone under any circumstances.* And I started carrying pictures of our children. (Once, at a convention center where I was speaking, every time I would go into the reception hall, the same attractive woman would come up and speak to me in a sexually aggressive way. Each time, I played dumb, pretending not to understand what she meant. Finally she got three of her friends to ask me point-blank if I would go to her room. I immediately pulled out the pictures I had of John—Jordan wasn't yet born—and their reaction was like vampires recoiling before a cross.)

· IRONICALLY, MY THIRD RULE WAS TO LOOK FOR A WEDDING RING.

Most of my affairs were with married women, but after I became aware of how many breakups I had contributed to and the trail of suffering and chaos I was leaving behind me, a wedding ring became an instant turnoff.

· MENTALLY JUMP TO HOW YOU WILL BE LOOKING AT THIS PERSON WHEN INFATUATION ENDS.

If I discovered that my sexual or romantic interest was beginning to grow, I would step forward mentally with my judgmental magnifying glass. I would reverse the falling-in-love process from one of generalizing to one of scrutinizing. Infatuation backlights and blurs. It surrounds its target in a haze of wonder and beauty. Whereas the defatuated mind looks at every enlarged pore and blemish as if through a microscope. It closely notes personal hygiene habits, bodily imperfections, signs of aging, taste in music and movies, differences in religious belief, and so forth.

We do this same mental flip over our public personalities as quickly as we do over our partners. Everything we come to dislike in a person manifests itself in the way we view his or her body and especially face. Thus a universally acclaimed beauty can look ugly to us when we find out that she abused her children, or a politician who only months before had "an honest face" looks very dishonest after we have heard some shocking revelation.

This reversal of attitude is also easily accomplished in our imagination—because we have had so much practice being judgmental! The average adult weight gain is about a pound of fat a year, so imagine this person ten years older and ten pounds heavier. Or pretend that you now know some unpleasant secret about him or her that you would learn later. (Probably one unpleasant discovery for each year of marriage is about right.) Or pretend going through a nightmare divorce with this person. (Your chances of staying together would be worse than fifty-fifty.) Any mental trick that allows you to stop the infatuation process can't possibly hurt you, and it may save many people needless suffering.

˙ THE LAST RULE WAS SUGGESTED BY GAYLE: DON'T TRY NOT TO NOTICE.

She had noticed that I was trying not to. She said, "I look at bodies. I even look at women's bodies. I'm not attracted to women, but I find big boobs and all that stuff fascinating. How could you not notice the parts of the body that an entire nation is obsessed with? I even

think it's all right to fantasize and masturbate about
what you saw. Why not?'' This last statement led to an
approach that I not only tried but that we have taught
many others to use. It can be a useful supplement to
one's protective program.

a program of guided fantasy and masturbation

When we have suggested various forms of masturbation as an aid
to meeting their sexual needs, a surprising number of people have
said, ''I can't masturbate, that would be wrong.'' Or simply, ''I
couldn't do that.'' But to risk betraying their life partner, destroying their children's home, and possibly killing both themselves
and their spouse with a sexually transmitted disease is somehow
more acceptable. Not that this is the only alternative to masturbation, but if you can get past centuries of prejudice on this subject,
a little ''self-abuse'' (as it was called as late as the fifties) can be
helpful to most potential cheaters.

It also isn't ''right'' to destroy possessions out of anger, but
when we were working with batterers, as a first step and as an
alternative to beating up their wives, we began instructing these
men to immediately destroy a good piece of furniture when they
felt the urge to attack their wife, and if necessary to keep destroying possessions until the urge passed. Naturally, they first had to
acknowledge that this was better than beating up their wife, and
their wife had to agree that the expense was a small price to pay
for helping end this problem.

The batterers quickly discovered that **the ego sees little difference between a possession of value and a person.** Interestingly,
attacking furniture also allowed some men to recognize very
quickly that they had no more use for battering. In these cases,
their first step became their last. (However, a great deal more work
was usually needed beside this step.) The furniture didn't say or
do anything unhelpful, and so they could see how they generated
and acted out these feelings much more clearly. Likewise, your

body doesn't know who or what brought you to orgasm and doesn't care.

A woman who later came to us for help with her second marriage told us that during her first marriage she had started attending one of the separation psychology–type groups. Every time she was away, her husband would masturbate while watching MTV. One day she discovered this and that it had been going on for over a year. When she reported it to her group, they told her that he was obviously a very sick person and that she should leave, which she eventually did. This was the same group that was now advising her to have an affair because her current husband was in a protracted period of impotency.

This attitude is not unusual in our culture. The ego part of us wishes to preserve its autonomy and will oppose simple solutions to problems that keep people separate. Masturbation is far from being the solution to infidelity, but it can help. And it's certainly simple: It hurts no one. It holds the sex drive down to manageable levels. It's a release of tension. It's inexpensive. It helps keep older men's reproductive systems functioning properly. It's a safety valve for those who have homosexual desires within a heterosexual relationship (or the reverse), as well as for any person who might have an affair. And it doesn't transmit hepatitis B, antibiotic-resistant gonorrhea, AIDS, or the twenty other sexually transmitted organisms.

One wonders why separation psychology hasn't embraced it as an expression of self-sufficiency.

The program we have recommended is very simple:

· NEVER TRY TO STOP YOURSELF FROM NOTICING ATTRACTIVE BODIES.

In a culture in which parts of the body are used more than any other symbol to attract attention, your attention will be attracted, and attempting to override this reaction is a battle you won't win. Once you have noticed, however, you do have a choice about how you behave. Obviously, if "looking" makes your spouse uncomfortable, then don't do it around her or him. Look, but don't attract attention to yourself or make others uncomfortable by being flagrant. However, it is helpful if couples will simply admit that we all like to look and allow each other this very harmless freedom. Strangely enough when it is shared, it can actually bring you closer. Flirting, or "making eyes" across a room, or in any other way coming on to someone—even someone you will probably never encounter again—is *not* what we are speaking of here and is a behavior you want to eliminate, whether your spouse is around at the time or not.

· MASTURBATE SYSTEMATICALLY.

What you want here is a good, sound maintenance program. You are systematically releasing sexual tension, just as you systematically eliminate waste from your body, shave, shower, clip your nails, and many other daily maintenance activities. How many times it will be helpful to bring yourself to orgasm may vary upward with the periodic swings in your libido, and naturally you don't want to masturbate too close to the time you would ordinarily have sex with your partner, or so often that it affects your sexual performance. However, **it is a myth that masturbation decreases the desire for marital sex**—unless it is done to excess. But it *can* burn up left-over sexual energy, and this you want to do. Although the number of masturbations is individual, your basic maintenance program should be very consistent. If

you settle on a minimum of twice a day, or three times
a week, then stick with this minimum. The regularity is
an important aspect of the approach, both as a safety
valve and as a mental symbol of your devotion to your
partner and family and of your determination to bring
this risk to them under control.

• FANTASIZE FREELY.

Place no restrictions on your sexual fantasies. In fact,
when you masturbate, it is especially helpful to fantasize
about those you are currently attracted to as often as possible. This activity slowly "uses them up," just as affairs
more quickly use and discard people.

To consciously and deliberately fantasize is a type of
awareness exercise that harms no one. **Affairs occur
because of a confusion between illusion and reality.
When you *intentionally* fantasize, you are practicing
seeing the difference.** You wish to develop a strong
demarcation between what you merely dream and what
you actually do. When you are in the physical presence
of someone about whom you have fantasized, look very
closely at this person and see just how different he or
she is from a fantasy. Prove to yourself that you can
imagine anything and yet be very disciplined about any
action that could harm others.

Decide quite specifically on the steps you will take to protect
your family. Make your program reasonable and well within your
willingness to carry out. As you practice in little ways being the
kind of person you want to be, you will feel noticeably stronger
and better. In many ways self-control is a more practical concept
than self-esteem. Being responsible is a decided pleasure, as well
as a gift to the world.

ELEVEN
Families

a half-century of structural change   Basic family composition has changed dramatically during the last half of the twentieth century, and this has put great stress on relationships. From a nation of large extended families living in stationary communities and neighborhoods, where people knew each other by sight and it was not uncommon for a family home to be passed down from one generation to the next, we divided ourselves into nuclear families that lived apart from their relatives, moved every five to six years, and consisted mostly of a stay-at-home mother, working father, and two or more children. This structure has continued to break down even further into families in which both parents work, blended families, single parents who work or receive welfare, single parents with a straight or gay lover, single parents with latchkey children, and so forth. And all of this happened within two generations.

At the same time, the media has focused considerable attention on the disintegration of the family, and we have been inundated with conflicting information about causes and solutions, most of them centering on who is more to blame, mothers or fathers. On one hand we are told that 90 percent of us came from dysfunctional families and are likely to create dysfunctional families ourselves; on the other hand we are presented with unworkable pictures of family life in "realistic" movies, wistful magazine articles, romance novels, "real-life" television dramas, and all-in-fun put-down humor.

Unquestionably we live in a house divided. This comes not only from our inflated expectations about what a nourishing family should look like but also from the inescapable recognition that there is little love or stability anywhere. We have seen few examples of how to care for each other and endless examples of how to disregard everyone except ourselves. Our priests, ministers, televangelists, and other spiritual leaders have preached rectitude but acted with extreme disregard for the moral welfare of their followers. Our politicians, who promised to govern responsibly, have squandered blood, money, and resources to enhance themselves. In many parts of the world, in the name of national sovereignty and ethnic purity, we see neighbors raping and murdering those they have known for a lifetime. And in the United States it is estimated that a woman or girl is raped every eight minutes, and very little is done about it.

Standing against this grim picture are a thousand judgments about who or what is to blame. Unfortunately these attacks just add to the separation that most families feel and result in remarkably few solutions or even attempted solutions. And so we end up in stasis, unable or unwilling to act, just hoping that things might get better and in the meantime only halfheartedly protecting ourselves and those who are in our care.

This is not a society of real families. We are a society of divorcers, adulterers, and leavers. Children are the one great hope of the world. They come to us surprisingly free of malice. They start out with a far greater measure of happiness and gentleness than adults. And yet they are very small and vulnerable and must rely on the world they come into for protection. And this the world has failed to give. If it gave it, wars would cease and famine would be halted before it could grow. Crime would not be tolerated, and couples with children would understand the moral necessity of working things out.

Children are easy to love, and yet only when the media singles out the tragic circumstances of a child here or there for occasional attention are we momentarily moved to compassion. It is difficult truly to love one's spouse, but if we are afraid to love even children, then we are clearly afraid of love itself.

We think that love will take away our individuality and freedom and merely set us up for prolonged unhappiness ending in almost certain abandonment. And indeed, a belief in love seems insane against the evidence of a loveless world. Especially the quality of love that heals. All that is beginning to dawn on us is that selfishness has not made us whole.

Love *can* heal, but not by giving us a partner who is just like us, not by giving us children who outperform other families' children. It heals by presenting us again and again with the opportunity to become whole by making those who are in our care whole.

the "normal" family   We both grew up in Dallas. We were always near grandparents, aunts, and uncles. We played with cousins and lived in neighborhoods where the same kids rode bikes, "played guns," and went to school together. We remember summer evenings with endless games of hide-and-seek and kick-the-can and days spent climbing trees and playing baseball. Homes weren't fenced, and neighbors didn't seem to mind children running through their front yards.

Because we live far from Gayle's parents, John and Jordan see very little of them, wouldn't recognize her brother and his wife on the street, probably wouldn't recognize Hugh's father or brother, and have met one little cousin of theirs twice. We live in a suburban development where it's common for neighbors to know nothing about each other and where it's difficult for Jordan to find anyone to play with during school vacations or summertime because all the children are in camps, day care centers, or other organized activities.

But as strange as this neighborhood seems to us compared with our childhood neighborhoods, we also live in a country where approximately 25 percent of the children are at or below the poverty line, primarily in one-parent families. Many of these kids are in neighborhoods that are remarkably similar to war zones, where walking to and from school or playing outdoors can be life-threatening, where witnessing classmates dying violently is not uncommon, and where these same children, when asked about their future, begin their sentences with, "*If* I grow up, I think I want to be . . ."

We live in a society that appears to have become not only uniformly cruel, but uniformly indifferent to cruelty; where special interest groups compete for power and money and promote hatred against any who disagree with them; where the races have become more prejudiced and combative rather than less; where many of the elderly, instead of wanting to protect and assist, have organized against a younger generation; where teachers and schools are woefully underfunded; and where parents seem to have found a thousand new ways to abandon their children.

We are living out the plot we have written, and it is not a happy one. It's a story that encompasses every race and every socioeconomic level, from poor men who take pride in the number of children who have their genes but not their commitment, to wealthy men who treat their children as mere extensions of their egos; from crack-addicted mothers who allow their daughters to be sexually abused for a quick buck, to society women who shun the mess and chaos of child care and desert their children emotionally.

It seems that it would be impossible for this story to change, but our personal belief is that if enough men and women, regardless of how they form themselves into families, will simply begin saying, "The insanity stops here," it will slowly begin to reverse itself. So rather than argue about who's to blame for where we find ourselves, there is one small thing we can do right now. We can commit to the people in our lives—to our parents, to our children, to each other.

beginning with the family we have   The firstborn child of close friends of ours had difficulty when he started school. He was hyperverbal, was always touching the other children around him, had trouble maintaining concentration on schoolwork, and didn't like being confined to a desk. At the same time, he was also bright, happy, intuitive, and amazingly thoughtful of other people. His mother described him as being like a puppy—you might get a little irritated because he keeps jumping up on you, but you know it's because he loves you.

His second-grade teacher suggested that he be tested for learning disabilities. She was fairly old-fashioned in her approach, and he began to feel self-conscious about his inability to stay seated and to concentrate on the numerous worksheets she passed out. His parents decided to take him to a local psychologist, who did extensive testing on him. At the end of this period the psychologist told them how much he had grown to like their boy and what wonderful qualities he had, but he said that he did recommend drugs for his hyperactivity. He also suggested that they see a local pediatric neurologist for a second opinion.

While it was clear that the psychologist had a genuine fondness for their son, the second doctor appeared to have little or no interest in him or them. After a series of difficult tests, he said that on a scale from one to ten, their son's hyperkinesis was about a seven and that now all he could do was "determine which of the six drugs available will make him manageable." He dismissed their concerns about drug therapy, told them they had no other viable choices, and gave them a prescription for the drug he wanted them to try first.

Even though they were hesitant, they gave their son his first dose—which made him considerably worse. When they reported this to the neurologist, he told them that this reaction was not uncommon and offered to call in a new prescription for something else. At this point the parents decided to search for someone who was a specialist in hyperkinesis.

Although it was a fairly long drive, they found such a man at the University of California Medical Center in San Francisco. He too was a pediatric neurologist, as well as a researcher and teacher. He spent half a day with the three of them, observing and getting to know their son and listening closely to them. At the end of that time he said, "I know it's a challenge to be the parents of this child, but I don't believe he needs drugs." He went on to explain that he definitely recommended drugs in situations in which a child was unable to function or was very unhappy, but since that was not the case here, he encouraged them "to become his advocates, to protect him from situations he can't handle, and to keep him away from people who aren't tolerant of kids." Then he paused for a moment before adding, "You know, I watch litters of rats, and in almost every litter there'll be one or two rats that move more than the others. They'll be all over the place, climbing over their brothers and sisters, and I just figure that that's okay, that they just need to move more."

In her gratitude and happiness, the boy's mother cried much of the long drive home. Finally here was an authority telling her that it was okay to love her son as he was, that rather than attempt to change or correct him, they could simply try to find situations that were a little easier for him. This boy is now fifteen and has none of the problems that made life difficult for him when he was younger. And he is still happy and considerate of others. In fact, his mother told us that his teachers usually tell her they wish all of their students were like him.

•   •   •

This book is not a plea for a return to the family relationships of the past, even if that were a possibility. And we should be grateful that it isn't, because family life then was often extremely lonely for women, who had essentially one role they could play. Therefore it is essential that, just as this mother took into her heart the boy she was given, we must begin with the family we have. And as a nation, it is time that we accept the way families are today and let this be our starting point.

It's as if mentally we haven't quite caught up with all that has happened, and because things obviously aren't working very well, all we know to do is blame. It becomes difficult for men and women to always be encountering new demands—new attitudes they are now expected to adopt toward each other, new health hazards to their family, new ways kids relate to adults. But it's important that we continue trying, because through family life we can heal our individual pasts and learn what love is and how to open our hearts to receive it.

In our rush toward personal fulfillment, we have forgotten what families are for. As they have evolved, we have narrowed and limited their definition. But no matter how small we make them, we still seem to carry with us the belief that they should somehow be different, that the one we have at the moment is not the right family. And perhaps in many ways they should change. Without a doubt we should live in a world that places the welfare of children above most if not all other concerns. At the very least, no child should go without food, clothing, education, medical care, and a loving home. But nevertheless, the family we live in is a sufficient place for us to start.

We know our discontents, but for too long we have been trying an unworkable solution. Once divorce was considered a tragedy. As a child of what was quaintly called a "broken home," Hugh can remember being whispered about and, because it was so un-usual, being openly referred to as "poor little Poncho" (his nickname then). Divorce is now commonplace, but it's no less destructive. There is a growing body of evidence that it is far more damaging to children's mental health than was formerly believed, even though the symptoms may not manifest for many years.

We must begin taking this into consideration when we grow weary of trying just one more time to get a breakthrough in an unhappy relationship. How many tries are our children worth? "Sticking it out for the sake of the children" is a wholly inadequate response, but the struggle, the unremitting toil, to get a breakthrough, is an example of the right kind of effort that will remain with our children—even if no breakthrough comes.

The children of this world are its greatest resource. There is no other that even comes close. And yet we obviously view them as an endlessly renewable resource, so that while we may feel momentary discomfort over each new barrage of tragic TV images, we don't believe there is much we as individuals can do. But there is. We can commit now to the children who are in our personal lives, even if we have none of our own; we can see to it that teachers are well paid and honored for their profession; we can insist that this country's deficit be reduced because of the burden it will later place on children; we can do our part to clean up the environment, because this is the land our children and grandchildren will walk and the air they will breathe; we can urge our companies to continue investing in more and better daycare facilities for their workers—because this will benefit children. In a word, we as individuals must become generative, which Allan B. Chinen, in his wonderful book *In the Ever After . . . Fairy Tales and the Second Half of Life,* describes as "the ability to transcend one's own needs and desires" and develop an altruistic concern for the next generation. This is a very different approach from attempting to mold children into living ego extensions so that parents with lesser children will feel uncomfortable.

It's essential that we also widen our definition of families to include all varieties of groupings that share the common purpose of loving and helping each other—homosexual couples with or without children, networks of close friends, long-term devotional groups, small businesses that embrace their employees and their employees' families. A close friend of ours, a single mother with one birth child and three adopted children, has long been a part of a network of other single mothers with adopted and foster children. They celebrate Thanksgiving, Christmas, and other holidays together, and on these occasions the adults assume responsibility for all the children in the group, just as members of extended families once commonly did. Throughout the year, if one mother is having difficulty coping with a child, she can call on one of the other mothers to come to her house to help her out, even to take her children for a weekend if necessary. This, also, is a family.

children as threats to marriage   There is no question that a baby is a beautiful and extraordinary gift, but it's a gift that comes with the *potential* for causing havoc in a relationship. The routine the partners have established—their evenings out, their meals together at home, their favorite TV programs, the rhythm of contacts within their circle of friends—all can be joltingly swept aside for the seemingly insatiable needs of the baby. There may be many sleepless nights (some children don't begin sleeping straight through until they are three or four), and if both parents come home from work already tired, a level of exhaustion can begin to build that can make parenthood seem like an unnatural state.

Just when it gets a little easier, it's time for the child to begin preschool, and suddenly there is a new set of problems. This pattern continues into the teenage years, with all of its attendant fears and frustrations. But this is not a book about how to get your baby to sleep through the night, how to choose a school, or how to get your teenager to listen to you. It's a book about a new way of approaching relationships, and one of the basic precepts is that the form will always matter less than the content. How you see your child is more important than whether you choose to breast-feed, buy toy guns, or send your children to camp. Despite the tremendous fear that is presently in the air about the hundreds of mistakes—physical or psychological—that you could make, **your enduring commitment to this child from infancy until the day you die can outweigh almost any other decision you make about upbringing.**

Part of that commitment is your willingness to accept your children as they are *today* and to work unceasingly to be fond of them as they enter each new stage of development. Assuming that your baby is healthy, that your life is not too chaotic, and that you get a reasonable amount of help, it's usually easy to love infants and cute little toddlers, but it can become much more difficult to remain a constant friend as your child develops a strong personality and grows older. And if you didn't have an adequate period of bonding during your child's infancy or you are not the birth parent, it can seem an impossibility.

But isn't an unshakable belief in a child what we all want for ourselves as adults? Isn't that what we don't think our parents gave us? And surely it's apparent that our inability to give it to the children in our lives is simply the perpetuation of an injustice. We don't have to be perfect. In fact, we won't be perfect. Even the attempt to avoid all mistakes is not beneficial. But endurance is. Persistence is. And the willingness to start over is.

If we believe that we are a victim of a dysfunctional family, having children carries a fearful prospect, because we know that soon the tables will be turned and we will be the topic of discussion in some group or counseling session that our grown child is in. Today, very little effort is spent seeing that the parents of our generation were victims also, and someday very little effort will be given to understanding why we brought up our children the way we did. In the culture we live in, sooner or later everyone must be judged. Being right is our national ideal, and the instant opinion has become more important than the problem itself.

As would be expected, this is also the atmosphere in many traditional families. When you add to the family picture stepparents, step- and half-brothers and sisters, visitation periods, late child support payments, and someone's new lover, it requires great vigilance to remember one's basic purpose, and this is why having a family today is a growth formula concentrate, a crash course in spiritual development. Where else can so many problems be found on a daily basis?

the danger of blaming parents   Many couples, even those who had very few disagreements before, may suddenly find that their ideas about raising children conflict. We are now all aware that mistakes in parenting can have disastrous consequences, but we are not aware of all the mistakes that *could* be made; nor were our parents.

In the late forties and early fifties, when we were children living in Dallas, there were no seatbelts and most mothers, when they drove around doing errands, would let their kids stand up on the seat. The few parents who made their kids and their kid's friends sit down were thought of as overly cautious if not mean. On the Fourth of July, children would throw cherry bombs and hold "baby fingers" between their fingers until they went off. When playing guns, kids who had BB rifles would often shoot them at each other and were merely warned by their parents not to aim at the face. Children rode their bikes all over town and rarely were asked where they had gone.

Our parents were not indifferent or neglectful—they simply hadn't thought much about a number of the dangers that people are so aware of today; and of course, there are now many new dangers, some of which this generation has not yet thought of.

Today parents are held responsible for almost everything that occurs in the life of their child, whether they were aware of the danger or not and whether they were directly involved or not.

Naturally, there has to be personal accountability, but as a nation we have gone to a damaging extreme in our attempt to discover every possible way that parents can be blamed. And if we continue to hold our parents guilty for all our difficulties, we also have to take responsibility for every problem our own children will ever have—and we know how hard we try.

It's easier to blame our parents than to change. It's easier to point backward than to begin the work that would make the world a little safer for children. However, giving up blaming parents is difficult in the present climate because it has become something of a national pastime. For example, in many public schools the teachers and counselors are now given special training on how to detect physical and sexual abuse. This would be an excellent step toward protecting children if these courses also emphasized how central to children's mental health is their attitude toward their mother and father. Parents are in many ways part of a child's being, especially very young children. They think of their parents and themselves as a team, a single unit, that moves through life, and in their memory that is the way it has always been. Their parents received them into the world; they carry the blood of their parents; in many ways they look and act like their parents; and their parents have been the gods that determine where they live, what friends they play with, what time dinner takes place, even what clothes they wear.

Unfortunately, though, the role that mothers and fathers play in holding the child's mind together is usually not sufficiently stressed. Instead, the signs of abuse are often unreasonably broad, and as a consequence, like so many other areas that have been influenced by separation psychology, the actual practicing of the protection often causes separation and in this case sometimes extreme and wholly unnecessary damage to the parent-child relationship. Much abuse is of course detected, but the number of false alarms is also substantial, and in the course of playing them out, deep doubts are planted in many children's minds.

Schools are just one area where this vague, widespread assumption that all parents are guilty has entered. It can be plainly seen in children's programming on commercial TV, in sitcoms, in children's movies, and in cartoons. For the first time there have been attempts to pass laws automatically charging parents if their children commit certain crimes. Certainly many fathers treat their significance in their children's lives far too lightly when they forget birthdays, skip important athletic events, or wait to be asked before they give praise. And of course, divorced mothers and fathers often see enormous guilt in each other and work quite hard to poison their children's minds against the other parent, not realizing that the children are being asked to turn against a part of themselves.

Here in Tucson we have recently seen two startling examples of how important parents are to their children. The first concerned a good friend of Jordan's. This boy had been to our house to play, had spent the night, and had even come to the hospital when Jordan broke his leg and given him his crutches to use. He was also special to Jordan because he was his first friend from another country. When he was at our house, he had often talked about how much he and his dad were alike, even having the same long name. A few weeks after the last time we saw him, a neighbor across the street from the boy's apartment building put up a sign saying that the boy's father had robbed her. At about the same time, his father was charged with that crime and was put in jail pending trial. Within a few days, the boy had committed suicide, hanging himself in a tree that the neighbor could plainly see.

Another example is a story, recently in the papers, of a Tucson man who was under his car working on the transmission, when suddenly the jacks holding it up collapsed. His sixteen-year-old son lifted the car off of him long enough for the boy's sister and mother to drag him out. Except for some broken bones, he was not seriously injured. The next day the boy again tried to lift the 2,900 pound Ford Granada and couldn't budge it.

•   •   •

Your parents are part of your being, the ones who brought you into the world. Unless you forgive them for all their errors and not only acknowledge their God-given innocence but accept them completely as your mother and father, you will not mend your childhood damage, you will not experience permanent love with another person, and you will not be a whole parent to your own child. There is no exception to this law of healing.

CHILDREN

do children need both parents?   Obviously, children can overcome not having one or both parents, but this does not change the fact that having both makes many aspects of growth easier for a child. When John was an infant, Gayle used to leave him with Hugh, along with a list of instructions about what and how Hugh was supposed to feed him, when he should be put to bed, and admonitions about being sure John didn't get too cold or hot and that Hugh didn't become preoccupied with some idea and start writing about it while John languished in his crib.

Hugh never paid much attention to these lists, especially Gayle's instructions about how babies are supposed to be held while you feed them. He would plop John into his little carrier and stick the bottle of prepumped breast milk into his mouth. This drove Gayle crazy, and she pointed to study after study that showed how babies who weren't held and cuddled grew up to be sociopaths and in extreme cases actually died. Hugh, in turn, kept telling her that this was how he liked to feed John. He liked to look at him and play with his little toes and talk to him and jiggle the carrier. He said that in his opinion John enjoyed it as much as being held.

One day, after one of these discussions, we decided to sit quietly and pray about this conflict, and when we did, Gayle suddenly remembered the time when a male cousin of hers brought his little girls to meet Gayle and her mother. His grandmother and mother had also come, and the minute they walked in the door, they started describing how Gayle's cousin had actually washed the little girls' hair that morning *by himself.* The entire time they were there, they laughed about this, made comments about how he probably hadn't gotten out all the soap, and then the two of them went on to regale us with the astounding news that his wife was out of town and he had actually *fed the girls and put them to bed.* During all of this my cousin knew his role and played it: he looked sheepish and made weak humorous protests.

Remembering that scene, Gayle realized that this little area of sanctioned attack had been present for many generations, and that not only did it create wedges between wives and husbands, it had the effect of turning men off from involving themselves with their children.

If we are to form complete relationships, we must support each other's parenting efforts. Males and females bring different strengths—and different weaknesses—to child care. Just as it takes a female and a male to create a baby, that same baby does not outgrow its need for those differences after conception. As a very young boy Hugh can remember how special were the times he was left in the care of his dad and his male friends. They didn't insist on Hugh's mother's set of rules. In fact, they basically left him alone, but there was something very reaffirming about being accepted into the company of men, hearing their kind of conversations, their kind of humor, and knowing that they trusted him to see them as they were, because he too was male.

absent children and blended families   It may be easier or more natural for most women to parent than most men, but women certainly don't help their children when they attack the way men do things. We have heard many fathers say that they didn't feel needed or even wanted in their families, that they felt as if they were living outside the home. In families in which both parents work, it's essential that fathers and mothers participate equally in child care when they are home. If an ex-husband or birth father is not active in the child's life, the single mother must reach out to the men around her—be they brothers, fathers, cousins, co-workers, friends, or Big Brothers—to find those who are willing to provide a masculine presence. And men who are single parents must also provide steady female companionship, not just a string of lovers.

Fathers or mothers who live apart from their children must not give up their parental roles, no matter how difficult, embarrassing, or even humiliating the gauntlet they must run to get to their daughter or son regularly. Teenagers can become extremely angry toward a parent for leaving—for example, toward a father who left "to find himself," or a mother who left to be with a lover. And it's easy for these parents to turn their backs on their teenager by saying that they are merely acceding to the child's wishes. But just as with a three-year-old screaming, "I hate you, I wish you were dead!" this anger must not be taken to heart by parents of an older child.

You must refuse to go away, no matter how difficult the situation becomes and no matter how often you have expressed your love on previous occasions. If the child continues to refuse to see you, then you must write or phone regularly if he or she will speak with you, send presents on birthdays, graduations, and other occasions, and continue letting your child know how much you love him or her. If you don't do this, you will not only confirm your child's assessment of your love, you can rest assured that you will not truly "find yourself"—because true self-knowledge does not come from the ashes of desertion.

No parent is dispensable, and divorced couples must work hard to put their children's needs above their own anger and disappointment. The only children we have seen who appear to have survived divorce undamaged are those whose parents have accomplished this. For some time we have been following the progress of two well-adjusted, happy boys from two different homes whose parents are remarried, and who have stepbrothers and -sisters and half-brothers and -sisters. The key in both cases appears to be that the boys see their birth parents regularly, and the stepparents love them as deeply as their birth parents. They are also completely welcome in both of their homes. In one case the parents broke up over an affair and there is still bitterness between them, but they are able to put it aside for the welfare of their son. In the other case, both the father and stepfather coach their son's Little League team and attend all of his sporting events and school activities together.

We are also intimately connected to many children who are not truly welcome in either one or both of their parents' homes. In most of these cases their birth parents obviously still love them. But their stepparents view them as liabilities, little negative reminders and added nuisances that unfortunately were included in the package with their new love. We have often heard stepparents say, "Oh, he's great, we get along great, everything's great—except for his kid. What a manipulator!"

In California we lived down the street from a couple who had two children: the older one, Kyle, was from the mother's previous marriage, and the younger one, Nancy, was from the current one. Kyle became friends with Jordan even though he was nine and Jordan was seven. He and his half-sister played at our house almost daily for two years until we moved. Kyle was never allowed to come to our house unless he brought his half-sister. In fact, it quickly became apparent to all of us that Kyle was essentially the girl's babysitter. Nancy, who was a perfectly nice kid but one who also knew a good situation when she saw it, would threaten to tell his parents if Kyle didn't do what she wanted him to and would often blame Kyle for things he hadn't done, knowing that she was the one who would be believed. Jordan naturally thought this was very unfair, but Kyle, who was remarkably easygoing, seemed resigned.

Several months after Jordan, Kyle, and Nancy began playing

together, Jordan told us that he was missing several Nintendo games, and John said that he was missing some money. After watching him carefully, it became clear that Kyle was taking things. This was a tremendous shock to Jordan, who considered him a best friend. Hugh gently confronted Kyle, who at first would barely talk, made no eye contact, and denied taking anything, but after Hugh promised that he wouldn't tell his stepdad, he finally admitted taking even more things than John and Jordan had discovered. He promised to return everything, which he immediately did.

Several months passed, and again Jordan began missing things. Hugh again confronted Kyle, who this time denied more strenuously taking anything, but eventually confessed and returned the items. This time Hugh told him that he would have to talk with either his mother or his birth father (with whom he spent every other weekend). Kyle chose his father, because he said that his mother would tell his stepdad.

Kyle's father turned out to be very loving, very concerned, and virtually powerless to help Kyle. He and his ex-wife were unable to have discussions about Kyle that went deeper than what time the father would pick him up and return him.

The stealing didn't stop, and Hugh continued to talk with Kyle's dad. His job often required him to work at nights, leaving Kyle alone with his stepmom during many of his visits. One day when the father was gone, Hugh spoke with the stepmother. She made it clear that she thought Kyle was a manipulator (the universal complaint of stepparents), and was a burden on their relationship.

From the few occasions when Jordan had been to their house, we knew that he thought that his stepfather didn't like Kyle, but that his mother was "real nice." This was essentially the same impression we had gotten in our few contacts with them. So there it was, a common pattern we had seen in counseling many times: an essentially good kid who was not welcome in either of his homes, with two birth parents who loved him but were basically powerless to protect and help him. No wonder he was acting out! And no wonder he found it so difficult to trust adults.

What are this boy's chances of growing up and forming a lasting, committed relationship based on love and trust? If he marries, what kind of father will he be? And this is a child from a middleclass family, living in a safe area with wonderful schools, and having two stable stepparent families to go between. How much more difficult is it for children who don't have love from both parents, who are in constant conflict with stepsiblings, or who live in areas where they also have to deal with drugs and gangs?

children as pawns   If blended families are going to work, your children from your previous marriage must be viewed as assets rather than liabilities. You may believe it was a mistake, but the children from that marriage have not failed you or anyone else. Yet this is often how they are consciously or unconsciously viewed within the new setting, and they grow up feeling vaguely misplaced, the product of a mistake that was somehow their fault. This will make it very difficult for them to commit deeply to a relationship as adults. In fact, commitment is often more frightening to them than alienation and loneliness.

When divorced parents use their children as leverage, or as a tool of revenge, they wound the one positive product that they believe came out of their marriage. A good example of this is a couple we know who have six children between them. The father, Tony, was offered a wonderful opportunity to advance in his career if he would be willing to relocate in a nearby state. At first he refused because he didn't believe that his ex-wife would agree to allow the one child of theirs who lived with him to leave, and he was reluctant to move farther from his other child, who lived with her. He also loved his stepchildren, and his wife, Lisa, would also need her ex-husband's permission to take their four children out of state. Eventually Tony realized that not moving would stymie his career, and he took his family to visit the city where his company wanted him to move. Everyone liked it, and so as a family they made the decision that if they could all get permission to go, they would accept the promotion.

Tony's ex-wife had always used all of her visitation rights and had supported the boy emotionally in many other ways. In the months leading up to the move, she not only agreed to the move, but whenever Tony would waver, she encouraged him to go because she knew it would be better for their son. She easily agreed to new rules for visitation, which gave her large blocks of time for the boy to visit her and for their other child to spend time with her dad.

Lisa's ex-husband, who shared joint custody of their children, had moved away after the divorce and had always used only a part of the visitations allotted him, sometimes canceling at the last minute. His response was to use their desire to move as an opportunity to reduce child support payments, even though they weren't high; he had an excellent job; he didn't have any other birth children; and his new wife received substantial child support payments from her ex-husband. The move, promotion, and large raise would benefit his children, because Lisa would only have to work part time and could act as a Girl Scout leader for their daughter's group and participate more fully in their three sons' activities. But he resisted the move—not because he didn't love his children, but because he was still very angry with his ex-wife, and the anger blinded him to their welfare. They were the only weapon he had.

Realizing that, even with less child support, the children and the rest of the family would still be better off, Lisa instructed her lawyer to settle. She and Tony tried to keep the support payments issue quiet, but the children somehow found out, as children often do, and they mistook their father's desire to reduce payments as a sign that he was not truly interested in them. This is a very common reaction when children hear this kind of news, and wise parents never involve their children in issues over child support.

We include this story not because it illustrates the pattern of a mother acting with love and a father acting with anger. The sexes could easily have been reversed. Rather than seeking to come together to work toward a solution, women and men have turned against each other over what to do about the abandoned children of our society. Much of what is presently wrong would be corrected if mothers would struggle to uphold the father's value in their children's eyes, and if fathers would support their children financially and emotionally. And unless it becomes financially impossible to maintain, fathers should probably not seek to lower payments. However, all too often men have been made to feel that their financial contribution was the most important element in their parenting, whereas their presence and their commitment have decidedly more profound and far-reaching effects.

What we are talking about in this book is not a new set of behaviors, but a new attitude toward growth and fulfillment that recognizes the practicality of putting our primary relationships above even our immediate ego interests, whether they are relationships with our spouse, our birth children, our stepchildren, our adopted children, or our foster children.

stepparents   Stepparents must strive to treat their stepchildren with the same respect that they give their own children. Favoring one's birth child is not an act of love. For example, a women may be protective of her own children if she feels they aren't being treated fairly at school, and she should also stand up for her stepchildren even though the school may know that she is not their real mother. Most men discipline in a firm, persistent way that can be very affirming to their children. It says, "I know you are capable of this, I know you have it in you, and that is why I am insisting." But with their wife's child they may think, "I'll just let her handle it—after all, it's her kid." A good stepfather will work closely with his wife to find ways acceptable to them both to bring an equal measure of male firmness to her children also.

This kind of evenhandedness is not only possible, love is also possible, and this approach is essential to the stepparent's happiness and spiritual growth. It is accomplished the same way that any achievement is accomplished—by refusing to give up, by study, by experimentation, by working at it.

If a stepparent cannot easily attain a bond with a stepchild, too often he or she merely gives up, or condemns the child, or blames the other birth parent for "causing trouble." And certainly many of the adults in children's lives do cause trouble. But if they knew what the results of their lack of maturity would be, if they could project their behavior into the future and see their stepchildren unable to love or be loved, unable to commit or accept commitment, perhaps they would stop emphasizing what was done to them as children and see that here is a chance to wipe out a generation of mistakes. When stepparents do this, miracles can result.

The task does not lie beyond one's ordinary talents. It doesn't require an advanced degree, previous experience, a status job, or lots of money. It requires only the willingness to hold your stepchild innocent within your own heart. If this wasn't done for you—if you grew up in a divided home where you felt abandoned or even abused by one or both of your parents; if you are "the product of a divorce" and were poisoned against one parent by the other; if you were a member of a blended family that didn't blend; and if now all around you people are saying that the only way to combat the effects of selfishness is to become selfish yourself— you can still do it for your stepchild. But only through compassion and generosity, only through giving to those in your care what you were not given.

If your parents didn't give you a deep sense of self-worth, you cannot give that to yourself by withholding from your family. In a thousand years you will not heal your pain through separation. But you *can* heal through commitment to your children and stepchildren—by getting rest in order to love, getting "time out" in order to love, getting "a little space" in order to love, "getting your needs met" in order to love. You don't want these things so you can have them for your smaller self alone, but so that you can give of your abundant self and extend it. If you will do this, and if we all will do this, not only will the residues of our childhoods be healed, there will be fewer lost childhoods; there will be real families.

A FEW WORDS ABOUT IN-LAWS

As any devoted reader of Dear Abby and Ann Landers knows, the relationship between couples and their in-laws has a long and troubled history. At one time mother-in-law jokes were an institution. It's not that the problem has gone away but simply that we have become more politically correct in our humor.

Sometimes it's simply not possible for your spouse and your parents to have a good relationship. This places you in the very uncomfortable position of trying to defend each side to the other. Naturally, this is a role you are reluctant to assume, because both sides become angry at you. Your partner may come to feel that you are not wholly supportive, while your parents express sorrow and bewilderment that their constructive criticisms aren't being received with the proper respect. This dynamic is further complicated if there are grandchildren, because kids quickly pick up on tension.

Like many problems, it is first helpful to simply see and accept the situation the way it is rather than waste time wishing it were different. Your parents may never like your spouse and vice versa, but you can minimize the impact of these feelings on your marriage if you will do one thing. If you see that your parents are beginning to form the habit of complaining to you about your partner, gently but firmly let it be known that you **never discuss, defend, explain, or apologize for your spouse.** It is not only useless to try to change their minds, the mere attempt is harmful to your marriage. Their criticisms are not harmless because they are felt even if not heard by your partner, and for you merely to give them audience will, to some degree, also give them legitimacy.

If this dynamic is already in place, your sudden refusal to continue playing the role of your partner's apologist may cause a temporary rift in your relationships with them. You can approach this subject in a loving way, and for your peace of mind you should. Certainly you don't wish to say more than is necessary. Your purpose is to extend love to your spouse, not to make your parents feel guilty or wrong. And perhaps if you are very thoughtful in the approach you use, there will be no rift. But you must be consistent whatever their reaction. For example, if they bring up something entirely new about your partner—saying that this is not a criticism but merely a point they want you to explain—simply say that you no longer wish to have these discussions and that you will not listen.

You are merely saying to them that this is the person you married, this is the one with whom you have pledged to walk through life. And you must be willing to do what is necessary to uphold this new policy, even if it means hanging up the phone or walking out of their house. When they express their hurt and their confusion because "we are just trying to be helpful and you have always been so honest with us," you must affirm your love for them yet also remain strong in this decision.

Naturally this same approach applies if you have remarried and your grown children are the ones expressing the criticism. You definitely want to understand their confusion, their pain, their anger, and to discuss these emotions with them if that seems helpful, but you must not get involved in an ongoing dynamic of defending your partner with anyone.

The other side of this coin is to work to accept your partner's parents as they are, even though it's socially acceptable to dislike them and to voice this dislike openly. You won't be hurt if you do this, and you will be extending a degree of honor and respect to your partner. And of course it's also helpful if parents will work to accept and even like the person their son or daughter married, even though this is an individual woefully inadequate and unworthy of their progeny. The time has simply come for us to stop throwing away relationships.

TWELVE
Money

WHEN IS MONEY MORE IMPORTANT THAN YOUR RELATIONSHIP?

attitudes toward money   Have you noticed that people will tell you about their sex life before they'll tell you how much money they make? In counseling couples, we've noticed that partners will reveal the most intimate details about each other—personal hygiene, "nasty habits," unusual sexual and criminal desires, body odors, even how often underwear is washed—but will withhold the important details of their finances. Since we don't charge, there is no advantage in keeping this information quiet, but emotionally there would appear to be ample reason for never discussing it.

From a spiritual standpoint, the world could be looked at as a bag of substitutes for God. Among the "other gods" that various religious beliefs admonish one not to worship are pride, position, power, sex, fame, possessions, and in our case, chocolate. But the one that is on almost *every* list is money. In "paper, rock, scissors," the children's game of decision, scissors cuts paper, rock breaks scissors, and paper covers rock. In the "game of life" money knocks out everything else, and as an issue that can come between you, it's perhaps the most subtle and devious one you will encounter, because it is hard for most of us to admit in what ways and especially to what degree money is important to us.

The body can evoke desire, but so can money. (Have you seen the bumper sticker "If you're rich, I'm single"?) Possessions can evoke jealousy and so can money. Power can evoke anger, but so can money. Affection can evoke jealousy, but so can money. And so forth. Money can stir up every ego emotion and stir each one up almost as strongly as anything else in the world.

Actually, money is just strips of paper with funny faces. Yet despite its inherent emptiness, it symbolizes many things: safety, power, desirability, freedom, respect, intelligence, accomplishment, even the ability to govern. And among the issues couples cite as causing divorce, not having enough of it ranks right up there with constant arguing, abuse, and affairs. **In most marriages money symbolizes love and caring even more than sex.** It may come as a surprise to many couples that an *abundance* of money can also generate sufficient fear, suspicion, or jealousy to break up an otherwise sound union.

Perhaps the central reason that money—whether we think we have too much of it or too little—is such a penetrating and disturbing symbol is that we are so totally conflicted in how we view it. We acknowledge that money is very desirable yet think that it *shouldn't* be. We want more and more of it—yet the more we have, the more tainted we feel. Prominent people who eschew money often take on an aura of purity, even saintliness. Likewise, when we discover that our heroes spend more money than we thought they did, they fall in our estimation.

Most of us believe quite deeply that money reveals who and what we are—our value in the world, the quality of our marriage, how well our adult children are doing, how "fine" a home we have, and the direction our life is heading. We don't want other people to have this window into our soul. We believe that we are not all we should be, and the financial details of our life would quickly reveal this to everyone.

We allow ourselves to suspect that there is a correlation between our income and how spiritual we are. We allow ourselves to suspect that if we are "right with God" it shows up in our finances. But is, for example, a member of the Perot family closer to God than a homeless person? Is there any evidence that the saints and holy ones of old were rewarded with money? Does either money or the lack of it have *any* power over how deeply we can feel God's peace?

Likewise, money has nothing to do with how much your partner loves you, is concerned about you, is attracted to you, or wishes to protect you. It has nothing to do with your prospects for true happiness as a couple. It flatly has nothing to do with the quality of the bond between you. And yet you must not ignore the deep beliefs that you both may have that money has a great deal to do with all of these things. In a real relationship, you don't really deal with money but with the meaning, the symbolism, it has for both of you. And this you should do openly and honestly and with tremendous understanding and compassion.

the fear behind the issue   Your attitude about what role money should play in your marriage can be generated outside the relationship, and you must be alert to these influences, talk about them, and not allow your opinion of each other to be poisoned by anyone. In their first marriages, both Hugh and his sister were too young and inexperienced to know to do this.

When Hugh, at age twenty, married his first wife, many people thought the Prather family was wealthy. This was not the case, nor was it a tradition for the men of that family to help their children financially in any substantial way. After the marriage there was great bitterness on the part of some of Hugh's in-laws when they saw that one of their own was now strapped with a penniless young man. Many people who knew the couple were convinced that this bitterness was strongly imparted to Hugh's wife and eventually became a deep source of discontent in their marriage and one cause of their divorce.

Hugh's sister also had a close relative who consistently opposed her staying in her first marriage, because she too was with a man who made very little money, much less than Hugh's sister earned. She recently told us that at her young age, this opposition from someone she had always looked to for counsel became a principal factor that led to the breakup of a marriage that otherwise had few problems and once had much love.

It's certainly understandable why so many couples believe that now more than ever they must look to money to protect them and their children from the chaos and danger of life. We live in a world filled with new diseases, new forms of violence, new forms of theft, and sudden homelessness. We also live in a culture that honors and defers to those whose sole achievement is the acquisition of money, with little concern for how they got it. And in matters of the heart it would appear that one gets sooner and keeps longer a better class of spouse if one has money. In short "there isn't anything money can't buy," or so it would seem. Little wonder that the desire for money can grow stronger than the desire for goodness and peace, which do not appear to offer protection, stability, worldly honor, or even to attract the best mates. And little wonder that relationships that don't generate "enough" money begin to have questionable value in many couples' eyes.

Money can buy health. It can protect you against loneliness. It can protect you against unhappiness. It can protect you better than God! At least these are the not-so-unconscious beliefs most people have. Because of its seemingly limitless protective qualities—protection against bad neighborhoods, bad schools, bad doctors, bad retirement, bad treatment in restaurants—fights about money usually have fear at their core, and it's helpful to be alert to this so that effort and goodwill are not wasted in battling the mere symptoms of the fear. For example, if the wife handles most of the grocery shopping and the husband wants the household allowance reduced, the argument may really be about the husband's growing fear that he is trapped in his present job and that his wife values him only for what he can earn, versus the wife's fear that since this is the area he has singled out to cut back on, she has become unimportant to him. Or it may not be so much the way the husband backs into parking places that is the issue, as the wife's fear that if there is an accident, the expense will threaten the security of the family, as opposed to the husband's fear that deep down his wife doesn't really respect him.

No fear is irrational given an individual's makeup and history. **It is always a mistake to attempt to reason away your partner's anxieties.** It doesn't matter whether the spider really is harmless, whether one really does save money driving, whether the coat really will look cheap, or whether coupon-cutting is actually time-efficient —arguing is not a proper response to fear. We aren't in a position to know all the factors that feed into our own anxieties, and certainly not in a position to tell our partner what he or she is really afraid of. "You're afraid of nothing" will not increase the trust between you.

Two people who love each other give one another the gifts that truly reduce fear: love, understanding, and support. Naturally this must include working diligently to earn money and to spend it wisely. Being "gainfully employed" is a symbol of caring and responsibility that should not be ignored in the name of idealism. Your function is to bring comfort to your partner, not to decide how he or she should think about paying cash versus charging. Of course, you always work through the issue at hand, and using the ten steps in arguing that we outlined in Chapter Eight is an efficient way of doing this, especially steps 8 and 9 that deal with fear. But remember that you gain nothing by *opposing* your partner because your partner is afraid.

PLANS AND AGREEMENTS

the heart-to-heart money talk   Money issues affect more areas of their relationship than most couples realize and sometimes completely control the attitude one partner has toward the other. As a first step, it's helpful to sit down and talk about what money means to each of you. It is especially useful to bring up lessons from childhood, admonitions about money one heard growing up, and also what one's pattern toward such things as bills, gifts from parents, savings, budgets, bank accounts, and large-ticket items tends to be. If a couple would do this before marriage, they could head off a number of potential problems, yet because of how well they get along during the honeymoon stage, most couples think that they will have no trouble working things out as they go along. Thus it is usually after marriage that their first serious financial discussions take place, and unfortunately, these tend to revolve around major issues that have already come between them.

Once you have each taken positions on a money issue, it is difficult to talk freely about your families' belief systems and the other influences on your attitudes toward money, because of the fear that whatever you admit will be used against you in the issue at hand. Therefore, early in the relationship, or at a time when you don't feel deeply divided over this subject, have a free-ranging conversation about money, and gradually, perhaps even over several days or weeks, try to come up with your first tentative plan for how you will approach obvious trouble areas. This kind of conversation may have to be repeated from time to time through the years until complete trust is finally established.

During the years that Hugh's first three diaries were being published, we had a series of fights over money, each seemingly more disturbing than the last (we were still several years away from working out our "How to Have a Real Argument" guidelines). These centered on the question of how much control Gayle should have over the money Hugh was bringing into the relationship, which was virtually our entire income.* One evening we were having still another fight, the latest of several that we had had over the last few days, during which we had been trying to resolve what was clearly beginning to destroy our marriage. Hugh can remember thinking, "Nothing is worth *this*," then he surprised us both by saying, "As far as I'm concerned, from now on there will be no his-and-her money. Everything—even if I inherit money—will be entirely yours and entirely mine." As he said these words, he was gripped with the terrible certainty that Gayle would soon spend them both into destitution. What actually happened is that Gayle turned out to have far more sense about money than Hugh did.

This is not a solution we recommend to other couples. It merely illustrates that *even if two people have bad arguing techniques,* if they stick with it, if they keep talking, and above all, if they at least *try* to remember that their relationship is more important than any issue, they will find a way.

prenuptial agreements   Naturally there can be circumstances under which a formal understanding about some of their financial concerns would help ease a couple's fears and reduce the possibility of future misunderstandings. For example, there might be questions of how to keep an inheritance intact for children from a previous marriage. Or if one partner will have to give up a job or alimony in order to get married, there could be questions about how to make the new financial situation balanced and fair.

The damage these agreements cause comes primarily from their emphasis and timing. They are formal documents that are so important that they must come before the marriage agreement. This

---

* In those days neither of us was acknowledging how important Gayle's contributions of editing and ideas were to those early books, or that the books would have been *impossible* to write without our relationship.

is quite different from two people trying to sort out and clarify their future plans, an exercise that could just as easily come after the wedding as before. The agreements are formalized before because there is a lack of trust over money, which means, of course, there is a lack of trust. This is further reinforced if provisions are included that apply in the event of divorce. Here the option of divorce is acknowledged as a prior condition to marriage. In this way the prenuptial agreement often formalizes doubt.

It doesn't follow, though, that these agreements should never be used. A couple we know wanted to get married, but the man, who was by far the wealthier of the two, was so fearful about money that every time they got close to the wedding date, he would panic and cancel. He wasn't doing this as a way of forcing the woman to sign an agreement—in fact, he was opposed to the idea—but his fear was so great that it would take control of him. The woman was a very kind and intuitive person, and she drew up a document herself in which she declined any right to his property or income and renounced any right to inherit from him if he died. This agreement, however, expired in three years. She said, "That is time enough for love to heal all—if it's going to."

This little document allowed him to go through with the marriage. And a few months later he made a tiny Zozobra-like figure out of it, and in a very humorous ceremony, they burned "Old Man Fear."

Our overall experience is that, although there are exceptions, these agreements cause marriages to begin with the scent of failure. One partner usually wants it more than the other and often must resort to "sign—or else" tactics to get it. The message to the more financially dependent partner is, "My money will remain more important than you." Indeed, those who want a prenuptial agreement might consider looking at their fear of the motivations of their partner and consider deeply whether they believe this person is entering the relationship to acquire money. If they are convinced that is the reason, they definitely should not proceed with the marriage.

All partners have some ego involvement in a marriage. Our egos participate in everything we do. No matter how pure a decision we make, if we look closely at all parts of our mind, we will see other motives. The question we must ask ourselves is, "Are we basing our choices on the better side of our nature or on the darker side?" and not, "Do we have a darker side?" for of course we do.

MONEY AND THE MIND

can motives ever be pure?　We have two sources of motivation, one is peaceful, the other is conflicted, and these urgings of the heart and of the ego can be heard anytime we care to listen. If you are to some extent wealthy, beautiful, famous, or have other characteristics that the world places great value on, you can't expect your partner to have no excitement about that or not to have some other purely human reaction. And if you are the one marrying or are already married to such a person, you will not have only neutral thoughts about your spouse. Don't assume that you can remain completely unaffected by what our culture is caught up in. Look closely at your fantasies, write down your thoughts, or in some other way bring your feelings about these more glamourous. aspects of your partner fully into consciousness. Once you see these feelings, you can decide for yourself how extensively they have affected you, what your true motives are, and whether there is anything you need to do to connect more strongly with your core.

Because of the fear and guilt that surround the subject of money, we can almost always become conscious of hidden motives that don't seem completely pure whenever financial questions arise. A friend of ours, a single mother with three children, came to us because she was concerned that she didn't really love the man she was going to marry. On a number of occasions she had caught herself thinking how wonderful it was going to be not to have to worry anymore about money. At the same time several friends had congratulated her on landing such a "good catch," and while they hadn't come right out and said she must be marrying him for his money, she felt this was implied.

She grew to doubt her motivation, even though she had fallen in love with this man before she knew how large his salary was, and now she was worrying that she wasn't being completely honest with him. She told us that trying to figure out what she felt and what to do about it was driving her crazy. It was also beginning to create distance between the two of them. He had even asked her if anything was wrong, and she had just put him off.

Most of us have had similar experiences. We take something happy and fortuitous and use it as an opportunity to attack ourselves. It's always possible to get in touch with some selfish or even cruel thought, but that doesn't mean we are being controlled by it. And yet we worry that in some way it is influencing us, or once influenced us, or might influence us in the future.

We asked her if she was happy about the fact that he made a good living and that she and her children wouldn't have to pennypinch. She said she was, but maybe she shouldn't be. "Money shouldn't be an issue, should it?" she asked. We pointed out that in this situation money was an issue only in her mind, nowhere else. Then we asked her a series of questions to help her pin down her ego thoughts and clarify her real feelings.

Did she want to break up with her fiancé and go out and look for a man who was broke? Absolutely not! she said.

Did she want to cancel the wedding because her fiancé had too much money? No, she didn't want to cancel it.

Did she want to postpone the wedding until she was certain that not a single strand of doubt about her motivation existed? No, that would be silly, she said.

Did she want to postpone the wedding until her friends had no doubts? No.

Did she believe that her fiancé could read her mind? No.

Did she believe that he could tell her with complete and perfect accuracy what her motivation was? No.

Did she believe that he could *make* her certain that she had nothing to worry about? No.

Then did she want to pass her doubts along to her fiancé and get him to worry about her motivation also? No.

So what did her ego want her to do?

She thought about this for a minute, then she said that it wanted her to worry and to feel guilty because the man she loved also made a good living and could provide a better life for her and the children. In other words, she saw what we all see when we look closely at an ego thought: that the logic is faulty, and that the effect is always to cause distance.

Our friend married her fiancé, and except for the usual problems of growing accustomed to living together, of fitting her children into their new routine, and so forth, they have been remarkably happy ever since. She said to us recently that having gotten over the fears, one night when they were reminiscing about the wedding, she had told him about having had them in the days leading up to the ceremony. After he got through laughing—because he had thought at the time that her preoccupation was over his being too old—he said that being able to provide her children with all the things they hadn't had before was one of his greatest pleasures in life. He said that before they married, he had actually been looking forward to helping her children, and it had never occurred to him that she might be marrying him just for his money.

thinking less about money   The attitude you both want is the willingness to seek creative solutions that fit the two of you and that can move your relationship past money preoccupations. This usually requires a little experimentation. Many couples have separate checking accounts, keep close track of expenditures, share the rent or mortgage payments, and always pay each other

back. For other couples, everything is shared and a strict accounting may not be necessary. We have some friends who, except for a
small checking account to pay utility bills, keep all of their money
in the house and pay cash for everything. Another couple we
know appear to live almost entirely off of coupons. They also go
to bed before they need to turn on a light; they flush the toilet only
every few days, they never finance a car, and they take their own
trash to the dump.

The key to achieving financial harmony is to understand what
money means to each of you and then to work out a way of
dealing with it that considers the fears and desires of both of you.
These of course will probably conflict. But you are not trying to
achieve some kind of perfect compromise. What you want is a
balance, a harmony, a way of proceeding that allows both of you
to think as little about money as possible.

For many years we shared a "well-matched" need to be spontaneous and free, especially with money. Sometimes our reaction
to the financial trouble this would bring was to become overly
anxious and penurious. Instead of merely adopting a more prudent
approach to spending, we would worry over every expenditure.
We would buy clothes, tools, or appliances that were so cheap,
they would end up falling apart, and how long we lectured John
and Jordan on what they had lost or broken would depend on how
expensive the item was.

Eventually we learned to look carefully at the thoughts and
feelings that constituted our desire to save money, and then to
explore ways that could satisfy this urge simply and harmlessly.
For example, instead of never buying the more expensive organic
fruits and vegetables that were good for us, we were more careful
about not letting things spoil in the refrigerator and brought home
fewer prepared foods. Instead of automatically taking the boys to a
movie every time one of them was bored, we began playing more
baseball, basketball, and tennis with them.

The most drastic step we took came about in part because of

the distress we felt over making John and Jordan cut back on the various little expenditures that meant a great deal to them—being able to play video games when we were at a convenience store, being able to get "The Big Slurp" at a movie, even though they never finished it—as well as some larger expenses. We called a family meeting in which we asked them which they would rather have, a large house like the one we lived in at the time, or a smaller house and more money to do the kinds of things they loved (roller-skating, skiing, remote-control car racing, collecting baseball cards, going to baseball card shows, attending special baseball camps, and so on). This was not an easy decision, because they both liked where we lived, but they were clear that they would rather have the freedom that the extra money would bring. As a result of this meeting and because we too realized that we would rather have this extra freedom for ourselves, we decided to sell our house and to rent.

Shortly after the meeting, and possibly because we had made the decision out of love, some people we had never met called and asked if we would be willing to sell our house. They said they would offer us a profit and that there would be no agent's commission. We have moved several times as a family, but this turned out to be the easiest one of all, and it had the happiest results.

The difference between this approach and the one we used to have is that we didn't waste time blaming each other for our common problem. We also didn't spend time blaming our parents for creating financially irresponsible children. We accepted the situation, discussed alternatives, and when we had one that we thought might work, we discussed it with our children and decided to try it. The process actually strengthened our relationship at the same time that it allowed us to become less fearful financially.

but surely money can make money problems disappear

Most couples believe that their financial problems would go away if they had "enough" money, but we have never known a case in which this belief was borne out. Until you change your thoughts about money, your financial problems only switch wardrobes. We have worked with several couples who had tremendous amounts of money, which simply created a different set of problems every bit as disturbing to their marriage as those of the average relationship. Stories of people who suddenly become famous and rich, win the lottery, or develop a booming business, seldom end happily.

One woman we knew had inherited a large estate, had a girl by her first marriage, and was on her fourth marriage when we met her. She could not shake the belief that her husbands had been attracted to her for her money, and yet she was the one who always left them, dragging her child along with her. After her third divorce she became suicidal and her drinking problem became more pronounced. And while we could see that her fourth husband was a thoughtful caring man who loved her and her daughter, she could not accept this. They are still together, but her fear about money, as well as her multiple divorces, are making it difficult for her to form a deep commitment. Her estate has grown, and so she has even more money than ever, yet she is also more unhappy and lonelier than ever.

Another common money problem that only changes form is seen in the lives of some couples who struggle for years to achieve their goal to become financially and socially successful, only to break up when the goal is achieved. Suddenly the partner who supported you while you were on the way up isn't good enough for the pinnacle itself. What is needed now is a trophy partner, someone who wouldn't be with you if you weren't rich and prominent. How many of these trophies are still around when the person they attached themselves to becomes old and tired?

EVERYDAY MONEY ISSUES

the path you walk is composed of problems   There is no end to the problems that can arise between partners and certainly this holds true for money issues. Many of these will center on the question of how money should be spent. In one marriage we encountered, the wife was critical of the husband for buying Häagen-Dazs ice cream instead of a less expensive brand, yet she insisted that they lease a Lear jet whenever they traveled. Even though he would not have chosen to fly by private plane, the husband could afford the expense, and with great good humor, routinely made this concession. He also continued to buy the brand of ice cream he wanted and would simply laugh off his wife's objections. The issue over ice cream remained a minor one because the partner who indisputably had the financial power within the relationship exercised it gently and fairly. However, we were told of another marriage that did break up over a minor food expenditure. The wife bought an extra head of lettuce against her husband's wishes and this, he explained to us, had been "the final straw."

Both the wife who objected to Häagen-Dazs and the husband who objected to extra lettuce argued their positions to us quite seriously and well. Both of them are considered by their friends and associates to be mentally normal. However, most of the problems that you will encounter that revolve around how money should be spent will seem more substantial to you than ice cream and lettuce, especially at the time they arise. Does one of you "need" a cordless drill; does the other one "need" a pasta maker? How many times should you eat out or go to a movie? How expensive should your vacations be? When is a new car really necessary, and how practical a model should it be? Has the time come to replace the living room couch or could it simply be reupholstered? Does one of you "need" cosmetic surgery; does the other one "need" a full membership at the spa? Should you move your child to a private school? Should you buy him or her new shoes simply because the style has changed? And so forth.

Each of these plus a thousand other what-to-spend-it-on issues can become a sufficient problem between the two of you that your relationship is seriously threatened. Yet within the normal course of a marriage, many other money issues can arise that seem even more charged than these. For example, the question of how income, debt, and assets are to be divided between the two of you: Will there be an exact accounting of everything or should all expenses be shared? If they are shared, will this include cigarettes, which one of you may feel is killing the other? Will it include food, in which one of you may feel the other is overindulging? Will it include child support, a prior circumstance one of you had no part in creating? And so forth.

And if all expenses arc shared, will all income be shared as well? What if one of you makes substantially more than the other —should a value be assigned to career encouragement and moral support, to housework and child care? Should sharing include cash birthday presents, bonuses, inheritances, and the like? Should it include the winnings from a contest that one of you thought was silly to enter? Perhaps it should include having a joint banking account. But if so, what kind of account? Would it be wise to open a separate savings or investment account as well?

This leads into another area of special difficulty, the question of future financial security. Should money ever be borrowed? Should credit cards be paid off immediately? What about lottery tickets or risky investments? Should both of you work? If so, should both jobs be traditional salaried positions providing regular income? What of the hard feelings that may come from one of you earning more than the other? Should you have insurance on your household possessions? Is life insurance a good idea? If so, should a child from another marriage be listed among the beneficiaries? Would it be wise for one of you to set up payroll deductions for a pension plan, and if so, should the other partner be required to match this in some way? And on and on.

Perhaps you can see or already know from experience that trying to negotiate each of these questions on the grounds of what your separate egos think is reasonable will inevitably lead to one of you feeling slighted and resentful, perhaps even terrified. It may also be clear to you that each problem settled in this way merely generates new questions for the future, since no agreement can anticipate all the ways that the present decision will play out. A forced agreement or even a purely negotiated one provides no real groundwork for unanticipated difficulties. Marriage, like life, is "just one thing after another." **A successful relationship is not one in which there are fewer problems, but one in which an ease of facing problems together has developed.**

We have already explored some of the reasons why money issues have a life and death quality to most people, and we will discuss this even further under "wills and inheritances." Insights into the causes of your particular money problem can be helpful, but to recognize that here is an area of special difficulty for you personally is enough to begin. You shouldn't think that you have to uncover all the antecedents of this problem before you can deal with it effectively.

The money issue before you today, just as any other issue would be, is a problem only because it has become more important than your relationship. Your overall goal is to restore the love between you to its proper place in your life. Once you have done this, this particular issue will be solved through a change or will simply cease to matter.

Issues over money should not be approached differently than other issues. In fact, this is an essential key to all problem resolution: **Do not take a problem out of context and treat it as special with rules all its own.** There are several areas of difficulty that are often approached in this mistaken way—sex, children from another marriage, illness, and in-laws are four common examples. But money is perhaps the most poorly handled issue of all.

Money is not a reasonable subject because the world has been wrapping it in layers of insanity for centuries. And indeed this insanity comes close to being "the root of all evil." You can't expect one another to somehow be immune to attitudes that are so deeply embedded in the human psyche. This is why it's important that you not insist that your partner be calm and rational about *any* money issue. You simply must take each other where you are and be a true friend.

As we have stressed throughout this book, we live during a time in which one's partner is expected to be ideal in all ways, that is, to meet *our* needs and live up to *our* expectations perfectly. Little wonder that most marriages fail whereas most friendships don't. Friends see each other clearly and make accommodations for differences. Surely some of your personal friends have behaved quite bizarrely at times, yet still you remain loyal. "That's just the way they are," perhaps you say to yourself. Obviously this is also the most helpful position to take toward your spouse. Having done this much, you are now in a position to see what mutual accommodations are possible. There is always a way around any issue, and that includes money.

a general procedure   The approach to all relationship problems includes awareness, open-mindedness, creative application, and stillness. We recommend the following six steps as one method of identifying and moving your relationship past a money issue. You will notice that these are merely a special adaptation of the "How to Have a Real Argument" section found in Chapter Eight.

1. Regardless of how often you have argued about this subject, you can be certain that you are not fully aware of all the ways the issue enters your mind and every reaction you have to these

thoughts. For two weeks, carry a small notebook wherever you go. Any time you find yourself thinking about money or anything that you have associated with money in the past, write down a few identifying words about the main ideas and feelings you are having. As you go through the day, be especially alert to your internal reaction to circumstances that symbolize money—hearing a stock exchange report on the radio, noticing the bills that are mixed in with the mail you pick up, driving past a bank, seeing a store that is having a sale, walking past a homeless person, and so on.

2. At the end of each week, review all of your entries at one sitting. You will notice not only certain patterns of thinking but also the operation of your prime thought in all of this.* For example, if your prime thought is "I will always be alone," you may recognize it in the entry you made when you drove by an automatic teller machine and saw someone of the opposite sex getting money. Perhaps the fleeting thought was a fantasy that this person was getting the money to buy a gift for his or her lover and that there would never be anyone who would love you that deeply. Or when you saw a group of well-dressed people outside an expensive restaurant, you recorded the feeling that this part of society would never welcome you, that you would always be an outsider to moneyed people. Or while balancing the checkbook one evening, perhaps you caught the thought that if you were ever in really desperate circumstances, there would be no one in the world who would be willing to sacrifice their money to bail you out.

3. Share these insights but don't read each other's notebooks. Be very understanding and supportive but don't give each other advice. The purpose of this sharing is to practice listening deeply and being each other's friend.

4. Divide the issue into its separate parts and take up only one of them. For example, instead of trying to decide whose money and how much of it should be spent on a child from another

---

* See Chapter Five, "Prime Thoughts—Core Dynamics."

marriage, consider only whether, for instance, one visit to the dentist should be paid for now. Would each of you contribute and if so, in what proportion? Do not get into whether something should be done about the other ways this child is expensive, whether this child has been manipulative about money in the past, whether other money grievances between the two of you are valid, and so forth. Concentrate on one small question that can be decided today.

5. Because fears are easier to let go of than wants, put your exchange of ideas in terms of what you are afraid of rather than what you demand. You have just established the groundwork for this in steps 2 and 3. You should now be able to express feelings you have already identified such as "I'm afraid this dental expense is just the next step toward uncontrolled spending." Or "I'm afraid that by not sharing this expense with me you're demonstrating that you don't realize how important my child is to me." Rather than "I want you to go to court and get the medical part of your divorce agreement expanded to include dental." Or "I want you to make my child's teeth more important than a new sound system for your car."

6. Before you each offer suggestions on how you can join together and move your relationship past this one issue, first take a moment to remember how important is the love between you. You can do this silently or if you wish, play some game such as listing out loud six or eight pleasant memories that you have of each other. Use any procedure or mental process that jogs your memory of what is really going on here between you. You are not merely solving a money issue; you are building a friendship that can last a lifetime and beyond.

WILLS AND INHERITANCES

the aftermath   We recently heard a minister say, "If there's a devil, he appears in the form of wills." After a parent or close relative dies, after the personal items are distributed, and after the will is read and probated, it is almost inevitable that one or more of the heirs will feel cheated. The anger and frustration generated by the dispersal of a loved one's possessions can create enough animosity to split families for a lifetime. Brothers and sisters who have always been close will stop speaking and assume the worst about each other's motivations. The rest of the family will often divide into warring factions, support different sides, and escalate the hostilities by reporting what one sibling said about another. If the heirs are not in conflict with each other, they are likely to feel cheated by the lawyers involved. All of these resentments can endure with surprising force.

It also rarely matters how large an estate is, because relatives can separate over what may seem to an outsider a trivial issue. We both grew up hearing tales of familial battles that would make good soap opera fare. Gayle's mother told her about a family she knew in the little town where she grew up. When the matriarchal grandmother was dying, her three daughters began sneaking things out of the house. This was extraordinarily distressing to this elderly woman, but no one would discuss it with her or even admit that it was occurring. Instead, they tried to convince her that she had just forgotten giving the things away. She had been a strong woman who had always been able to control her own affairs, and this made her final year a miserable and lonely one. According to Gayle's mother, who knew all three, the daughters hadn't really intended to act this way, but they couldn't just "sit back" and let another sister "take everything." After their mother's death they couldn't even remember how it had gotten started, but they were so afraid that they would be cheated that they hadn't been able to stop. And of course, it drove a wedge of guilt between them that remained the rest of their lives.

Even an individual who recognizes the insanity and doesn't get physically involved can come away feeling cheated. After Gayle's grandmother died, her grandfather married a young woman who survived him for many years. When she in turn died, all of the possessions that had belonged to Gayle's grandmother and grandfather went to her stepgrandmother's family instead of to Gayle's father. There were not a large number of possessions and there was no money, so her father chose not to contest, even though he would very much have liked to have a few remembrances of his mother and father. Gayle doesn't know how her father continued to feel about this, but she, who didn't really want anything of her grandparents', felt resentful of the family for how they had deprived her father and carried this little bit of mental poison around for many years.

prevention and correction   In a society in which people are willing to kill each other over a slight on the freeway, it's probably unrealistic to expect the division of property to be harmonious. And so it's important to acknowledge the difficulty and not fight the feelings you have. There isn't some magical approach to handling wills and inheritances, but being very conscious of what you are doing with your mind is necessary if you are going to keep from bringing a polluting thought into your relationship. As in all situations, you can choose to react from the peace of your heart rather than from the small-mindedness of the ego. Choosing peace does not mean that you must act out a particular role—i.e., that of the selfless sibling who sacrifices all for the welfare of the family.

If you know that a relative's property will soon be dispersed, you can take several steps to protect your mind and, thus, your marriage:

- Remind yourself of the basic innocence of each member of your family, of the lawyers, and of anyone else who will be involved, and build your determination to

keep this truth in mind during the upcoming events.
Do this before the dispersal begins, because once people start taking positions on money, it is very difficult
to remember innocence.

· Acknowledge how fearful most people are about possessions and money, and specifically acknowledge
which members of your family are likely to be most
fearful and in what ways. Fantasize about some of the
things they might do, and picture yourself responding
from the core of your being. This is not an exercise of
deciding beforehand what actions you will or will not
take. It is more important than that. You wish to
imagine yourself going through all that is to come
deeply connected to who you are, so that you will be
more likely to act accordingly.

· Make the decision *now* that you will not overreact,
that you will not do more than is necessary. When
you do more than you want to do or say or do more
than you need to, it becomes very difficult to stay
focused. However, if you make a mistake, prepare in
advance to forgive yourself and to return to your single purpose, which is to come out of this with your
peace intact and carrying as little bitterness back into
your marriage as possible.

As difficult as it is to contemplate death, there is one practical
gift each of us can leave our children: a clear and unequivocal will
that goes beyond the so-called liquid assets and also allots personal possessions to specific people. These personal possessions
often evoke the most emotion because they represent one's history
and childhood. They have a symbolic value that can overwhelm
any decision for "rational, adult behavior" by brothers and sisters
who have always been close and who never believed they could
fight over their parents' things.

Gayle's mother had a friend who, as she neared the end of her

life, began to write the names of her children on adhesive tape and
put these on the bottoms of all of her nicest possessions. After her
death this did not prevent them from getting upset about who got
what, but rather than getting angry with each other, they got angry
with her, which, in a sense, was her last sacrifice and gift to them.
Before this woman died, she told Gayle's mother that she had not
mentioned to her children that she had done this, so that they
wouldn't lobby for specific things and also so that she wouldn't be
tempted to punish them by threatening to withhold something. All
of this can seem quite petty until we remember the symbolism.
What we inherit from our parents is their last tangible gift to us,
but the kind of thoughtfulness that this woman showed can be
more valuable than money and possessions alone.

When thoughts of money take a dominant position in the mind,
the relationship one is in begins dying from lack of thought and
attention. This is true whether the amount of money is too much,
too little, or as we have seen, "enough." The more one's life
revolves around a thing that can't feed the soul, the deeper the
disturbance it will bring. This is why you never want to take
money issues out of the context of problems in general and raise
them to some untouchable position. Instead, you want to treat
them as you would any other issue that comes between you. That
is, you want to understand each other's positions; you want to feel
each other's fears; then you want to open your minds to any possible way that you can move beyond the difficulty, discarding what
doesn't work, starting over as often as necessary.

THIRTEEN

I Will Never Leave You: The Six Promises of a Real Relationship

"I PROMISE NOT TO QUESTION YOUR NEEDS."

This is the opening commitment in the vows we use when we marry a couple. Before two people can recognize in what ways they join, they must see and accept the ways they do not join—not as eternal truths, but as deeply held beliefs about themselves and each other. Accepting your partner's needs removes the first block to oneness.

During the honeymoon stage, lovers have little difficulty not questioning each other's needs. For example, the decision of what movie or restaurant to go to is made easily. It's almost as if they knew beforehand which one it would be. If one partner needs to be held and reassured, this is asked for and given effortlessly. Then, as the energy of the honeymoon stage lessens, and as the partners begin to withdraw more and more into their separate interests, even little decisions can become enormously difficult. Now they have different needs, and their needs conflict.

A husband may come in from a hectic day at work and want to rest and be quiet, whereas his wife, who has been home all day, is ready to get out and see other people. Or the wife may also work, but when she comes home, her husband expects her to cook, clean, and take care of the children, as if it were her duty to return to a traditional role for this one segment of the day.

As we have indicated before, a real relationship will eventually enter a second honeymoon, one that will not fade away. This honeymoon is based on the fulfillment and love that come after two people have struggled long and successfully to break out of their separate egos. Now the partners find that making decisions is once again easy and that meeting each other's needs is a pleasure.

a more practical approach to needs   Please do not misconstrue what we mean when we say that you should not questions your partner's needs. Naturally, we don't mean that you should blankly accept whatever your partner wants to do, or that you should condone addictions, abusive behavior, or destructive urges— alcoholism, gambling addiction, sexual disorders, drug abuse, battering, and so forth. These special problems may require an extreme response, and fortunately twelve-step groups that specialize in most of these difficulties, as well as other organizations, centers, and individual therapists, are available to help you decide what to do or how to treat your spouse. Be certain, though, that the behavior your relationship has to deal with is truly abusive or self-destructive. Almost every human trait has now been dubbed by some expert as addictive or abusive, causing many couples unnecessary concern.

Bodily needs are among the many common needs that your relationship will be called upon to deal with. A need to rest, a need to eat, a need to withdraw, and a need for sex are a few of the easier ones to understand. But your childhood also sets up certain needs that you would be better off accepting rather than blindly classifying as pathological. Obviously all of our families were dysfunctional in some ways, and we all show the results. But here we are.

Is it really helpful to our relationships to look on common human traits as shame-based codependent illnesses? Many, many people have a strong need to get away frequently and be by themselves. Why must this be classified as a "toxic preoccupation with privacy"? Many, many people love to shop. Why must they be called "shopaholics"? And why must someone who will argue about anything be called "verbally abusive" and someone who will never argue be called "passively abusive"? In our experience, very few people have a partner with a true psychological disorder. We are all a little screwed up, and that's just the way it is. It is simply easier and more practical for you to be relaxed about the human condition, to take each other the way you are, and to begin the work of carefully removing the blocks to love.

The journey to oneness, which we have been pointing to throughout this book, must be undertaken as an act of faith, because you have not yet fully experienced it. If you wait to see your way through to the state of permanent compatibility that awaits you, if you hold back your commitment and devotion until you are certain that you will attain a real relationship with this particular partner, then you will never begin the journey. Perhaps the observation that every journey begins with a single step is a cliché, but many of the simple facts of marriage have been rejected today on the grounds that they have been too well known for too long. Better to have a new belief than an old truth. Yet love offers you truth, and to have love you must begin. An excellent first step is to acknowledge that you each have separate needs, to see and accept those needs, and to commit to helping each other meet them.

the substance and form of a need   For partners to try to classify each other's needs as either "legitimate" or "inappropriate" often sets in place judgmental feelings that can last as long as the needs last—and needs can last a very long time. Perhaps a more helpful distinction is between the need and the assumption of how it must be met. For example, many people have a need to conserve money, a need for carefully and thriftily managed affairs. Their need is *not* to leave a small tip on all occasions—that is merely one way they may choose to meet it.

Needs can be met in ways that do not hurt others, but until we are ready to relinquish them, they must be met, otherwise we may end up creating a far greater problem for the relationship. A time comes when we have seen through a need and now can safely resist it. If we are correct in our assessment, the need melts away in the face of our resolve. But until that time is reached, needs must be recognized and nondisruptive ways of satisfying them must be found. Whenever we neglect to do this, we risk being swept up in an overall ego revolt, depression being a common signal that this has occurred.

One very common need that often goes unmet, especially in the West, is the need to withdraw, to rest, to slow down. People bolt down their food, return early from vacations, force their bodies to sleep less, risk accident trying to make a light, shorten conversations through abruptness, and skip important family events. The results, especially in terms of illness, are perhaps most obvious during winter, when the body's rhythms shift to a slower pace, as they do with most of Earth's creatures. Yet this natural rhythm is ignored by industrialized humans in their attempt to carry on business as usual, especially in any activity that involves money. As a consequence, many people feel bad during the colder months, and this of course affects their attitude toward their partner and children.

Ignoring your own needs for calm and rest will definitely hurt your relationship, but this doesn't mean that you should force each other to conform to some mental picture you may have of the perfectly paced person. In all areas of your life, you must accept that your needs for time off and for limits, and even your metabolisms, will differ. One partner may be more of a "morning person"; the other may get a burst of energy in the evenings. One partner may like to take naps; the other may like nonstop activity. One may walk faster, talk faster, clean house faster, and so forth.

Like all differences, the need for action and the need for rest can complement each other—if the partners will begin to form the habit of helping one another be happy.

can you make your partner happy?   Don't be fooled into thinking that you can make each other angry, but you can't make each other happy. And yet the insane idea that we are not responsible for each other, that we are not able to nurture positive feelings in each other although we are capable of nurturing countless negative ones, has been repeated so often that most people now accept it as a universal truth.

If we can make dogs happy, children happy, and even cats happy, certainly we can make adults happy, especially an adult we know very very well.

This is not to say it's easy. But it's always a possibility. During an argument, we know exactly what buttons to push. The same tactics would not necessarily work on anyone else. Another person might even laugh at the very words that make our own partner cry. We can affect our partner because we know our partner—but we have little practice in using this knowledge to encourage, to comfort, to warm, to make laugh, to make happy. Learning how to reverse a long habit of misusing knowledge definitely requires study and effort, but it can be done.

When Jim, an old friend of ours, first began trying to make Betty, his second wife, happy, it seemed as if his efforts were always being misinterpreted. He was continually being caught off guard by her reaction to his "perfectly innocent" remarks and actions. What he didn't realize was that he got these results because he was trying to get *results*. He was trying to change Betty, not to see her and love her. He was approaching making happy the same way he had approached making unhappy—that is, he was acting at a distance instead of from oneness.

At our suggestion Jim made two lists, one containing everything that he thought *should* make Betty happy and the other, everything that he had seen or that she had told him made her happy. This exercise was not as easy to complete as Jim had expected, because his irritation about how his wife *should* react kept getting in the way of his honesty. Frequently he had to close his eyes and mentally "feel" her reactions to past situations, and on several points he had to experiment. He would say or do something and observe closely her response—even though he had been married to her eleven years and should have known her reactions as well as his own!

Betty was an attorney—in fact, one of the most successful trial lawyers in the state. "One would think," Jim later said to us, "that she would like to talk about deeper things than the weather and the he-said-she-said stuff from the office." Jim had finally acknowledged that his wife liked to chit-chat, that she really did want his opinion on her nail polish, that she liked flowers and romantic settings, that she liked their doing things on the spur of the moment, that she wanted to be left alone when she was upset, that the pictures and mementoes she had kept from the past meant a great deal to her, and that she did not want to be kidded. Even more deeply, Jim realized that Betty had to some degree lost herself in his expectations that she be mature and profound on all occasions. Only then did he remember that the very qualities that he thought were somehow beneath Betty as a professional woman were actually the ones that had attracted him to her in the first place and were what he still loved about her the most.

We make our partners cry, scream, pout, fume, and withdraw because—for the moment, at least—we don't like them. The dislike takes our knowledge of our partner and informs us what to do with it. We don't even have to think about how this is done. If it seems that an argument isn't going our way, we instinctively begin attacking our partner's weak spots—and often get the results we want.

Likewise, **making someone happy becomes a possibility only when we like them.** Jim, for example, would try to manipulate

Betty into a better mood when she was angry. His words and actions were calculating rather than caring. He finally learned that he made Betty happy, not by cajoling, cheering her up, or turning her on, not by deciding what would make "any reasonable person" happy, but by identifying with Betty, knowing her, becoming her, being her, liking her—which is something we all do naturally with a good friend or a young child. Notice that parents who deeply love their kids *act* like kids when they play with them. They don't think this out; it is simply the natural outcome of empathy. *Love* is the focus we need to make our partner happy, not technique.

meeting each other's needs   A partnership begins with
total, absolute acceptance. You simply look at each other and say,

> You are my partner.
> This is your mood today.
> This is how you are acting today.
> This is how you look today.
> Everything about you is my partner.

So what do you see? One of you has a need to control, but not always. One of you has a need to watch sports, but not always. One of you has a need to talk on the phone, but not always. One of you has a need to sleep late, but not always. One of you has a need for cleanliness, but not always. One of you has a need to prepare special dinners for guests, but not always.

So here is where you begin. As you look a little deeper, perhaps you discover that some of these are needs and some are ways to satisfy a need. You don't necessarily make a decision about this, but you do remain tentative and flexible, and always willing to experiment. And thus you set about building an accommodation for all aspects of your personalities within the relationship, like a

mother bird building a strong nest to encircle each little demanding beak that will soon be there.

We don't have to continue buying into the current philosophy
that you should grasp and claw and step over anyone necessary to
get whatever you can think of having, the philosophy that if
there's the slightest chance it will make you happy, regardless
how it affects someone else, "just do it." Surely we can look at
the devastation around us and see that this approach to life has not
worked. And there is one very good reason: **Happiness cannot
survive unshared.**

"I PROMISE TO SEEK YOUR PEACE."

This is the second commitment. It supplies the reason for not
questioning another's needs. When two seek each other's peace,
they find their own, because peace is a single reality. But when
they question one another's needs, they falsely assume that they
can see their own peace without seeing their partner's. This splits
the mind and makes the experience of peace impossible. *A Course
in Miracles* states: "The ark of peace is entered two by two."

"Seek your peace" has two meanings. The first is literally to
locate it. You already know where each other's discomfort lies;
now you must search for each other's peace. There is no greater
treasure, yet you will have to struggle to find it.

The second meaning is that you seek to be a source of peace in
one another's life. For too long you have been a burden; you have
made life more difficult for each other. To become a comfort will
take practice, but it is a lovely art that rewards deeply. Your temptation will be to wait until the other begins, thinking that if you go
first, or if you do more, you will lose. Yet how can becoming the
person you want to be cost you anything but failure?

Finding peace and giving it are accomplished the same way—
by making peace the single goal in all that you do: drive in peace,

get up with the kids in peace, eat in peace, argue in peace, clean the toilet in peace, hire and fire in peace, get sick in peace, win the lottery in peace, get depressed in peace. You feel your stillness and you don't let go. And if you lose it, you pause long enough to regain it. Just a little inner quietness is enough.

Being at peace does not mean acting or looking peaceful. It doesn't mean shutting down the emotions or placing a limit on enjoyment. It has nothing to do with rigidity or phoniness. Peace is not an affect but rather a conscious connection with your core. It does not mean speaking softly, having long eyelashes, wearing pastel colors, smiling a lot, or being above it all. It is simply a quiet decision about who you are, which you do not forget.

"I PROMISE TO PUT OUR HAPPINESS FIRST."

an ancient approach   Those who do not really believe in a reality that endures, who think of themselves as separate and apart, and who have not yet felt the safety of a complete relationship may find this third promise a threat to individuation and self-esteem and thus a danger to themselves and others. And yet to carry out this promise is merely to practice the way love *feels*. Those who walk in love *want* to give to each other; it is their greatest pleasure. They blossom, not wilt, from their acts of joining.

Today much lip service is given to the importance of relationships. It is pointed out by many that each of us is a product of a relationship, that our identities were formed by relationships, and that we never cease to exist in relationship to others. Yet side by side with this line of thought is another that places the limits on the usefulness of relationships, for you are also told that you are ultimately alone, that your happiness and fulfillment are solely in your own hands, that you should not take on other people's problems, and that most people suffer from fuzzy boundaries and inadequate individuation.

Behind our house is a big paloverde tree that evidently took root under the large rock that breaks the desert surface just beside it. The early growth of the tree was shaped by its need to circle around the rock to reach the sun, and now its trunk is twisted and its entire branch system leans to one side. As its roots have grown, they have begun to enter the rock and are slowly splitting it.

The tree and the rock have a relationship. Some today might even say it's a codependent relationship. And yet because they can't escape their identities, the tree and the rock have not given birth to a third reality that encompasses them both and is stronger and more beautiful than either of them alone. That third reality is what we have been referring to in this book as a real relationship, and it begins forming whenever two people struggle to walk past their egos—in other words, to walk beyond their fear that love will diminish their separate selves, discount their dreams, ignore their needs, and block their growth and fulfillment. And to keep walking until they know a love that has no fear.

Today, too many couples are not getting beyond their fears. In fact, they are being encouraged to cling to them like a safety line that will catch them when love inevitably fails. Proceeding from fear, naturally they form a restricted relationship, one with clear boundaries and safeguards. They agree to share only those moments of intimacy that will end, in order to give them time to withdraw and build back their separate selves. They agree only to a cautious friendship, one that they vigilantly monitor and continuously reappraise. They do contract to marry, but only with the "right" of separateness included—the right to come together when they prefer and withdraw whenever they elect. Thus they protect their alliance against the treachery of love, which waits below them like a giant blender, its blades furiously spinning, ready to make of them an indistinct mass of agreeableness, sweetness, and mindless harmony.

Although today selfishness is trusted and love is feared, the grounds for this remarkable attitude do not exist. Even on the simplest level, most of us know that it's usually more fun to give a present than to get one, but we don't then carry this to the extreme of refusing to receive. And when we look back at those people who trusted love to guide them in all aspects of their lives, we see that they were not weak and indistinct figures, and certainly they were not unfulfilled. Love's influence on those who devote themselves to it is celebrated in virtually all sacred scriptures. It is singled out as the one path to heaven or Everything and *not* as a distant reward that comes after a life of sacrifice and drudgery. Saint John wrote: "If we love one another, God abides in us and his love is brought to perfection in us. . . . God is love, and those who love dwell in God, and God dwells in them."

Nowhere in the wisdom of the ages is it stated that "you can only make yourself happy" or that "you are responsible for yourself and no one else." In fact, so confident were these holy ones in the safety of love's effect on those who practice it that many of them, as Mother Teresa has done, stated their way of life even more radically than "love one another." If asked to write this third commitment in the wedding vows, they probably would word it, "I promise to put *your* happiness first," and would be confident that by each pledging to do the same, no possible damage could result to anyone. Saint Paul wrote, "Each must seek, not his own good, but the good of his neighbor. . . . Even Christ did not please himself." The *Bhagavad Gita* states, "The gift given to one who does nothing in return . . . is a pure gift."

The Prayer of Saint Francis, believed by many to have been written over seven hundred years ago, is one of our favorite expressions of this ideal. Several versions of it exist; here is one:

Today, let me be an instrument of Thy peace.
Where there is hatred, let me sow love;
Where there is injury, pardon;
Where there is discord, union;
Where there is doubt, faith;

Where there is darkness, light;
Where there is sadness, joy.

May I not so much seek
To be consoled, as to console;
To be understood, as to understand;
To be loved, as to love.

For it is in giving that we receive.
It is in pardoning that we are pardoned.
And it is in dying to self
That we are born to eternal life.

unbalancing the two needs   The lovely progression spelled out in this prayer is descriptive of the stages of a relationship. Every line is a line about how to relate. And it is striking that love and forgiveness (pardon) are mentioned twice, and that the entire prayer begins with the word *today*.

The prayer's promise is that as we de-emphasize our ''need'' to be always getting and instead emphasize our ability to give, we die to smallness and awaken to our limitless nature. In marriage, for example, to focus on nourishing ourselves first feeds the conviction that we are merely a needy body, a damaged and lacking self, whereas to shift our focus to extending the best of ourselves to our partner acknowledges our abundance, our boundless spiritual resources.

As we have said throughout this book, you must never *ignore* your needs, but at the same time, you don't wish to make satisfying them the driving purpose of everything you do. To paraphrase an Eastern saying:

Learn to meet your needs with your left foot.

If we are to move past the unequal and often loveless relationship pattern of the mid-1900s and past the uncommitted and frequently selfish relationship pattern of the last few decades, we will need a radical approach, something that will allow us to experience a reality that lies beyond both the illusion of stability and the illusion of freedom.

This third promise that you give each other is such an approach. However, by using it you will attempt to throw yourselves into the arms of something that you may not know is there, and in doing so you can expect very little approval from others for your efforts. Why then would you do this? Because nothing else is working.

So make this promise to each other now, and begin the work of learning how to carry it out. Start simply by *guessing* what you think would make your marriage happier, and put it first. Take excellent care of your body and your emotional needs, yet still put your relationship first. Eventually you will find that these do not conflict.

Break down your life together into every tiny event and circumstance, and as each one arises, ask yourself, "In this situation I am in now, what is our happiness?" In all the little decisions you make throughout the day, ask yourself, "What is the most loving, the kindest, the most nourishing thing I can do for our life together?" And do it.

Obviously you will not be consistent about this. There will be long periods when you will not want to put your marriage first and won't put it first. We are speaking here of a goal, of an option, that will take you forward each time you exercise it.

It is our sacred responsibility, our spiritual practice, and our holy path, to give to something outside of our smallness, but it is also the key to personal happiness and to a good, sound, healthy, growing relationship. As you practice this approach and grow in understanding of what it means and does not mean, you will see that it never asks you to sacrifice anything but fear. Love is the blessing that shines in every heart, demanding no reciprocity, demanding not even acknowledgment. You will not harm yourself by becoming more like Love.

"FOR IT IS IN GIVING THAT I RECEIVE,"

the present can't receive from the future   We can look out on the cities and towns where we live and see thousands of people walking on sidewalks, crossing streets, moving inside office buildings, driving cars, taking buses. . . . As we watch, it becomes clear that, although they are purposeful, very few seem happy. Those who do often stand out as somewhat odd or out of step.

Sadly, most people do not drive to be driving, walk to be walking, work to be working, or have relationships to be having relationships. Everyone is going somewhere, but the "where" is just out of reach. They do what they do for an uncertain outcome. Meanwhile, they are confined to the cages of their toil, hoping someday to be released into the bright sunshine of results.

We went to a car wash recently, and a woman who had come in several cars in front of us was at the counter complaining when we went in to pay. She was telling the cashier that the last time she was there, no one had come back to the waiting area to tell her that her car was ready, that instead "they" had parked it. The cashier said that most of their customers waited out front where the people drying the cars could signal when theirs was ready, but that the woman was right, they did have the policy of coming back to the waiting area if no one claimed a car. The woman said that she certainly hoped they would do that this time because she did not have any time to waste.

After sitting for a few minutes, the woman quietly went up to the window that looked out on where the cars were being wiped off and stood there until she saw the car-wash people signaling to those waiting outside that "the blue Pontiac" was ready. Even though this was her car, she went back to her seat. A minute or two later, she again went to the window, saw that they were still signaling, and returned to her seat. When a boy finally came into the office and yelled that the blue Pontiac was ready, she didn't respond until he came closer and called out again, at which time she acted surprised that her car was ready and was loudly approving of having been informed, an act that was lost on everyone in that very busy office—except for the two alert authors who had a book to write.

This woman had set a goal, the goal of being right. She had focused; she had worked hard; and she had stayed overtime at the car wash to complete the task. And remarkably, she had gotten the outward results she wanted, which very often doesn't happen. Yet because she was trying to get rather than trying to give, she was clearly not happy during the process, nor did she make the people around her happy. Which left only the outcome that could possibly compensate her.

Was forcing the young man to come to the waiting area fulfilling? Did she drive off satisfied? Was she or the world better off for her efforts?

doing it to be doing it   Which brings us back to the fourth line of the marriage vows. This of course is borrowed from Saint Francis, who makes clear in his prayer that it is *in* giving, not *from* giving that we receive.

Saint Francis was describing an entirely different approach from the one taken by most of us—to do something just to be doing it, to bring light simply because there is darkness, to bring joy simply because there is sadness. He could have said to God, "If I bring faith, please build me a church. If I bring unity, please draw more followers to me." Not only was he willing to love, pardon, and console for no reward, he made it clear that he was not particularly interested in reward, even the more spiritual ones —"May I not so much seek . . . to be understood, as to understand; to be loved, as to love." He was interested only in the pure act of giving. He knew that "in giving we receive" and that "in dying to self . . . we are born to eternal life," but these he states as mere facts, not as requests. All that he asks of God is that he be allowed to give.

And so it is within a real relationship: In *having* the relationship, moment by moment, day by day, we receive it. But even to ask ourselves if we are receiving it is not the most helpful approach. The practical way to proceed is simply to have it—to be a real partner, to be a real friend, and if the circumstance arises, to be a real parent. It is impossible to relate and not have a relationship, but **it is possible to have a marriage and yet wait forever for the relationship you want to come to you.**

Please remember that in our own case Gayle was faithful and devoted to Hugh for fifteen years—and yet Hugh did not heal. Gayle's devotion to Hugh strengthened her immeasurably, but it was not until Hugh began to devote himself to Gayle that he healed the wounds of his childhood.

"AND IT IS IN HELPING YOU AWAKE THAT I AWAKE."

unreceivable gifts   With this line of the vows, we move from when to give, to what to give. In a relationship only one gift can be received at the same instant it is offered, and that is love in all of its unlimited expressions. As the woman in the car wash demonstrated, being right can't be given, and certainly it can't be received. But can codependence be given? This is the great contagion that so many fear catching if they enter a relationship. And can one partner's quest for personal enhancement and empowerment be a gift to the other partner—or as a spokesman for separation psychology recently said to us (without smiling), "When you put your own needs and happiness first, you will radiate confidence and become more attractive to your partner"?

We were in some heavy traffic the other day and noticed a city bus putting on its brakes about ten or twelve cars ahead of us.

Gayle, who was driving, saw a sufficient gap in the lane on her left and began pulling over, but the driver in that lane who had fallen back realized what she was doing and gunned his car to fill the space. He had been so far back that all he managed to do was to pull partway up beside her and glower. (He was a good glowerer and never wavered in his attitude for the next ten minutes that we saw him in traffic.) Gayle was between lanes when this happened and almost had a wreck trying to move back out of his way. As soon as she got out of danger, she became very upset. Hugh, who wasn't having to brake and swerve, was able to get upset even a few seconds sooner.

Gayle's immediate impulse was to speed up and try to cut in front of the man, then perhaps slow down just to torture him. If she had done this, she and the other driver might have formed a little codependent relationship that could have gone on for miles.

This man had tried to make Gayle feel guilty or to teach her a lesson or something along those lines. He had in a sense tried to give her something. And she had reacted, at least emotionally. But this kind of giving is actually the opposite of the kind that Saint Francis described in his prayer and is not really a gift or extension of oneself that can be received.

The ego tries to give by not giving—that is, by withdrawing, by not empathizing, by attacking, by pulling back, by separating. After the man saw Gayle try to pull into his lane, he felt more separate from her than before, and by putting us in danger and glowering at Gayle, he withdrew even further. His speeding up and glowering were *acts* of separation. Our reaction, which first had to "sink in"—unlike love, which can be felt immediately—was to separate from him. If either of us had tried to act this out, we would have separated even further. People don't actually "take on" negative vibrations, they react to them with negative vibrations of their own—which continue for as long as they choose to continue them.

receivable gifts   A real gift is always a joining, a uniting. A part of me enters you and a part of you enters me, and we feel closer—because we are. In 1989 the 7.1 earthquake that killed more than fifty people in the collapse of highway structures and buildings in the San Francisco–Oakland area was actually centered near Aptos, just three miles from our house. The evening it hit, the boys were there with a teenage babysitter, and we were driving toward Half Moon Bay to meet friends for dinner.

Our car was not damaged, and we immediately turned around and started the sixty-mile trip back. After we had worked our way through the rock slides that covered parts of the highway, we finally reached the Santa Cruz–Capitola–Aptos area, where city lights were out, bridges cracked, many homes were off their foundations, and where the older downtown section of Santa Cruz had been virtually destroyed.

All the way back, we had been listening to the only local radio station that was still on the air, and the stories of death and devastation had brought us close to panic by the time we came to the first series of city intersections. Naturally, no stores or restaurants were open, and so most of the other drivers were just like us— they were trying to get back home or to where they last saw some loved one.

It would be impossible for us to forget what happened at those intersections. Although there were no stoplights functioning, all of the drivers—without exception—were patient and thoughtful. Most people who live in that area have always driven that way— slowing to let other cars enter traffic, stopping for pedestrians no matter where they step off the curb, seldom honking—but on this tragic night they seemed even kinder than usual, and so by the time we located Jordan and John near a neighbor's house—physically unharmed but emotionally traumatized—we carried with us some of the calmness and kindnesses these drivers had extended.

is marriage more likely to generate codependence? As we have said, in our opinion most of the concepts out of which separation psychology grew are sound, but their application to relationships in tapes, books, and workshops is often destructive. For example, except in the form it appears in some of the more extreme definitions, codependence is unquestionably a part of most relationships. However, the impression that many people teaching codependence theory leave is that, although it is present in other areas of our culture, it is more present in marriage, and that if you marry or stay in a marriage "too long," you are more likely to become codependent than if you merely date, cohabit, or have no romantic relationships at all.

Obviously it would take several more books to point out all the ways that unmarried individuals are codependent with friends, their lovers, the mailman, co-workers, people who cut into line, relatives, the Rottweiler next door, their boss, and the bluejay that fusses at them every time they take out the garbage. Until you outgrow it, **your capacity for codependence remains constant whether you are married or unmarried.** There are many effective ways to advance beyond this capacity, but there is no way *more* effective than commitment to a marriage. Marriage simply does not put you in greater danger of being codependent than you already are, but it is an ideal tool for curing it.

can personal enhancement be shared? Taking care of yourself, being happy, meeting your needs, and working on your own growth are not only good things to do, they are an essential part of your contribution to a real relationship. The trouble comes when the word *first* is added to these concepts. If I say, "Our happiness comes before my own," I may be insane or I may be a masochist. *Or* I may want to practice a spiritual reality—that when I give my blessing to you, I am blessed in the same instant. This is the way love is experienced, and the reason is simple: On a heart level we are already joined.

However, if I say, "My happiness comes first," unless I mean that you are already a part of me—which we have never known anyone to mean when they said this—then I believe that I can act and think without affecting others, that I have a separate mind, a separate life, and a separate destiny. And for the ego this is true —but we are more than an ego. And we have far more to give each other than the occasional sharing of a common ego interest.

marriage as a spiritual path   In the seventies, when Hugh first came across *A Course In Miracles,* Gayle saw him go through several months of soul-searching before he came to a surprising conclusion. He had underlined the books extensively (in those days it was published in only three volumes) and had pages of objections to what he had been reading. One day he said to Gayle, "You know how all my life I have been skipping from one spiritual path to another? Here, now, is another path, and I can see that although it's highly flawed, it's adequate. It would get me to God if I followed it. I have made the decision to stop spending my life being a searcher and simply make this my path until the day I die."

Then he asked Gayle if she would join him and make it hers. After looking the books over, she agreed that it *was* sufficient, and it has been our family's path ever since.

Marriage must be like a spiritual path. You find someone who is adequate, and you simply make the decision to stay with that person until the day you die. You will suffer, you will go through one hell after another, but you will not leave. Your back will go out and you'll get migraine headaches, but you will not leave. Your sleep will become disturbed and you'll lose your ability to sustain long lovely meditations, but you will not leave. You will become more accident prone and take longer to get over the flu, but you will not leave. One of you will become infatuated and perhaps even have an affair, but you will not leave. And maybe one night there will be a fight so violent that one of you will strike the other, but even then you will not leave.

And gradually the relationship will begin to get better. It will take time and forgiveness, but it will happen. You will move to levels of peace that you didn't know were possible. Your partner will become your companion, the person you most want to talk to and be around, the one with whom you cannot wear out your welcome. Now you have a partner with whom you can grow old; a real mate who accepts your wrinkles, your loss of hair, your loss of memory, and still blesses you; a friend in whose presence you can even die.

A relationship of that quality may be many years in coming, but with effort and willingness it always comes. This promise is not broken by your spouse failing to work as hard as you do. It is, however, dependent on your trying to see your partner's deep innocence—trying until that vision becomes permanent. Once you see your partner as God sees your partner, your basic happiness is invulnerable.

"I LOVE YOU; I BLESS YOU; I WANT TO WALK HOME TO GOD WITH YOU."

A real relationship is perhaps the quickest and simplest path to the top of the mountain. There, in stillness and humility, Love shows us a great splendor that covers everything and embraces all. In the warm light of God, the mist of separation vanishes and we no longer make distinctions between our needs and those of our mate. In the sweetness of God's peace we see only one Self and feel only one Fulfillment. This experience is in the hands of our partner and is held out to us. To take our partner's hand is not a weakness, but salvation.

Through the centuries, we have walked in many directions trying to find love. But we have not yet walked home. We have tried walking dutifully by each other's sides—but free of the inconvenience of helping one another along the way. This was a journey to a heartless and lonely house. We have tried walking away from each other as a means of loving and indulging ourselves. This was a journey to a house of chaos and pain. In this new century, let us try walking together, giving our hearts as well as our hands, and the path we travel will become the home we seek.

Permissions

About the Authors

Hugh and Gayle Prather are writers, ministers, and marriage and family counselors. They live in Tucson, Arizona, with their two youngest sons, John and Jordan.